A Practical Guide to Content Delivery Networks

Second Edition

A Practical Guide to Content Delivery Networks

Second Edition

Gilbert Held

CRC Press
Taylor & Francis Group
Boca Raton London New York

CRC Press is an imprint of the
Taylor & Francis Group, an **informa** business

AN AUERBACH BOOK

CRC Press
Taylor & Francis Group
6000 Broken Sound Parkway NW, Suite 300
Boca Raton, FL 33487-2742

First issued in paperback 2019

ISBN-13: 978-1-4398-3588-3 (hbk)
ISBN-13: 978-1-138-38202-2 (pbk)

Library of Congress Cataloging-in-Publication Data

Held, Gilbert, 1943-
    A practical guide to content delivery networks / Gilbert Held. -- 2nd ed.
        p. cm.
    Includes index.
    ISBN 978-1-4398-3588-3 (hardcover : alk. paper)
    1. Computer networks. 2. Internetworking (Telecommunication) 3. Internet. I. Title.

TK5105.5.H444 2011
004.6--dc22   2010030232

Visit the Taylor & Francis Web site at
http://www.taylorandfrancis.com

and the CRC Press Web site at
http://www.crcpress.com

Contents

Preface

The development of the World Wide Web has had a considerable effect upon how we purchase items, review financial information from the comfort of our homes and offices, and perform numerous work-related activities. Today, it is common for people to check their stock and bond portfolios online, use the facilities of a price-comparison Web site prior to initiating a work-related purchase, check the latest results of their favorite sports team, examine weather predictions for a possible vacation getaway, and perhaps even book airfare, hotel, and a car rental online. Although many people consider such activities to be confined to the use of personal computers (PCs), within the past few years the Apple iPhone, Blackberry Storm2, and other "smart" cell phones incorporating browser software now allow these activities to be performed while on the go. In addition, a new generation of small Wi-Fi devices, ranging in size from mini-notebooks that weigh a few pounds to devices that can fit in your shirt pocket, enable these activities to be performed from coffee shops, sandwich shops, airports, and hotel rooms and lobbies without incurring the cost of monthly data plans. While we now consider such activities as a normal part of our day, what many readers may not realize is that our ability to perform such activities in a timely and efficient manner results from a hidden network within the Internet. That network and its operation and utilization are the focus of this book.

Since the publication of the first edition of this book, the growth in the use of video over the Internet has been nothing short of astounding. Today you can view the highlights of *Dancing with the Stars, American Idol*, and other reality types of programs; watch your favorite TV program; download a movie; post videos to many social-networking sites; and, of course, view hundreds of thousands of videos on YouTube and similar sites. Given the importance of video, this author would be remiss if he did not include information in this new edition showing how organizations can incorporate so-called new media into Web pages as well as how they can use content delivery networks to assist in the delivery of these pages.

In this book, we will examine the role of content delivery networking to facilitate the distribution of various types of Web traffic, ranging from standard Web pages to streaming video and audio as well as other types of traffic. Because content delivery networking operations are normally performed by independent organizations, the appropriate use of facilities operated by different vendors requires knowledge of how content delivery networks operate. Thus, in this book, we will describe and discuss how such networks operate as well as the advantages and disadvantages associated with their utilization. In addition, because an appreciation of content delivery networking requires an understanding of Web architecture and the TCP/IP (Transmission Control Protocol/Internet Protocol) suite, we will also examine both topics. Understanding Web architecture, including the relationship between Web clients, servers, application servers, and back-end databases, will provide us with the knowledge required to ensure that the use of a content delivery network satisfies all of our organizational requirements. By understanding the TCP/IP protocol suite and the manner by which different applications are both transported and identified, we can obtain a base of knowledge that enables us to appreciate how content delivery networks operate.

Because we can learn from the past, this author believes that the evolution of technology represents an important aspect of any technology-related book. Thus, we will examine the development of a variety of technologies that have evolved over the past decade as mechanisms to distribute various types of Web content. By understanding the advantages and disadvantages associated with different types of content distribution technologies, we will obtain an appreciation for how we can use the networks within the Internet operated by various Internet service providers (ISPs) as a mechanism to deliver our organization's Web-server-based information in a timely and efficient manner to both actual and potential users located around the globe. Last, but certainly not least, we will examine how we can code Web pages to facilitate the delivery of various types of media in an effective manner. In doing so, we will periodically refresh our knowledge of HTML coding as well as turn our attention to the number of bytes required to deliver certain types of media. Many cell phone operators as well as Wi-Fi hotspot operators are placing limits on the amount of data that can be delivered for a basic monthly fee. With ISPs now billing companies based upon traffic generated, additional usage is costing considerably more. Thus, it is becoming beneficial to optimize the delivery of content for both the recipient and the generator of such information.

As a professional author who writes on technology-related topics, I am interested in and highly value reader feedback. You can write me either via my publisher, whose mailing address is in this book, or you can send an e-mail directly to me at gil_held@yahoo.com. Let me know if I spent too much or too little effort covering a particular topic, if I should have included another aspect of content delivery networking in this book, or share any other comments you wish with me. Because I frequently travel, I may not be able to respond to you overnight, but I will make every effort to respond to your comments within a reasonable period of time. Many previous comments and suggestions concerning other books I have written have made their way into subsequent editions, it's quite possible that your comments will have a role in shaping the scope of coverage of a future edition of this book.

Gilbert Held
Macon, Georgia

Acknowledgments

The creation of the book you are reading represents a team effort, even though there is only the name of this author on its binding and cover. From the acceptance of a proposal to the creation of a manuscript, from the proofing of the manuscript to the printing of galley pages, and from the correction of galley page typos and errors to the creation of cover art and the printing of this book, many individuals have contributed a considerable amount of time and effort. I would be remiss if I did not acknowledge the effort of several persons as well as the Taylor & Francis Group's publication team that resulted in the book you are reading. Once again, I am indebted to Rich O'Hanley, publisher of Taylor & Francis' Information Technology Division, for agreeing to back another one of this author's research and writing projects.

Due to a considerable amount of travel, this author many years ago realized that it was easier to write a book the old-fashioned way, using pen and paper, rather than attempt to use a laptop or notebook. Pen and paper were more reliable in the face of circular, rectangular, square, and other oddball electrical receptacles that could vary from one side of a city to another. The use of a few pens and a couple of writing pads was preferable to the uncertainty of the availability of suitable electrical plugs to power a portable computer. Once again, this author is indebted to his wife Beverly for her fine effort in converting his handwritten chapters into a professional manuscript.

In concluding this series of acknowledgments, I would like to take the opportunity to thank all of the behind-the-scenes workers at Auerbach Publishers and Taylor & Francis Group. From the creation of galley pages to printing, binding, and cover art, I truly appreciate all of your efforts.

1

INTRODUCTION TO CONTENT DELIVERY NETWORKING

The purpose of any introductory chapter is to acquaint readers with the topic or topics covered by a book, and this chapter is no exception. Commencing with a definition of a content delivery network (CDN), we will describe and discuss its evolution. In doing so, we will examine several types of networking technologies that were developed to deliver specific types of content as well as the rationale for the development of the modern content delivery network.

1.1 The Modern Content Delivery Network

The modern content delivery network can be defined very simply as follows: A content delivery network represents a group of geographically dispersed servers deployed to facilitate the distribution of information generated by Web publishers in a timely and efficient manner. Of course, this definition does not mention the capacity of dispersed servers. Less than a decade ago, the transfer of digitized video was in its infancy. Today, YouTube and other sites are making the use of video commonplace. When you add in the growth of smart phones and their data delivery—which, according to an article appearing in the Technology section of the October 30, 2009, edition of the *Wall Street Journal*, entitled "Unraveling In-Building Wireless Networks," AT&T experienced a growth of data on its network that expanded by 4,932% between the third quarter of 2006 and the second quarter of 2009—the capacity of servers becomes extremely important. This is a subject we will revisit numerous times in this book.

Although the prior definition of a content delivery network is simplistic, it tells us a significant amount of information about what a CDN represents. That is, a CDN is a group of servers that facilitate the distribution of information generated by Web publishers in a timely and efficient manner. To accomplish this task, the servers must be located closer to the ultimate consumer or potential client operator than the server operated by the Web publisher.

Although there are several third-party organizations that offer content delivery services, it's also possible for organizations to build their own network. In doing so, they can either position servers at multiple sites or use third-party data centers to create their own content delivery network. Thus, there are certain trade-offs associated with the development and use of a content delivery network that must be considered, and we will examine these in this book.

1.1.1 Advantages

There are two key advantages associated with the modern content delivery network. Both advantages result from the fact that making multiple copies of the content of a Web publisher and distributing that content across the Internet removes the necessity of customer requests traversing a large number of routers to directly access the facilities of the Web publisher. This in turn reduces traffic routed through the Internet as well as the delays associated with the routing of traffic. Thus, a content delivery network can be expected to reduce latency between client and server. This can become a significant issue for the delivery of real-time video to clients; however, it's important to realize that most video we watch on the Internet is presently being buffered, and the delay resulting from buffering permits a relatively smooth delivery to occur. Because it has been over a dozen years since organizations began experimenting with pay-for-use models that have been less than successful, most content is distributed freely, which means that many organizations will continue to use buffering, as it represents an economical method to deliver video.

Figure 1.1 illustrates an example of how pervasive video has become on the Internet. In this example, this author went to Yahoo News the day after the 2009 election results occurred, that is, on November 3, 2009. In the original window under the heading POLITICO, you will note a picture of the governor-elect of New Jersey as well as a button labeled Play Video. Clicking on that button results in the display of an advertisement for Crest toothpaste before the video of the news occurs. If you carefully examine the background window shown

Figure 1.1   Viewing a Crest advertisement prior to the video about the off-year election being displayed.

in Figure 1.1 you will note that there are three additional videos you can view from a common Web page. Thus, this single Yahoo page allows viewers to select from four videos concerning a recent election.

Turning our attention to the foreground window where the Crest toothpaste advertisement is shown, note that the version of Yahoo News at the time the screen was captured shows the label "Advertisement" above the Play button on the left of the window as well as the time into the video and its length in the right corner of the display. From this screen, you can view other videos, which can result in a large amount of traffic being directed toward your computer. If you were accessing a site that did not use a content delivery network (CDN) or did not have distributed servers, then a person accessing the video would obtain a data stream from the server to the client that could be at opposites ends of the globe. This in turn would significantly affect the flow of data through the Internet. In comparison, if you were accessing a video from an organization that either used a content delivery network or maintained distributed servers, your request for viewing the video might only travel to a nearby city or server farm, where the video would then flow directly to your computer without having to traverse a significant number of routers on the Internet. Thus, this hypothetical example illustrates two key advantages associated with the use of a content delivery network or the distribution of servers. First, it may significantly reduce the response-time delay associated with client-server requests. Secondly and most important for video, it can reduce the latency or delay in the delivery of packets containing portions of the video requested.

1.1.2 Disadvantages

Because the Internet is, in effect, a world wide network, a Web publisher can have hits that originate from almost anywhere on the globe. This means that it would be impractical for almost all organizations to maintain duplicate servers strategically located around the world. Thus most, if not all, organizations with a large Web presence need to rely upon third-party content delivery network (CDN) operators that have globally distributed in-place networking equipment whose facilities are connected to the Internet. Because most organizations need to use a third party, this results in those disadvantages associated with the use of any third-party technology provider, including cost and support as well as the need to ensure that the CDN provider can update the Web publisher's server changes in a timely manner throughout the content delivery network operated by the third party. Last, but far from the least, you need to verify that the CDN provider has locations that, as best as possible, correspond to the locations where potential groups or clusters of Web clients that will access the organization's server reside. For example, persons accessing the *New York Times* might be expected to primarily reside in the eastern United States, while the online readership of the *Seattle Times* might be primarily in the northwestern United States. Thus, one newspaper would more than likely have a significantly different requirement for the characteristics of a CDN than the other newspaper.

Now that we have a general level of knowledge concerning what a content delivery network actually represents and a few of the advantages and disadvantages associated with its use, let's probe more deeply into this topic. In doing so, we can consider the "history" factor, whereby we can learn from the past and examine the evolution of different content delivery methods.

1.2 Evolution

Although there were many technical problems associated with the development of the World Wide Web (www) series of servers created by academia, businesses, and government agencies, two problems were directly related to content delivery. Both problems resulted from the growth in the number of Web servers in which the total number of Web pages was increasing at an exponential rate.

The first problem resulted from the literal infinite availability of information, making it time consuming for individuals to locate information on the Internet. While search engines such as Yahoo! and Google facilitated the location of Web-based information, if a person required access to a series of data from different locations, he or she would need to spend an inordinate amount of time repeating the Web-page location processes on a daily basis.

The second problem resulted from the global location of Web servers. Because a client in Chicago could require access to a server located in London, Web queries would need to flow thousands of miles through a series of routers to reach their destination. As each query reached the destination server in London, the computer there would process the request and return an applicable Web page. That Web page would flow in a reverse manner to the query, through a series of routers back to the client. Because routers need a small period of time to examine the header of each data packet as a mechanism to determine where to send the packet, network delays are primarily a result of the number of router hops between source and destination computers as well as the traffic flowing through the router. Thus, as the number of hops between client and server increase, so do the expected delays between the client query and server response.

In Chapter 2 we will obtain an appreciation for the in-depth details of client-server computing. Until that chapter, we can simply note that the additional flow of traffic through the Internet and the delays due to packets having to traverse a series of routers are impediments that adversely affect the flow of data. Of the two problems mentioned, the first resulted in the development of "push" technology. Because push technology contributed to the flow of data across the Internet and pre-dated the establishment of content delivery networks, we will discuss their basic operation as well as the different types of content delivery. However, prior to doing so, let's refresh our knowledge by discussing the basics of client-server computing and note that it represents a "pull" technology.

1.2.1 Client-Server Computing

Although *client-server computing* represents a term we normally associate with the introduction of PCs during the 1980s, in actuality its origins date to the mainframe computers that were manufactured beginning in the 1950s and 1960s. Thus, in this section, we will briefly review data flow in the client-to-mainframe environment prior to examining modern client-server operations.

1.2.1.1 Client-to-Mainframe Data Flow   By the mid-1960s, many mainframe computers had a hierarchical communications structure, using control units that were also referred to as cluster controllers to group the flow of data to and from a number of terminal devices cabled to each control unit. Control units were in turn either directly cabled to a channel on the mainframe computer when they were located in the same building as the mainframe, or they communicated via a leased line to a communications controller when the mainframe was located in a different building or city. The communications controller, which was also referred to as a front-end processor, specialized in performing serial-to-parallel and parallel-to-serial data conversion as well as other communications-related tasks, in effect off-loading a majority of the communications functions previously performed by the mainframe.

In fact, when this author commenced his long career associated with computers, he initially worked at a location where cluster controllers were connected to terminals in a suburban Washington, D.C., location, whereas the mainframe was located in Minneapolis, Minnesota. As you might expect, the room where the terminals were clustered was called the terminal room. All was fine until one day someone answered the ringing of the telephone by saying "terminal room" into the headpiece, receiving the response "Oh my God" and a hang-up. Upon a brief investigation, it was determined that the emergency room of the local hospital was assigned a telephone number one digit away from the telephone number assigned to the telephone in our terminal room. To ensure that this situation was not repeated, we had the local phone company change the telephone number of the phone in the terminal room. While this story has nothing to do with cluster controllers nor directly with terminals, it does illustrate the fact that you need to consider that the unusual may occur and build some slack into your timeline for contingencies.

As previously noted, the use of cluster controllers connected to a front-end processor or communications controller enabled the architecture of the mainframe computer to be better designed for moving bytes and performing calculations. This in turn allowed the mainframe to process business and scientific applications more efficiently, since the communications controller was designed to process bits more efficiently, which represents a major portion of the effort required when taking parallel-formed characters and transferring them bit-by-bit onto a serial line or, conversely, receiving a serial data stream and converting the data stream bit-by-bit into a parallel-formed character that the mainframe would operate upon.

Figure 1.2 illustrates the hierarchical structure of a mainframe computer-based network. If you think of the terminal operators

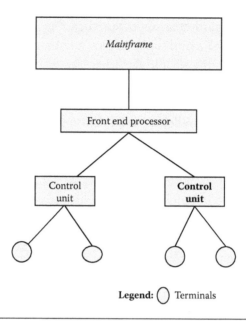

Figure 1.2   Terminal access to mainframes can be considered to represent an elementary form of client-server computing.

as clients and the mainframe as a server, since it provides access to programs in a manner similar to a modern-day server, then the terminal-to-mainframe connection could be considered to represent an elementary form of client-server computing.

In the terminal-to-mainframe environment, the terminal functions as a client requesting a particular service. The mainframe, which functions as a server, represents the provider of the service. Because the first generation of terminal devices had a limited amount of intelligence, it wasn't until the second and third generation of terminals appeared on the market during the later portion of the 1970s that terminals were designed to perform what we would now refer to as limited functions, but which at that time were in effect hard-wired electronics. Those hard-wired electronics represented an early version of firmware and included a sequence of operations that could be considered to represent a program. Thus, the later generations of terminal devices were more representative of client-server computing than the first generation of terminals that simply displayed data and provided a limited data-entry capability.

One of the key limitations of the mainframe environment was its original hierarchical structure. That is, all communications had to flow upward through the mainframe, even if two terminal operators sat next to one another and desired to exchange information electronically. This could cause significant delays, especially if the terminal operators were located in, for instance, a city on the East Coast and the computer was located in the West. This was especially true during the 1970s, when a high-speed communications circuit provided a data transmission rate of 4800 or 9600 bps. Although IBM attempted to change the hierarchical architecture of mainframes through its Advanced Peer-to-Peer Networking (APPN) hardware and software introduced during the 1990s, by then local area networking was dominant to include modern client-server communications.

1.2.1.2 Modern Client-Server Operations Although we previously noted that the relationship between terminals and mainframes could be considered to represent an elementary form of client-server computing, it wasn't until the introduction of the personal computer during the early 1980s that this term gained acceptance. The programmability of personal computers formed the basis for the development of modern client-server computing to include Web-based applications whose operations are improved by the use of a content delivery network.

In a modern client-server computing environment, the client represents a process (program) that transmits a message to a server process (program) over a communications network. The client process requests the server to perform a particular task or service. The client operates a program that normally manages the user-interface portion of server programs, although it may also perform other functions. In a Web environment, the PC transmits Uniform Resource Locator (URL) addresses indicating the address of information the client wishes to receive. The server responds with Web pages that include codes that define how information on the pages should be displayed. The client program, which is the modern-day browser, deciphers the embedded codes to generate Web pages on the client's display.

Figure 1.3 illustrates the relationship of several aspects of modern-day client-server computing in a Web environment. In the upper-right corner of the main window of the Microsoft Internet Explorer browser program, you will note the address http://www.yahoo.com. This address represents the URL transmitted to the Yahoo server from the author's client PC. In response to this query, the Yahoo server

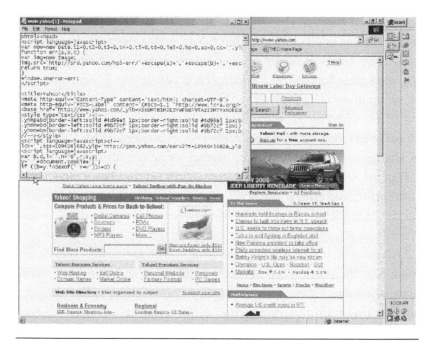

Figure 1.3   The relationship between an URL query, HTML code response, and client display of a requested Web page.

transmitted its home page that corresponds to the URL address it received. In actuality, the client PC receives a sequence of HTML (HyperText Markup Language) and JAVA or VBScript statements, a portion of which are illustrated in the window in the foreground that is located in the upper-left portion of Figure 1.3. By selecting Source from the browser's View menu, the source statements that were interpreted by the PC operating the browser are displayed in a Notepad window. Thus, in this single display, you can view the client request in the form of the URL transmitted to the server and the server's response that, when interpreted by the browser operating on the client, generated the Web-page display. In Chapter 2 we will describe and discuss in considerable detail HTML, including embedded programs coded in Java and VBScript.

Because the Internet and its assorted facilities, such as Web servers, are recent additions to the history of client-server computing, it should be noted that servers perform other functions besides generating Web pages. Some servers execute database retrievals and update operations. Other servers provide access to printers, while a server-based process could operate on a machine that provides network users access to

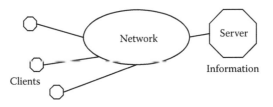

Figure 1.4 A generic information-delivery system.

shared files, resulting in a device referred to as a file server. Over the years, a number of different types of servers were developed to support a variety of applications. While a database server represents one common type of server, when the database is incorporated into a reservation system, the result is a specific type of reservation-system server, such as a car rental, hotel, or airline reservation system server. Another popular type of server that has recently emerged is the video server.

Figure 1.4 illustrates a generic information-delivery system where the network could be the Internet, a corporate intranet, or simply a local area network (LAN) without a connection to another network.

1.2.2 Use of Video Servers

As its name implies, a video server is used to store video content. To illustrate why the storage capacity of a video server is extremely important, let's assume that an organization is storing "How To" videos covering fixing a faucet, installing a light switch, and similar projects. If the video has a frame rate of 30 frames per second (fps) and if a resolution of 640 × 480 pixels is used with a 24-bit color depth, then a 1-second display requires the storage and transmission of 30 × 640 × 480 × 24 or approximately 221 million bits, which is almost 28 million bytes. Thus, a 1-minute video would require the storage and transmission of approximately 1.68 Gbytes of data. In a modern video environment such as the Web, there are several methods that can be used to reduce both the storage and transmission of video data. The major methods used to reduce the size of video files include reducing the length of the video; altering the resolution, frame rate, and color depth of the video; as well as the use of compression technology.

1.2.2.1 Video Length Obviously, the longer a video, the more storage is required as well as additional time for its transmission. Thus, one obvious method that can be used to reduce the data storage and transmission requirements of a video is to reduce its length. This is why, in a fast-changing world, the on-line news videos are normally only a few minutes in length.

1.2.2.2 Video Resolution   Full-resolution video dates to the VGA monitor, which had a resolution of 640 × 480 pixels, or 640 pixel dots across by 480 lines of pixels. Although there have been significant improvements in the capabilities of adapter cards and monitors with respect to resolution since the VGA standard was developed, full-resolution video is commonly used today. Other commonly encountered resolutions include 320 × 240, in which the width and height are reduced by a factor of two (which reduces data storage by a factor of four), and 160 × 120 (which is referred to as quarter-resolution and which reduces the total amount of data by a factor of 16).

1.2.2.3 Frame Rate   In the movie theater, the frame rate of a film is typically 24 frames per second. On a TV, due to the refresh rate, images are displayed at a rate of 30 frames per second. A slower frame rate can result in images having a jumpiness quality. In the distribution of images to computers, the initial use of video occurred at frame rates as low as 15 and even 10 fps to reduce data requirements by a factor of two or three. While this was almost a necessity a decade ago, advances in data storage capacity as well as the data rate of cable and DSL communications allows a 30-fps rate.

1.2.2.4 Color Depth   Color depth refers to the number of pixels used to represent the color of each pixel displayed. The use of black and white requires one bit per pixel, while what is referred to as "true color" and "full color" uses 8 bits each of red, blue, and green data; requires 24 bits per pixel; and represents the maximum amount of color the human eye can distinguish. The next-smaller reduction results in the use of 16 bits, which can represent thousands of colors and provides a one-third reduction in the quantity of data. Because video is typically shot using a 24-bit color-depth device, trimming the color depth from 24 to 16 bits, which is referred to as quantization, can distort transitions within frames.

1.2.2.5 Data Compression   Of all the techniques previously mentioned, data compression provides the largest reduction in the quantity of data used to represent a video. For full-motion video, there are several data-compression methods that are used. A few of those compression methods include Windows Media Video (WMV), which is based upon Microsoft's implementation of the Moving Picture Experts Group (MPEG) 4, Part 2; and Adobe's Flash Video, which in versions 6 and 7 used the Sorenson Spark, a codec (coder-decoder) for FLV files, while Flash Player 8 and newer revisions now support the use of ON2 Technologies VP6 compression as well as various versions of MPEG. While each version of data compression performs differently with respect to its support of low-, medium-, and high-bit-rate transfers and compression efficiency, in common, they all considerably reduce the size of data storage requirements as well as data transmission time. However, to effectively view a video, the client must have either a compatible browser or a compatible plug-in in the browser, two topics we will discuss in more detail later in this book.

1.2.3 Server Network Architecture

Similar to network architectures developed to expedite the flow of data, the use of servers resulted in an architecture being developed to facilitate processing. Initially, PC networks were based upon the use of file servers that provided clients with the ability to access and share files. Because the file server would respond to a client request by downloading a complete file, the server's ability to support many simultaneous users was limited. This limitation still exists today with Web servers and has been exploited through the use of denial of service (DOS) attacks, in which the nature of the Transmission Control Protocol (TCP) and its three-way handshake permits a DOS attack to occur. In addition to being subjected to potential attacks, network traffic occurring as a result of many file transfers could significantly affect communications.

The limitations associated with file sharing resulted in the use of database servers. Employing a relational database management system (DBMS), client queries were directly answered, considerably reducing network traffic in comparison to the use of networks when a total file-transfer activity occurred. Thus, the modern client-server architecture in many organizations results from the use of a database server instead of a file server.

There are two types of server architecture one must consider to expedite the flow of data. Those types of architecture are internal and external to the server. When we discuss internal server architecture, we primarily reference the arrangement and specifications of the components within the server, including processors, processor power, memory, channels to disk, disk capacity, and disk input/output (I/O) data transfer rates. When we discuss external server architecture, we primarily reference the subdivision of effort by having one server function as a preprocessor for another. Because this type of server relationship commonly occurs over a network, it's common to refer to this architecture as a server-based network architecture. In this section, we will focus our attention upon external or server network architecture. The two most common forms of server architectures are two-tier and three-tier.

1.2.3.1 Two-Tier Architecture   A two-tier architecture represents the direct communications between a client and server, with no intervening server being necessary. Here, the client represents one tier and the server represents the second tier. This architecture is commonly used by small- to medium-sized organizations, where the server needs to support up to approximately 100 users. It's important to note that when we discuss user levels, we are referring to the number of simultaneous users and not the population of potential users, which is normally considerably larger.

1.2.3.2 Three-Tier Architecture   In a three-tier server architecture, a server or series of servers function as agents between the client and server where the data or application they require resides. The agents can perform a number of functions that off-load processing that otherwise would be required to be performed by the server. For example, agents could provide a translation service by placing client queries into a database retrieval language for execution on a database server. Other possible agent functions could range in scope from functioning as a metering device that limits the number of simultaneous requests allowed to flow to a server, to functioning as a preprocessor mapping agent, where requests are distributed to different servers based upon

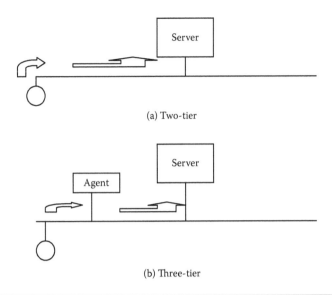

(a) Two-tier

(b) Three-tier

Figure 1.5 Two-tier versus three-tier architecture.

certain criteria. Still other examples of functions that could be performed by middle-tier devices include queuing of requests, request filtering, and a variety of application preprocessing that is only limited by one's imagination.

Figure 1.5 illustrates two-tier and three-tier architectures on a common network for simplicity of explanation. In the two-tier architecture, note that client-server communications flow directly between devices. In a three-tier architecture, data flow occurs twice on the network, first from the client to the agent and then from the agent to the server. Thus, in a local area networking environment, the additional network utilization needs to be compared with the off-loading of processing functions on the server. For example, assume that the data flow averages 6000 packets per second (pps), with each packet having an average of 1200 bytes of data. Then, a two-tiered architecture would have a data flow of 72 Mbps, while a three-tiered server architecture would result in a situation where the doubling of the data flow would result in a data rate of 144 Mbps. While this is insignificant if a Gigabit Ethernet network is installed, one would go from an overused network that could not handle the data flow if Fast Ethernet, which has a maximum data-transfer capability of 100 Mbps, was employed. Note that because the agent could perform preprocessing on data, it's possible that the data flow might be less when flowing to the server. However, it's also possible that the preprocessing could result in additional traffic. Regardless of the action of the agent, there will be more traffic on a three-tier network than a two-tier network, and you need to consider this when designing your network structure.

Now that we have an appreciation for the basics of client-server architecture, let's return to our discussion of the evolution of content delivery and focus our attention upon push technology.

1.2.4 The Road to Push Technology

Push technology is normally thought of as a new model of information distribution and data retrieval. In actuality, early versions of push systems occurred during the 1970s and early 1980s in the form of teletext systems and broadcast delivery videotext.

1.2.4.1 Teletext Systems   Teletext systems began to become popular in the late 1970s, especially in Europe. Information pages are transmitted in the vertical blanking interval (VBI) of television signals, with decoders built into TV sets becoming capable of capturing, decoding, and displaying "pages" selected by the consumer. As many persons who travel to Europe probably remember, most televisions in hotels include a teletext capability that enables a person holding a remote control to view the weather, TV schedule, and other information.

As illustrated in Figure 1.6, a teletext system transmits a sequence of information in the form of pages that are repeated at predefined intervals. The person with the remote control enters a request, which is transmitted to the television and results in the display of the desired information once the request is processed and the requested information is returned via the broadcast stream.

Because teletext operators noted that certain pages of information were more desirable than other pages, they altered the sequence or cycle of page transmissions from the pure sequence illustrated in Figure 1.6. For example, suppose that there are only three pages of

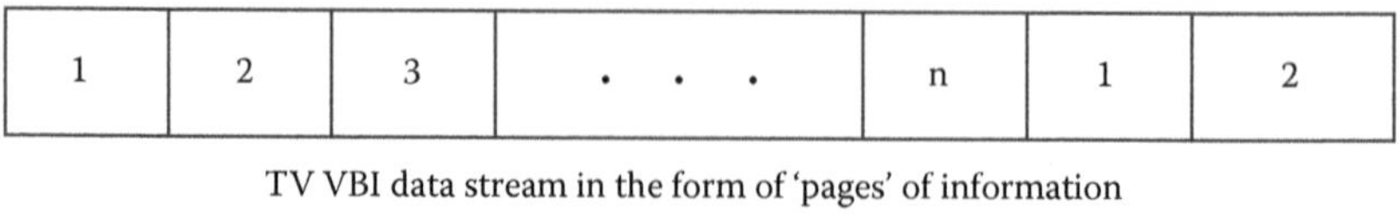

1	2	3	. . .	n	1	2

TV VBI data stream in the form of 'pages' of information

Figure 1.6   Teletext system operation.

...	1	2	1	3	1	2	1	3	1	2	...

Figure 1.7 An example of a possible optimal teletext cycle where pages 1, 2, and 3 occur 50%, 30%, and 20% of the time, respectively.

teletext information, and it was found that the information in page 1 could be requested 50% of the time, while the information on pages 2 and 3 might be desired 30% and 20% of the time, respectively. Then an optimum teletext cycle could appear, as illustrated in Figure 1.7.

1.2.4.2 Videotext While we can consider teletext as an elementary form of push and select technology, it was videotext that added block-formed pictures, such that the technology can actually be considered as the father of modern Web-based technology. Originally, videotext systems delivered information and transactional-oriented services for banking, insurance, and shopping services. Later, videotext technology was used by newspaper publishers, who made news and advertisements available through special terminals hooked up to television monitors. However, it wasn't until teletext systems were developed for operation with the growing base of personal computers that teletext, with block characters that provided what we would consider to represent elementary graphics today, became widely available. By the mid-1990s, prior to the availability of the Web, videotext systems were operated by America Online, CompuServe, Prodigy, and Genie. In fact, this author remembers countless nights his wife spent on the PC connected to CompuServe and Prodigy, communicating with other patrons of the theater while navigating through various system menus displaying what would now be considered as crude graphics. To obtain a more worldly view of teletext, we can consider the use of terminals to replace the weighty phone directory as well as save numerous trees from being made into paper. In France, Minitel terminals were distributed by the French government in place of telephone directories, and videotext was and still is in popular use in that country.

1.2.5 Pull Technology

Until the introduction of push technology, information retrieval was based upon what is referred to as *pull* technology. That is, a person would either have previously located an item of interest or used a search engine, such as Google or Yahoo!, to locate an item of interest. Once an item of interest was located, the consumer, acting as a client operator, would use his or her browser to point to the URL on a server to retrieve the information of interest.

1.2.5.1 Role of Caching   One popular method developed to facilitate client-server pull operations is caching. In a browser environment, which most readers are familiar with, caching occurs through the temporary storage of Internet files in a predefined folder on your hard drive. The stored files represent previously visited Web pages and files, such as graphics displayed on a particular page.

In a Microsoft Explorer browser environment, temporary Internet files are placed in a predefined folder located at: C:Documents and Settings\Owner\Local Settings\Temporary Internet Files\. A browser user can go to Tools> General> Settings in Microsoft's Internet Explorer to view cached files, adjust the amount of disk space to use for caching, change the location of the cache folder, as well as define how caching occurs.

Figure 1.8 illustrates the Settings Window selected from Tools> General> Settings on this author's computer when he used Microsoft's Internet Explorer 5. Note that, when you used that browser, you would

Figure 1.8   In Microsoft's Internet Explorer Version 5, you can use Tools> General> Settings to control the use of caching.

have several options concerning the manner by which caching updates occur. You can have the browser check for newer versions of stored pages on every visit to the page, every time you start Internet Explorer, automatically (browser default), or never. In addition, you can adjust the amount of space used for caching. While increasing the amount of disk space can increase how fast previously visited pages are displayed, it also results in additional processing, since additional pages need to be searched. In addition, an increased disk cache obviously decreases the amount of space available for other files on the computer.

The newer versions of Internet Explorer are conspicuous by their absence of an option for directly controlling cache. For example, in Internet Explorer 8, if you go to the Tools menu and select Internet Options, the dialog box will considerably differ from that shown in Figure 1.8 and will not provide any options for the controlling of cache. However, if you go to the Tools menu and then select Developer Tools or press the F12 key, the resulting dialog box will provide you with the ability to clear the Browser cache or clear it for the domain. This is illustrated in Figure 1.9.

If you use a different browser, your ability to control cache will depend upon both the browser used and its version. For example, this author also uses the popular Mozilla Firefox browser, with the latest version being version 3.6.3 when this book revision was performed. This version of the Firefox browser provides the ability to directly control cache similar to earlier versions of Internet Explorer. For example, going to the Tools menu, selecting Options, and then selecting Advanced results in the display of a dialog box with a series of four tabs. Selecting the tab labeled Network results in the display of the current setting for cache. In addition, the dialog box provides you with the ability to reset the value shown to another value if desired. Figure 1.10 illustrates how you can control cache via the use of the Mozilla Firefox browser, assuming you are operating version 3.6.3 or another version that provides a similar capability.

While Web caching is probably the most popular form of caching in use, it has certain strengths and limitations. Web caching is effective if documents do not change often, but it becomes less effective as document changes increase in frequency. Thus, there are several deficiencies and limitations associated with pull technology and the use of caching.

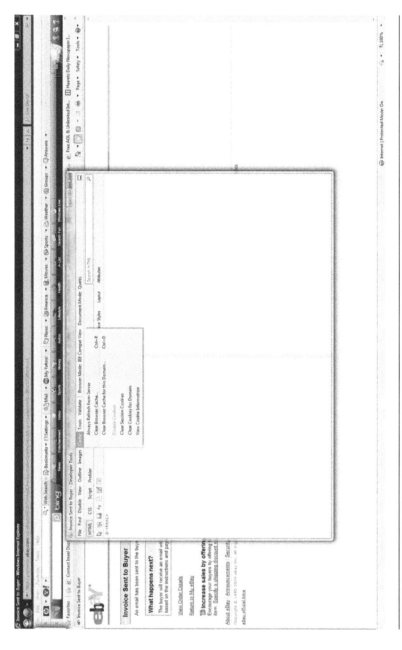

Figure 1.9   Using the Developer Tools entry from the Tools Menu provides two mechanisms for clearing the cache.

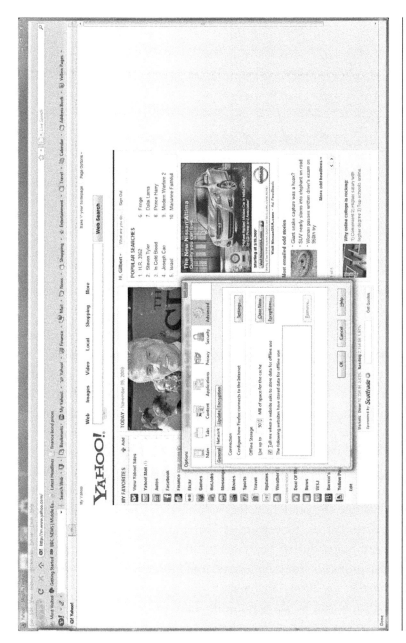

Figure 1.10 Controlling the cache using the Mozilla Firefox browser.

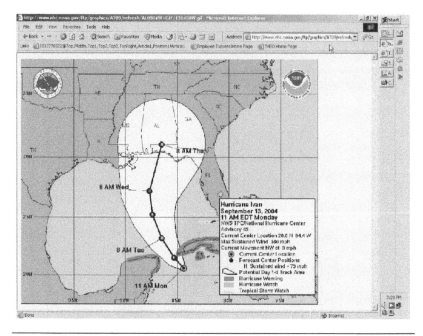

Figure 1.11   Using pull technology, a client has to periodically retrieve a Web page to determine if an item of interest has changed.

1.2.5.2 Pull Limitations   As anyone who has used the Internet to obtain information on a topic that is evolving knows from experience, to obtain frequently updated information requires the periodic checking of a server. For example, during 2004, information about Hurricanes Charlie, Francis, and Ivan were obviously of interest to persons living in the southeastern United States. Under the pull model, users interested in hurricane information would have to periodically query the United States National Hurricane Center Web site or a similar location to obtain a forecast of the current and projected movement of the storm of interest.

To illustrate the preceding, let's assume that you were interested in the projection of the movement of Hurricane Ivan as it raced toward the United States during September 2004. Figure 1.11 illustrates the three-day projection for the movement of Hurricane Ivan as of 11 a.m. on September 13, 2004. Obviously, if you lived in the projected path of this hurricane, you would periodically have to "pull" a new projection to see if the projected path was altered.

From a network viewpoint, there can be hundreds to millions of persons accessing the same information over and over, since they are not sure when a new forecast will be available. This means that the

Web server may have to periodically handle a volume of connections that can significantly vary. Depending upon the location of clients with respect to the server as well as the amount of traffic flowing to clients, latency can considerably increase. This may not only adversely affect persons accessing one or a few servers but, in addition, adversely affect other persons running different applications.

Because applications of interest to many persons have no efficient mechanism to avoid duplicated data, another limitation is the quantity of traffic in a pull environment. For example, suppose one user transmits a 256-byte packet representing a URL request to a server that elicits a 10,000 1024-byte sequence of packet responses. If 1000 users requested the same information, the server must respond 1000 times with 10,000 1024-byte packets! In addition to the server responding over and over again, the network traffic would be considerable. For example, if the server was located in Miami and clients located throughout the southeastern United States were accessing the server, network traffic would be directed throughout the Internet to clients located in each southeastern state. While Internet traffic would be perhaps reasonable for clients located in Florida, network traffic to Georgia residents would first flow through Florida and then through Georgia. Similarly, clients located in South Carolina would have traffic routed through Florida, then through Georgia to arrive in South Carolina. For clients located in North Carolina, the traffic would first flow through Florida, so the bandwidth capability of the Internet in Florida would be a major constraint to clients accessing weather information on a server located in Florida. Thus, a method to duplicate the content of the Miami server in other states could reduce the possibility of network bottlenecks and can be considered another advantage associated with content delivery networks.

During the 1980s and early 1990s, several attempts occurred to minimize the bandwidth required for the distribution of popularly requested information. Perhaps the most popular method that is still in use today is multicast transmission.

1.2.6 Multicast

Multicast communication represents a method to conserve bandwidth in a TCP/IP protocol environment. Under multicast, communication occurs between a single data source and multiple receivers that have joined a multicast group. To avoid potential confusion, note that there are three types of addressing that can occur on a network: unicast, multicast, and broadcast. A unicast address represents the address of a distinct entity. In comparison, a broadcast address represents a method to send data so that it is received by all members on the network. Thus, we can view a multicast address as representing more than one entity and possibly all entities on a network if each entity joined the multicast group.

Although multicast represents a 1990s technology, it provides several important advantages for group communications in comparison to traditional unicast and broadcast transmission.

1.2.6.1 Advantages A primary advantage of the use of multicast is that it enables the conservation of network bandwidth. For example, if 10 clients residing on a network subscribe to a multicast video, only 1 sequence of packets flows onto the network instead of 10 packet sequences. Another important advantage of multicast transmission is the fact that it scales very well to large user groups. That is, if the number of clients on a network desiring to subscribe to the multicast video increases to 100 or even 1000, the same sequence of packets would flow on the network.

1.2.6.2 Addresses In a TCP/IP environment, the range of IPv4 addresses from 224.0.0.0 thru 239.255.255.255 is reserved for multicasting. Those addresses are also referred to as Class D addresses. Every IP datagram whose destination address commences with the first four bits set to 1110 represents an IP multicast datagram. The remaining 28 bits in the address identify the multicast "group" that the datagram is sent to. Because multicast addresses represent a group of IP devices, they can only be used as the destination of a datagram; hence, they are never the source.

In an IPv4 environment, the 28 bits after the leading "1110" in the IP address define the *multicast group address*. The size of the Class D multicast address space is therefore 2^{28} or 268,435,456 multicast groups, of which certain portions of the address space are set aside for specific uses. Table 1.1 illustrates the general allocation of the Class D address space.

Table 1.1 IP Multicast Address Ranges and Utilization

ADDRESS RANGE BEGINNING	ADDRESS RANGE ENDING	UTILIZATION
224.0.0.0	224.0.0.255	Reserved for the use of special "well-known" multicast addresses
224.0.1.0	238.255.255.255	Internet-wide multicast addresses referred to as "globally scoped" addresses
239.0.0.0	239.255.255.255	Local multicast addresses referred to as "administratively scoped" addresses

Within the Class D address block, the range of addresses between 224.0.0.0 and 224.0.0.255, which are considered as "well-known" multicast addresses, are reserved for use by routing protocols, topology discovery protocols, and maintenance protocols. Within this address range are several well-known multicast groups. Two examples of such groups include:

224.0.0.1 is the all-hosts group: If you ping this Class D address, all multicast-capable hosts on the network will respond.

224.0.0.2 is the all-routers group: All multicast routers must join that group on all its multicast-capable interfaces.

The majority of the Class D address space is in the middle multicast range, which contains Internet-wide multicast addresses. They are similar to Class A, B, and C unicast addresses, which we will discuss in detail in Chapter 3 covering TCP/IP, and can be assigned to various groups.

The last address range shown in Table 1.1 is for local multicast addresses, more technically referred to as administratively scoped multicast groups. This address group represents 1/16th of the total multicast address space and is subdivided into site-local multicast addresses as well as organization-local addresses and other local multicast addresses.

1.2.6.3 Limitations One of the major disadvantages of multicast is the fact that users must register to receive a multicast data stream, which makes this technology more suitable for predefined events, such as video telecasts, rather than pulling different information off several Web servers. Another limitation of multicast is the fact that not all routers or hosts conform to the multicast specification. In fact, there are three levels of conformance with respect to the multicast specification, with level 0 indicating no support, level 1 indicating support for sending but not receiving multicast datagrams, while level 2 indicates full support for IP multicast.

1.2.7 Push Technology

The development of push technology was a response to the need to bring information of interest to consumers instead of having them retrieve data. Under push technology, a consumer signs up with a push provider to receive certain data that is transmitted over the Internet to the user's desktop. Information of interest is displayed either as a stream on the 25th line of the screen, or perhaps in a separate window on the display. The actual data sent to a user's desktop can come from a variety of Web sites, depending upon the information of interest to the user. When the user fills out a profile of data of interest with the push provider, that profile functions as a filter. The vendor's server searches a variety of Web sites, collecting information of interest to all subscribers; however, it uses each subscriber profile as a mechanism to determine the data to push to individual subscribers. Because selected information of interest is broadcast similar to a television or radio broadcast, the terms *streaming*, *channeling*, and *broadcasting* are sometimes used as synonyms.

According to some persons, the term *push* also derives from the term *push polling*, which was used during the 1996 U.S. presidential election, when unscrupulous polling personnel pretended to conduct a telephone opinion poll but, in actuality, used questions that "pushed" their candidate's strengths.

1.2.7.1 Evolution In a modern push-technology environment, PointCast represents the vanguard of a series of companies that developed push technology. Founded in 1992 to deliver news and other information over the Internet, during 1996 the company distributed approximately 1.6 million copies of its proprietary Webcasting software, which for its time period represented a tremendous achievement. During 1997, the hype associated with Push technology resulted in *Business Week* noting PointCast in its cover story on Webcasting, including a quotation from its then-34-year-old CEO, Chris Hasset, that "we are defining a new medium."

PointCast's run at fame was momentary. Although PointCast provided customers with the ability to receive advertisements along with specific requested information, push technology was literally shoved off corporate networks by organizations who found that employee use of the PointCast system was clogging their Internet connections as well as the local area networks connected to the mother of all networks. As more and more companies shunned the technology, the fortunes of PointCast considerably diminished. In addition, competition from Yahoo! and other Internet-related commercial firms resulted in the use of push technology via the use of nonproprietary Internet channels. Eventually, both Microsoft and Netscape incorporated Webcasting technology into their browsers, further diminishing the need for PointCast's proprietary software. Within a few years, PointCast was acquired by another company, and the use of push technology from the pioneer ceased many years ago.

The adoption of push technology was valuable for organizations needing a mechanism to deliver information en masse, such as automatic updating of business price lists, manuals, inventories, and policies. However, the mass market never actively used the desktop channel bar that became available under Internet Explorer Version 4.0. In fact, the more modern versions of Windows—such as Windows XP, Vista, and Windows 7—do not support the desktop channel bar or only support it for users who upgraded from Internet Explorer 4.0 or Windows 98. Instead, most persons today use Microsoft's Windows Media Player, RealNetworks's RealOne, or a similar program to view predefined audio and video. You can use either program to retrieve news; to play, burn, and rip audio tracks; and to find a variety of content on the Internet. Nevertheless, these modern Webcasting tools are more pullers than pushers. In addition, these modern Webcasting tools lack one key feature—a crawl capability—that was built into many push products and was included in Internet Explorer Version 4.0. We will briefly discuss this crawl capability before moving on to focus our attention on modern content delivery methods.

1.2.7.2 Crawling Under Internet crawling, users specify either the general type of information or a specific type of information they desire. Then, the client program performs a site-crawl of applicable Web sites, examining data for relevance as well as checking for updated content, and then notifying the user of changes. Users of Internet Explorer 4.0 could specify Web crawls up to three levels deep from a subscribed Web page as well as retrieve pages from nonsubscription sites.

To perform a crawl requires a specified starting Web page. Given that page, a browser crawls each link on that page and, if configured to do so, the browser can crawl multiple levels deep or restrict its operation to each specified page in a list. During the crawl operation, the browser will check to see if a page changed by comparing file size and creation date of stored and access files. Depending upon the configuration of the crawl, once a page is checked, either a notification of changes or actual page content is downloaded to the user. Today, Web crawling is primarily performed by search engines or users with older browsers, as newer browsers have replaced Web crawling with Atom and Really Simple Syndication (RSS) feeds, which we will shortly discuss.

1.2.7.3 Feeds A Feed can be considered to represent frequently updated content that is typically published by a Web site. Some common example of Feeds include news and blogger site updates; however, a Feed can also be used to distribute videos and audios, the latter commonly in the MP3 format and referred to as podcasting. Thus, a Feed can be considered as a modern push technology.

The most common Feed is the Really Simple Syndication (RSS) feed; however, similar to most software, there are different versions off RSS, such as RSS 1.0 and RSS 2.0. Versions of RSS as well as other Feeds are based upon the Extensible Markup Language (XML), which is a test-based computer language employed to develop structured documents.

If you are using a modern browser with a Feeds capability, when you visit a Web page, you will note a Feeds button that, when clicked upon, allows you to select one or more Feeds. On some Web sites, the Feeds button is prominently displayed, while on other sites a bit of searching may be required. For example, on the *New York Times* Web site (www.nytimes.com), you have to scroll to the bottom of the home page to find the Feeds button. This is illustrated in Figure 1.12, when this author scrolled down the home page of the newspaper to observe the Feeds button and the acronym RSS to the right of the button.

Figure 1.12 To select the Feeds button on the home page of the *New York Times*, you need to scroll to the bottom of the page.

Once you select the Feeds button, the Web site shown in Figure 1.12 will provide you with a list of Feeds you can select from. For example, at the time this author viewed the feeds available for selection, they varied from the Home Page to World, U.S., Regional, Business, Technology, and many other potential selections. Figure 1.13 illustrates the potential feeds available for user selection when this author browsed the *New York Times* Web site. Just as a matter of conjecture, perhaps providing a wealth of free information has resulted in the financial plight of the print media.

1.2.7.4 Advantages   Similar to most technologies, there are several advantages associated with push technology. From the viewpoint of the client, push technology permits predefined requests that enables items of interest to be received when such items have Web-page changes. From the viewpoint of the server, push technology enables common multiple requests to result in a single response to the push provider, which in turn becomes responsible for the transmission of Web pages to individual client subscribers. Due to this, push technology is potentially extremely scalable and can reduce the load on both distant servers and networks, which in turn can be expected to enhance response time.

1.2.7.5 Disadvantages   Previously, we noted that the main reason why early versions of push technology failed to live up to the hype was because its use was clogging corporate networks. Today, the replacement of 10-Mbps Ethernet LANs by 1-Gbps and even 10-Gbps LANs has allowed modern versions of push technology in the form of RSS and other feeds to be allowed onto many corporate networks.

Besides clogging corporate networks, two additional limitations—associated with early versions of push technology and its more modern replacement by feeds—are the common needs for clients to subscribe to a service and control. Concerning subscription fees, most Internet users rightly or wrongly view the Internet as a free service and always want cheap or no-cost information. Concerning control, many users prefer on-demand information retrieval (pull), where they control information to be downloaded. Because push technology was developed in an era where high-speed LANs operated at 10 Mbps, the traffic resulting from push had a significant effect upon corporate networks. When combined with the subscription nature of most early

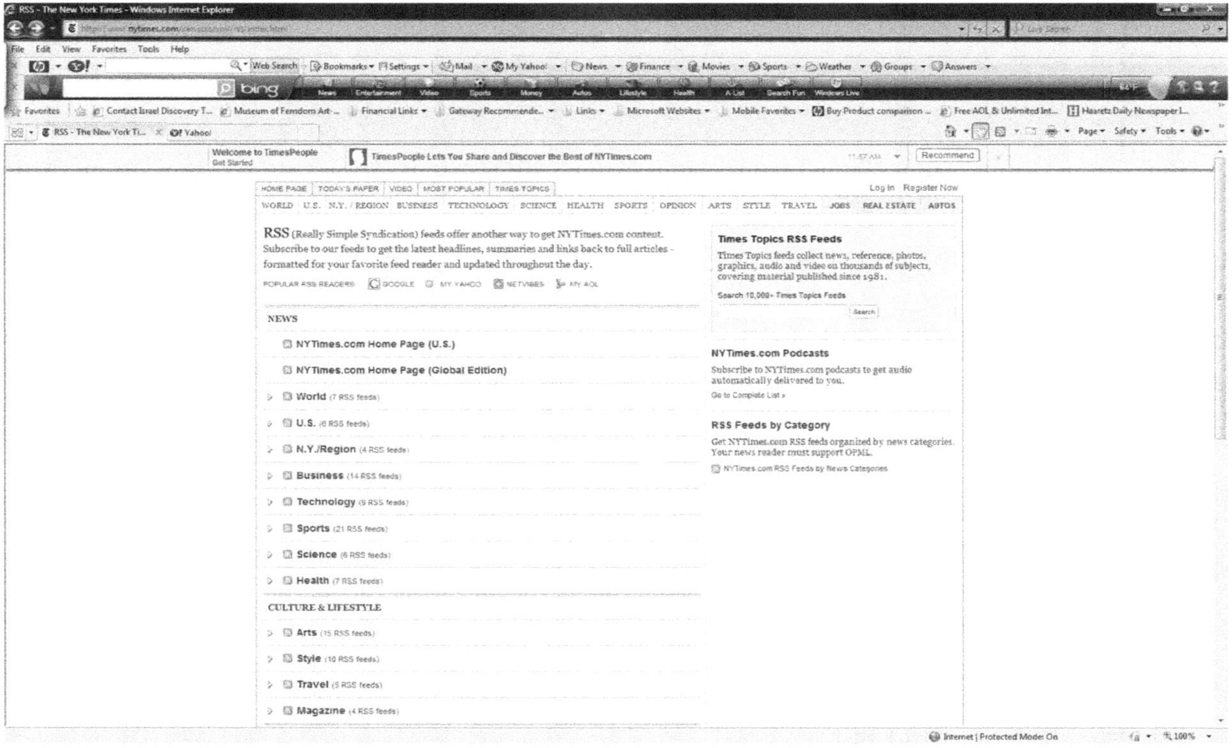

Figure 1.13 Viewing the feeds available from the *New York Times* Web site.

versions of push operators as well as user preference for control of Web-page retrieval, it's a wonder that push technology held the interest of Internet users for several years during the 1990s.

With the development of higher speed networking capability and the removal of subscription fees, push technology has been revitalized. Today, many persons subscribe to business-related feeds to find out information about favored investments, while other persons subscribe to certain types of news to be aware of the latest events.

Now that we have a general level of appreciation for the evolution of a variety of information-retrieval techniques that were developed over the past half century, let's examine the role of modern content delivery networking and how it facilitates many types of client-server communications, including push, pull, and Web crawling.

1.3 Content Delivery Networking

In the first section of this chapter, we were briefly introduced to content delivery networking (CDN) through an abbreviated definition of what the term means. Thereafter, we focused our attention on the second section of this chapter—the evolution of client-server technology, including caching as well as pull, push, and crawling operations. In this section, we will use our prior base of knowledge to obtain an appreciation for the manner by which content delivery networking facilitates the various types of client-server operations. Recognition of the benefits obtained from the use of a content delivery network requires some knowledge of the limitations of client-server operations as well as the general structure of the Internet. Let's begin our examination of CDN by discussing client-server operations on the Internet.

1.3.1 Client-Server Operations on the Internet

The Internet represents a collection of networks tied to one another through the use of routers that support the TCP/IP protocol suite. To illustrate some of the problems associated with content delivery as data flows across the Internet, let's first assume a best-case scenario where both client and server are on the same network. Then, we can expand the distance between client and server in terms of both router hops and networks traversed, introducing the point of presence (POP) and peering point used to interconnect separate networks to one another on the Internet.

1.3.2 Client Server Operating on the Same Network

When we speak in terms of the Internet, the term *network* represents a collection of subnets with connectivity provided by an Internet Service Provider (ISP). Thus, when we mention that both client and server reside on the same network on the Internet, the two computers can reside on the same segment or on different subnets that require one or more router hops to be traversed for one computer to communicate with the other device.

The delay associated with the delivery of server content primarily represents a function of network traffic, available network bandwidth, and the number of router hops from client to server. Because a "network" in terms of the Internet is controlled by an ISP, content delivery is more manageable than when data delivery has to flow between interconnected "networks." That is, the ISP can upgrade bandwidth and routers as it signs up additional clients as a mechanism to minimize the effect of additional traffic.

1.3.3 Client-Server Operations on Different Networks

When the client and server are located on different Internet "networks," traffic must flow through an access point where networks operated by different ISPs are interconnected. On the Internet, a point-of-presence (POP) is sometimes used as a term to reference an access point where one network connects to another. In actuality, the term POP has its roots in telephony and originally represented the physical location where the local telephone operator connected its network to one or more long-distance operators. While the term POP is still used to reference the location where two ISPs interconnect their networks, a more popular term used to reference this location is the *Internet peering point.*

1.3.4 Peering Point

An Internet peering point represents the physical location where two or more networks are interconnected. Such locations are based upon contractual agreements between ISPs and trace their origins to the original expansion of ARPANET, whose full name represented the Advanced Research Project Agency Network. As the Internet evolved, ARPANET was considered to represent a backbone network, with other networks linked to one another via one or more connections to the backbone. As the Internet has expanded and evolved, there is no longer a single backbone network in the traditional meaning. Instead, various commercial ISPs as well as private network operators entered into agreements whereby two or more networks were interconnected at a peering point under a peering agreement. Today there are two main types of peering: private and public. A private peering point results in an agreement among two ISPs to permit traffic to flow between two networks. In comparison, a public peering point, also referred to as an Internet Exchange Point, represents a location independent of any single provider where networks can be interconnected. ISPs with large traffic volumes, such as MCI (formerly known as WorldCom), are often referred to as Tier 1 carriers and usually establish peering agreements with other Tier 1 carriers without charging one another for the interconnection. Smaller providers with lighter traffic loads tend to use Internet Exchange Points, where they pay a fee for interconnection services.

One example of a peering point is MAE-East. The term MAE stands for Metropolitan Area Ethernet and represented an interchange constructed by Metropolitan Fiber Systems (owned by MCI prior to its acquisition by Verizon) for PSI, UUNET, and SprintLink during 1993. MAE-East was established at approximately the same time that the National Science Foundation was exiting the Internet backbone business, which enabled this peering location to become so successful that a similar facility was opened in Silicon Valley, referred to as MAE-West. By 2005, MAE-East had expanded to four sites in the Washington, D.C., metropolitan area and one location in New York City, with 38 members ranging in size from AT&T WorldNet and BT, to Epoch Networks, Equant, Hurricane Electric, Infornet, Swiss Com AG, UUNET, Verio, and Xspedius. By 2009, MAE-East offered Frame Relay encapsulation at Optical Carrier (OC) OC-3, OC-12, and OC-48 data rates using Packet over SONET as well as Gigabit Ethernet connections on fiber and ATM connections at DS-3, OC-3, and OC-12 data rates.

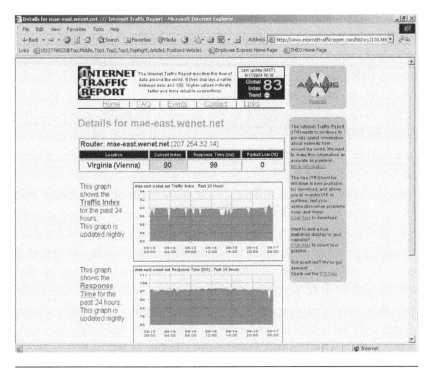

Figure 1.14 The top portion of a Web page that provides three metrics concerning the operation of MAE-East.

Today there are three major MAEs in the United States: MAE-East, MAE-West, and MAE-Central, with the latter located in Dallas, Texas. In addition, there are two central MAEs for frame encapsulation (FE) service that are located in Chicago and New York.

Figure 1.14 illustrates the Internet Traffic Report for MAE-East when the first edition of this book was written. Note that Figure 1.14 illustrates two graphs, each indicating activity for the past 24 hours. The top graph indicates a traffic index, which represents a score from 0 to 100, where 0 is slow and 100 is fast. The traffic index is computed by comparing the current response of a Ping echo to all previous responses from the same router over the past seven days, with a score of 0 to 100 assigned to the current response, depending on whether this response is better or worse than all previous responses from the route.

The second graph indicates response time in milliseconds (ms). The response time represents a round trip computed by sending traffic from one location to another and back to its origination.

If you could scroll down Figure 1.14, you would be able to view a third graph, labeled packet loss. That graph indicates the percent of packets dropped by the router or otherwise lost. Typically, routers discard packets when they become overloaded. Thus, this represents a measurement of network reliability.

The three metrics displayed by the Internet Traffic Report partially shown in Figure 1.14 can be considered to represent bottlenecks when information flows between ISP networks. That is, the peering point can be viewed as a funnel through which all traffic from one Internet "network" destined to a different "network" must flow. Because the flow of data between ISPs is usually not symmetrical, this means that, at a point in time, some ISPs may have more data to transfer through a peering point than the connection can handle. When the situation occurs, the connection becomes a bottleneck. Although the peering point could be upgraded, many times only a few customers operating servers experience a problem, and the ISP where the server resides may very well be reluctant to upgrade the peering point due to the cost involved. Similarly, the installation of additional peering points can represent a significant cost. Even if both existing peering points are upgraded and additional peering points established to provide extra internetwork connectivity, doing so takes time and may not appreciably decrease the delays currently experienced by clients on one network attempting to access servers on another network. The latter situation results in a fixed number of router hops needing to be traversed when a client on one network needs to access information from a server residing on another network.

In developing this new book edition, this author returned to MAE-East. In doing so, he realized that, over the past five years, considerable progress had occurred in upgrading the data rate of connections, but the total traffic on the Internet had also increased. Thus, it would be interesting to determine if the increase in capacity could accommodate the increased traffic.

Figure 1.15 can be considered as a return to MAE-East five years later, occurring in November 2009. In this illustration, note that while the Global Index remained at 83, significant strides had occurred at MAE-East due to its data transmission upgrades that apparently outpaced the increase in traffic. If you examine the traffic index, response time, and packet loss, you will note a line near zero for each.

Figure 1.15 Returning to MAE–East in November 2009.

Thus, MAE-East has made significant strides in processing data without losing data or having unacceptable levels of response time.

Because of the previously mentioned problems associated with packet loss and increased response time, another solution evolved during the 1990s. This solution was based upon moving server content from a central location to multiple distributed locations across the Internet. In doing so, Web pages were moved closer to the ultimate client requester, reducing both the number of router hops a request would have to traverse as well as the round-trip propagation time. In addition, since Web pages are now closer to the end user, traffic would not have to flow through peering-point bottlenecks, further enhancing traffic flow and minimizing traffic delays.

The effort involved in distributing Web pages so that they are available at different locations is known as content delivery networking, and that is the subject of this book. Thus, a portion of the increased performance at MAE-East can be attributed in part to the growth in content delivery networks. While we will probe much deeper into this topic in subsequent chapters, for now we can note that the role of the modern CDN is to facilitate the retrieval of Web-based information by distributing the information closer to the ultimate requester. In doing so, CDN facilitates a variety of client-server communications to include pull, push, and even Web crawling.

1.3.5 Video Considerations

In concluding this chapter, a few words concerning video are warranted. Although video was being incorporated onto Web sites when the first version of this book was written, both server storage and network bandwidth were constraints that severely limited its use. Over the past decade, data storage has grown by a factor of 10 to 100, depending upon the technology considered. In comparison, LAN transfers have increased from Fast Ethernet's 100 Mbps to 10 Gigabit, while wide-area networks that were primarily using T1 lines at 1.544 Mbps have, in many cases, been replaced by Optical Carrier (OC) data rates of 155.52 Mbps (OC-3), 622.08 Mbps (OC-12), and 2488.32 (OC-48).

Due to the increased storage capacity of servers and the ability of both wide- and local-area networks to handle a significantly increased data flow, video has significantly increased as an option on Web pages for users to view. In addition, it's now possible to download movies, view television episodes, and even connect your television to the Internet to view shows on the "big screen." In addition, in an era of terrorism, many cities now have extensive video camera networks, with real-time feeds from many locations displayed on a single console that the operator can toggle and expand upon when he or she needs additional information available from a full-screen image. While many city feeds bypass the conventional Internet, the relatively low cost of video cams has resulted in many Web sites providing viewers with views of a resort, scenes of sunrise, and other actions where a picture is truly worth a thousand words.

However, for video to be successful, Web developers need to consider the fact that not all potential viewers are similar. This means that Web developers need to consider the fact that some potential viewers may reside on legacy LANs operating at 10 Mbps, while other viewers could reside on cable or DSL connections or on Gigabit LANs. In addition, the flow of data from the server to potential viewers can take divergent routes, with some flows going through congested peering points while other data flows do not. Thus, Web developers that incorporate video should, at a minimum, provide end users with the option to select the type of Internet connection they are using. Other options can include the frame rate and resolution to use to view a selected video. By incorporating these options, you can tailor the delivery of video to the different networking and computer capabilities of potential viewers.

2
CLIENT-SERVER MODELS

In the first chapter of this book, we considered client-server architecture to represent a single model that varied by the manner by which data flowed between each computer. If data flowed directly from client to server, the architecture could be represented as what is referred to as a two-tier architecture, with the client considered to represent the first tier, while the server is considered to represent the second tier. If data flowed from client to server and, depending upon the request, then flowed to another server, we could refer to the architecture as being a three-tier architecture. As a review, in a two-tier architecture, the user interface is typically located in the user's desktop, while the database being accessed is located on a server that provides services to many clients. In a three-tier (also referred to as multitier) architecture, a middle layer was added between the client and the database to be accessed. The middle layer can queue requests, execute applications, provide scheduling, and even prioritize work in progress. When considering trade-offs between a two-tier and a multitier architecture, it is important to note that the latter will always increase the data flow on a LAN, and this increase needs to be considered, especially if the network is approaching congestion prior to implementing a multitier solution to a database retrieval problem. In addition, because a number of different types of software products can reside at each tier, this can result in a series of different client-server models, which is the topic of this chapter.

In this chapter, we will turn our attention to a core set of software products that operate on both client and server. The interaction of such products results in different client-server models, with each model having varying characteristics that are affected by latency as data moves across the Internet, by traffic on each Internet Service Provider (ISP) network, and by the traffic routed through any points of presence as data flows from a client located on one ISP network to a server located on a different ISP network, with a response that then flows back to the client.

To begin our examination of client-server models, we will follow a familiar tune and "begin at the beginning." That is, we will examine the three tiers that can be employed in different client-server architectures. In doing so, we will note different types of popular software that can operate on each tier. Once this is accomplished, we will use the preceding information as a foundation to probe deeper into the characteristics of different software on each tier, including their relationship with other software as well as the effect upon software operations as the distance between client and server increases from residence on a common network to computers located on different networks. Because of the role of images and video in the modern Web-page environment, we will focus our discussion of certain types of software to include the use of images and video technology.

2.1 Overview

Figure 2.1 illustrates, in a block-diagram format, the three tiers associated with modern client-server architecture. In this block diagram, potential software programs are indicated with respect to the tier where they would normally reside. In addition, the common operating systems used at each tier are indicated to provide readers with additional information concerning platforms that are commonly used in the modern client-server environment.

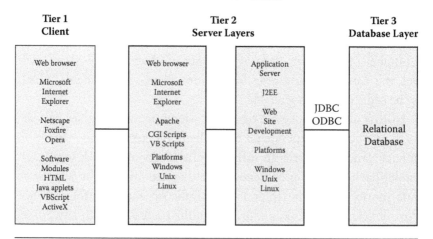

Figure 2.1   The client-server architectural model.

2.2 Client Operations

In the wonderful world of the Internet, the browser represents the client. The purpose of the browser, besides surfing the Web, is to enable users to request documents from a server as well as to display the serviced request. While Netscape Corporation developed the first commercially available browser, Microsoft Corporation's Internet Explorer now dominates the browser market, with approximately an 80% market share. Other browsers such as Netscape, the open-system Mozilla Firefox, Opera, and other products cumulatively hold the remainder of the market.

Browsers differ in the version of the Hyper Text Markup Language (HTML) they support as well as in their support of code modules, plug-ins, amount of customization users can perform, and caching capability. As we noted in the first chapter in this book, browsers are not static, and their capabilities can vary considerably based upon the version used. Because of the market share of Microsoft's Internet Explorer, we will primarily focus our attention on this browser when discussing client operations in this book. However, due to the rise in the popularity of the Mozilla Firefox browser, this author will periodically use this browser to illustrate certain browser operations.

2.2.1 URLs

Uniform resource locators (URLs) are short strings that identify the location of various resources on the Web. URLs are defined in Request for Comment (RFC) 1738, which was published in December 1994. While RFC 1738 does a good job of defining how resources are addressed, one persistent problem is the fact that it limits the use of allowed characters to a subset of the U.S. version of the American Standard Code for Information Interchange (ASCII). Because modern browsers commonly support the HyperText Markup Language (HTML) version 4, which is not only compatible with the International Standards Organization (ISO) 8859 code but also all Unicode characters, this means that there are some characters, specifically those above Hex 255 in the Unicode character set, that should not be used in URLs. In addition, there are certain characters that are reserved for special use, such as the dollar sign ($), ampersand (&), and question mark (?), while other characters such as the less-than (<) and greater-than (>) symbols have the potential of being misinterpreted when used in a URL. Thus, when constructing URLs, it's important to consider the fact that when you diverge from the use of alpha-numeric and defined special characters, you may need to reference material that illustrates how to encode them for use.

The resources defined by URLs can include documents, images, downloadable files, electronic mailboxes and even services. The general format of a URL is as follows:

Protocol://location

Note that the general format commences with a protocol, followed by a colon, which in turn is followed by two forward slash characters and a location. Two common examples of a protocol are http (HyperText Transfer Protocol) and ftp (File Transfer Protocol). The location can include a significant degree of variety, depending upon the actual location where information resides. For example, the home page of the Web server whose domain is popcorn.com would be accessed as follows:

http://www.popcorn.com

In the above example, the use of http tells the computer to use the hypertext transport protocol, while www references the host name at the domain popcorn.com.

Not shown in the above URL example is the port number used by http. By default, the port number is 80. If, for some reason, the port on the server being accessed uses a different port number, then the URL would become

http://www.popcorn.com:number

where number represents the port number.

The URL preceding this last URL would take you to the home page of the Web server at the domain popcorn.com, whose address is www.popcorn.com and which is configured to receive HTML queries on port 80. We should note that we can also specify a path to a par-ticular location on a computer, pass parameters to scripts via a query string, and even refer to a specific section within an identified resource through the use of a fragment. Thus, a more detailed URL format would be as follows:

Protocol://domain name[IP address]:[port][path][Query][fragment]

It should be noted that you can use either a registered domain name or an IP address for the destination location in a URL. For example, the relatively new search engine from Microsoft called Bing can be accessed by the domain bing.com or its IP address of 64.4.8.147. It should also be noted that the host name and domain name of a URL are case-insensitive, as the Domain Name Service (DNS) is programmed to ignore case. Thus, bing.com and BING.COM both reference the home page of the search engine. However, to add some confusion to addressing, the file path name used to specify the location of a document or program is case-sensitive; however, many servers will treat such data as being case-insensitive, especially servers running Microsoft Windows. Thus,

http://64.4.8.147/search?q=bing&go=&form=QBLH&qs=n

and

http://64.4.8.147/SEARCH?q=BING&go=&form=QBLH&qs=n

would direct you to the same search page results on Microsoft's Bing search engine, while modifying the two URLs for access to a different search engine might result in different results when different cases are used. One interesting Web site you might consider using is http://www.hcidata.info/host2ip.cgi, which converts host/domain names to IP addresses while also performing a reverse operation.

As an example of the use of an expanded URL, let's assume that we want to log onto the home page of the discount brokerage firm TDAmeritrade. You could either point your browser to the TDAmeritrade home page and select a menu entry that will prompt you to enter your user information, or you could go directly to the access log-on page. For the latter, you would enter the URL as

https://wwws.ameritrade.com/cgi-bin/apps/Main

From the preceding URL, note that the protocol was changed to https, where the s stands for secure. Also note that the CGI (Common Gateway Interface) represents a set of rules that describes how a Web server communicates with other software that can be on the client and the server. In our example, the TDAmeritrade access page will display a small form requiring you to enter your UserID and password. The CGI program will process the entered data. Later in this chapter we will take a more detailed look at CGI.

To specify a path to a particular document, file, or service on a server results in the use of one or more additional forward slashes (/) following the server address and optional port number. When the Web was evolving, it was common for some organizations to hide their presence by using a port other than port 80. Unfortunately, the use of port-scanning technology resulted in port hiding as a security mechanism being rapidly replaced by the use of encryption. Within the URL, a variety of special characters can be used to effect different operations. For example, the question mark (?) can be used to delimit the boundary between the URL of a queryable object and a set of words used to express a query on that object. For example:

http://www.popcorn.com/?bucketprice.dat

2.2.1.1 Absolute and Relative   In concluding our initial remarks about URLs, it should be noted that they can be absolute or relative. An absolute URL is one that directly points to the exact location of a file. Absolute URLs must be unique. Thus, if two absolute URLs are identical, this means that they must point to the same file. For example,

http://popcorn.com/taffy/bucketprice.dat

is an absolute URL.

In comparison, a relative URL points to the location of a file from a point of reference. That point of reference is commonly beneath the location of the target file and can be considered as a reminder of the role of the old Disk Operating System (DOS), which used the double dot (..) to identify changing a path down through the use of the Change Directory (CD) command followed by the double dot (CD..) or the use of a single dot (.) to indicate the current directory. Thus, if the initial absolute URL took us to http://popcorn.com, then a relative URL such as ../taffy/bucketprice.dat would reference the file bucketprice. dat in the directory taffy on the domain popcorn.com. If you were at that location, you could then use the URL ./salty/bucketprice.dat to reference the file bucketprice.dat in the directory salty, assuming that its location is presently under the current directory.

2.2.1.2 Shortening URLs With the need to specify relatively long URLs and the constraints of such services as Twitter, which limits users to 140 characters per post, a need arose for the significant shortening of URLs. Thus, this author would be remiss if he did not mention two services and briefly discuss how they can be used to shorten relatively long URLs as well as provide readers with the knowledge that, when viewing a URL, you might be viewing an abbreviated version of a rather lengthy actual uniform resource locator.

Two services that provide persons with the ability to significantly shorten URLs are Bit.ly and TinyURL.com. For example, using the latter, this author was able to shorten the URL

http://www.popcorn.com/files/html/special/dfg.mpeg

which has a length of 50 characters, into the URL

http://tinyurl.com/ye66ga7

which has a length of 26 characters.

If you are using Bit.ly, the 50-character URL previously mentioned would be replaced by the 20-character URL

http://bit.ly/6lKkiE

Thus, if you're viewing a URL and note the inclusion of "tinyurl.com" or "bit.ly," you are actually viewing a truncated URL.

2.2.2 HTML

The document typically requested by the use of a URL is more often than not encoded in HTML (HyperText Markup Language). HTML represents a markup language that defines a structure for a document without specifying the details of layout.

2.2.2.1 Versions The origin of HTML can be traced back to 1980, when Tim Berners-Lee, a physicist at CERN in Switzerland, developed a system for researchers to facilitate the sharing of documents. Berners-Lee used this effort, referred to as ENQZURE, as a base to develop HTML, programming both a browser and server software to facilitate the surfing of what became known as the World Wide Web. In 1991, Berners-Lee made available to the public a description of HTML that covered 20 elements, of which a majority are still incorporated into the latest version of HTML, referred to as HTML version 5.

The development of HTML was considerably influenced by the Standard Generalized Markup Language (SGML), which is an International Standards Organization (ISO) standard technology for defining generalized markup languages for documents. The first HTML draft specification was published by the Internet Engineering Task Force (IETF) in 1993, followed by an HTML+ draft in 1994. During 1995, the IETF HTML Working Group completed its HTML 2.0 specification, which was published as RFC 1866. Other notable versions of HTML include HTML 3.2, which appeared in January 1997; HTML 4.0, which was first published in December 1997 and then reissued with some editing in April 1998; HTML 4.01, which was issued in December 1999; and HTML 5, which was published as a working draft in January 2008. Because browsers must consider the fact that servers around the world will operate a variety of HTML versions, it's of critical importance that a modern browser be backward compatible to support various versions of the markup language.

2.2.2.2 HTML Documents   HTML documents are plain-text ASCII files that can be created using a text editor or word processor that enables text to be saved in ASCII format. The fundamental component of the structure of a text document is referred to as an *element*. Examples of elements include heads, tables, paragraphs, and lists. Through the use of tags, you mark the elements of a file for a browser to display. Tags consist of a left angle bracket (<), a tag name, and a right angle bracket (>). Tags are usually paired with the termination tag prefixed with a backward slash (/), such that <h1> and </h1> would be used to surround a header level 1 name. Similarly, <h2> and </h2> would be used to surround a header level 2 name, with up to 5 levels capable of being defined.

Although most elements have a start tag and an end tag, some do not. For example, a line break <br> does not have any content and does not have a closing tag.

An elementary example of a hypertext-coded document is presented in Figure 2.2.

```
<html>
<head>
<title>
Title of document
</title>
</head>

<body>
<h1>Header level 1</h1>
Some text goes here
After this text we add a line break<br>
<h2>Header level 2</h2>
Some text goes here
</body>
```

Figure 2.2 A brief HTML document.

2.2.2.3 Font Control Within the set of elements of HTML are markups that enable one to alter the appearance of text. For example, the pair of tags boldface indicate that the visual display should be rendered as boldface, while <i>italic</i> results in text being displayed in italics. Table 2.1 lists seven font-control elements available in HTML.

In addition to the font-control elements listed in Table 2.1, you can specify the type of font via the use of the <Font Face=> tag, the color of the font by the use of the <Font Color=> tag, and the size of the font by the use of the <Font Size=> tag, each of which is delimited by the </Font> tag. You can also mix various font-control elements, generating, for example, bold italic blue text in a particular size. However, it's important to note that the correct rendering of tags depends upon the browser used. While most modern browsers are fine, older browsers may represent a potential problem in displaying certain tags or combinations of tags.

Table 2.1 Font-Control Elements Available In HTML

...	**Bold**
<I>...</i>	*Italics*
<u>...</u>	Underline
<s>...</s>	~~Strike-through~~
<tt>...</tt>	Teletype
^{...}	Superscript ($E=MC^2$)
_{...}	Subscript (H_2O)

2.2.2.4 Hypertext Links   The Web can be considered to represent a set of network-accessible information resources constructed upon three basic ideas. Those ideas include URLs that provide a global location and naming scheme for accessing resources, protocols such as HTTP for accessing resources, and hypertext in the form of HTML that enables one document to contain links to other resources. Under HTML, a unidirectional pointer, referred to as an *anchor*, is used in a tag along with a URL to function as a hypertext link. The letter *a* is used in an anchor tag as an abbreviation for *anchor*, with the format for a hypertext link as follows:

   <a href = destination>label </a>
where the <a> and </a> tags represent an anchor, "destination" represents a URL, and "label" represents highlighted information displayed by the browser or selected results in the browser after retrieving and displaying information from the destination. That destination is hidden from view until you move the cursor over the label. At that time, the URL hidden in the anchor will be displayed on the bottom line of the browser. One example of the use of an anchor is as follows:

   See:<a href = www.popcorn.com/tasty> for tasty popcorn </a>
      information.

2.2.2.5 Adding Images   When using HTML, an image is embedded into an HTML page through the use of the <img> tag. The general format of the img tag is shown as follows, where attributes shown in brackets are optional.

   <img src="URL" alt="text displayed" [attribute]...[attribute] />

   Although the <img> tag supports a wide range of attributes, only two are required: src and alt. The first specifies the URL of the image, while the second specifies an alternate text for an image. For example, assume that you wish to incorporate a picture labeled "homeview.jpg" onto a Web page and display the text "Our Factory" if clients have configured their browsers such that they do not display images. Assuming that the picture is located on the server at www.popcorn.com/files/html, you would use the following <img> tag:

   <img src="www.popcorn.com/files/html/homeview.jpg" alt="Our factory" />.

Table 2.2   Optional <img> Tag Attributes

ATTRIBUTE	VALUES	DESCRIPTION
align	top, bottom, middle, left, right	Specifies the alignment of an image according to surrounding elements (deprecated)
border	pixels	Specifies the width of the border around an image (deprecated)
height	pixels	Specifies the height of an image
hspace	pixels	Specifies the white space on left and right side of an image (deprecated)
ismap	ismap	Specifies an image as a server-side image-map
longdesc	URL	Specifies the URL to a document that contains a long description of an image
usemap	#mapname	Specifies an image as a client-side image-map
vspace	pixels	Specifies the white space on top and bottom of an image (deprecated)
width	pixels	Specifies the width of an image

Table 2.2 lists nine optional <img> tag attributes and a brief description of their use. Note that the align, border, hspace, and vspace attributes are referred to as "deprecated." This means that these attributes
have been superseded by what many consider more functional or flexible alternatives and were declared as deprecated in HTML 4 by the
W3C, which is the consortium that sets the HTML standards. Most
browsers can be expected to support deprecated tags and attributes,
but eventually they are likely to become obsolete, and thus future
support cannot be guaranteed. The five deprecated attributes are still
commonly used, although style sheets provide more flexible methods
of manipulating images. However, since the primary purpose of this
book is to discuss Content Delivery Networks and networking, we
can use our knowledge of <img> tag attributes without resorting to a
discussion of style sheets.

2.2.2.5.1 Image Formats   From a technical perspective, all images,
including video, can be considered as a series of images occurring at
a particular frame rate, and these are stored as data files. However,
we can categorize images as being either in a raster or vector format.
A raster format results in an image being broken down into a series
of dots, with the dots referred to as pixels. The vast majority of
image formats used on the Web are raster format images, such as the
Graphics Interchange Format (GIF), JPEG (format developed by the

Table 2.3   Popular Image File Formats

BMP	Bitmapped images stored under Windows
CLP	Windows Clipart
DCX	ZOFT Paintbrush
GIF	Graphics Interchange Format
JIF and JPEG	Joint Photographic Experts Group Related Image Format
MAC	MacPaint
MSP	MacPaint new version
PCT	Macintosh PICT format
PCX	ZSoft Paintbrush
PNG	Portable Network Graphics file format
PSP	Paint Shop Pro format
RAW	Unencoded image format
RLE	Run-Length Encoding
TIFF	Tagged Image File Format
WPG	WordPerfect image format

Joint Photographic Experts Group), and bitmapped (BMP). In comparison, a vector image is created via a series of mathematical expressions, such as those used by CorelDraw (CDR), Microsoft's Windows Metafiles (EFW), and the Hewlett-Packard Graphics Language (HPGL). In this book, we will focus our attention on raster images. Table 2.3 lists 15 examples of image file formats. Of the 15 listed, the most popular formats used on the Web are JPEG, followed by GIF and BMP, which are encountered upon occasion.

The use of JPEG images is very popular because they provide a lossy compression capability that can significantly reduce data storage and transmission requirements. Later in this book, we will discuss the key advantages associated with both image and video compression.

2.2.2.6 Adding Video   There are three common methods associated with adding video to a Web page. One method involves using the <embed…> tag to display a media file. In actuality, the use of the <embed…> tag places a browser plug-in on the Web page. The plug-in represents a special program located on the client computer that supports viewing the file. The most common plug-ins are for sounds and movies.

The embed tag does not require a closing tag and operates similar to the image tag. When you use the <embed…> tag you must include a src (source) attribute to define the location of the video. You do this by specifying an applicable URL that, similar to other URLs, can be

Table 2.4 <embed...> Tag Attributes

ATTRIBUTE	MEANING
SRC	URL of resource to be embedded
WIDTH	Width of area in which to show resource
HEIGHT	Height of area in which to show resource
ALIGN	How text should flow around the picture
NAME	Name of the embedded object
PLUGINSPAGE	Where to get the plug-in software
HIDDEN	Specify if the play/stop/pause is visible or not; values are true and false
HREF	Make this object a link
TARGET AUTOSTART	Frame to link to specify if the sound/movie should start automatically; values are true and false
LOOP	Specifies if the media is continuously played; values are true and false
PLAYCOUNT	Specify how many times to play the sound/movie; value is a number
VOLUME	Specify how loud to play the sound; value is a numeric from 0 to 100
CONTROLS	Specify which sound control to display
STARTTIME	Define how far into the sound to start and stop
ENDTIME	Define when to finish playing

local or global. The <embed...> tag supports a wide range of attributes, most of which are listed in Table 2.4.

The default value for the CONTROLS attribute (Table 2.4) is CONSOLE. This value results in most browsers displaying a full-sized set of controls, including a start button, a pause button, a stop button, and a volume control or lever.

The general format of the <embed...> tag is shown as follows:

<embed src="URL" [attribute1][...attribute n] />

The <embed ...> tag uses the SRC attribute to indicate the location of the plug-in data file. Typically, it also includes a WIDTH and HEIGHT of the plug-in area. Unfortunately, different browsers render different media types differently, so sometimes selecting the height and width may require some trial and error as well as the use of different browsers. For example, the following code embeds a Motion Picture Experts Group (MPEG) video called Popcorn-Technology located on the server in the domain popcorn.com into the client Web page and immediately starts the video:

<embed src=http://www.popcorn.com/files/html/Popcorn-
   Technology.mpeg
autostart="true" />

Note that <embed …> is not a part of the HTML 4 specifications, but it is still widely supported by modern browsers. Unlike other tags, the attributes used by <embed …> depend on the type of plug-in being used. Perhaps this lax policy explains why <embed …> was rejected by the HTML standards makers.

A second method that can be used to place media files onto a Web page is by placing the URL of the media files into the HREF attribute of an anchor tag. HREF indicates the URL being linked to and makes the anchor into a link. For example, the following tag creates a link to view the Popcorn-Technology mpeg video and displays the message "View the Video," which when clicked results in the video being displayed in the client browser.

<a href=http://www.popcorn.com/files/html/Popcorn-
Technology.mpeg>View the Video</a>

Recognizing the role of video on modern Web pages, the developers of HTML 5 added a video element to the specification. The video element added under HTML 5 functions as a block-level element type, which means that it is within the body of an HTML document and makes up the structure of a document. Similar to the embed tag previously described, the video element defined in HTML 5 includes a series of attributes. Those attributes include autoplay, autobuffer, controls, height, loop, poster, src, and width.

Two of the previously mentioned attributes deserve a bit of elaboration. First, the autobuffer attribute, when specified, results in the video automatically beginning buffering. This attribute should be used when it's considered highly probable that a client browser will navigate to a Web page to view the specified video and not to a page that has video embedded along with other content, such as a news organization's Web page with multiple videos available for selection. Secondly, the poster attribute results in specifying a URL of a poster frame that is displayed until the client plays the video, and its absence results in nothing being displayed until the first frame becomes available, which is then displayed as the poster frame.

2.2.2.6.1 Video Formats   Similar to images, there are a number of video file formats in use on the Web. Some of the more popular file formats include the Apple Computer's QuickTime .mov and .qt files,

Microsoft's .avi (Audio Video Interleave), the SWF standard Adobe Flash file format, FLV which represents a special type of Flash video embedded in an SWFF file, MPEG-4 video files with the extension .mp4, Real Media .rm and .rmvb files, and Microsoft's Windows Media Video files with the extension .wmv. Unfortunately, at the time this book revision was performed, Microsoft's Windows Media Video support of MPEG-4 video was limited to a nonstandard MPEG-4 codec (coder-decoder) that is not compatible with a later version of MPEG-4 that was standardized. Similarly, there are various degrees of incompatibility between video files, which led to the popularity of video converters, some of which support over 30 file types.

2.2.2.6.2 Video Servers and Streaming Video A video server represents a computer typically dedicated to providing storage for video. One of the major applications provided by a video server is the support of streaming video, which represents a one-way video transmission over a data network. Streaming video is widely employed on the Web as well as on company networks to play video clips and video broadcasts. In the home, computers in a home network can be configured to stream video to digital media hubs connected to a home theater. Unlike movie files that are played after the entire file has been downloaded and stored, streaming video is played shortly after only a small amount is received and buffered, and the content downloaded is not stored at the destination computer

When the streaming video is broadcast live, such as the Victoria Secrets annual fashion show, it is commonly referred to as "real-time video." However, technically, real time means no delays, and there is a slight built-in delay in streaming video.

The streaming-media data-storage requirements can be significant and usually result in the need to employ a separate server. You can easily calculate the uncompressed data storage requirements by using the following formula:

storage size (in mebibytes) = length (in seconds) × length (pixels) × width (pixels) × frame rate (frames/second)/8 × 1024 × 1024

since 1 mebibyte = 8 × 1024 × 1024 bits.

If you have a 60-second uncompressed 420 × 320 video clip operating at a rate of 30 frames per second (fps), then the storage size becomes

MiB = 60 seconds × 420 pixels × 320 pixels × 30 fps/8 × 1024 ×
1024 = 28.839

for a single 1-minute video. When we think of the evolution of the
PC, less than a decade ago a 1-minute video would have required
most of the storage capacity of the computer's hard drive. Even with
the modern 1-Tbyte storage capacity available on many PCs, this
would allow only 30 minutes of video to be stored, which is why data
compression is critical when working with video images.

2.2.3 HTTP

The Hypertext Transport Protocol (HTTP) represents a stateless,
connectionless, reliable protocol. HTTP is used to transfer Web pages
from a Web server to a client's Web browser using TCP (Transmission
Control Protocol), usually on port 80. Here the term *stateless* refers to
the fact that each HTTP transmission occurs without needing information about what previously occurred. The protocol is connectionless,
which means that an HTTP message can occur without establishing
a connection with the recipient. Finally, HTTP is a reliable protocol,
as it uses the TCP transport protocol, which provides a reliable
error-detection and -correction facility. In Chapter 3 we will probe
more deeply into TCP/IP; however, for now we will simply note that
HTTP is transported by TCP within an IP datagram.

2.2.3.1 Versions   The current version of HTTP is 1.1, with previous
versions being noted as 0.9 and 1.0. The first line of any HTTP message
should include the version number, such as HTTP/1.1.

2.2.3.2 Operation   As previously noted, HTTP messages are stateless,
connectionless, and reliable. HTTP messages fall into three broad
categories: Request, Response, and Close.

2.2.3.2.1 Request Message   Every HTTP interaction between client
and server commences with a client request. The client operator enters
a URL in the browser, either by clicking on a hyperlink, typing the
URL into the browser address field, or selecting a bookmark. As
a result of one of the preceding actions, the browser retrieves the

```
Request=Simple Request/Full-Request
Simple-Request="GET" SP Request-URL CRLF
Full-Request=Request-Line
              *(General-Header
              | Request-Header
              | Entity-Header
              CRLF
              [Entity-Body]
```

Figure 2.3   HTTP request formats.

selected resource. To accomplish this task, the browser creates an HTTP request as follows:

```
Request Line    GET/index.html HTTP/1.1
Header Fields   Host: www.popcorn.com
User-Agent      Mozilla/4.0
```

In this HTTP request, note that the User-Agent represents software that retrieves and displays Web content. Netscape's browser is identified by the "Mozilla" user agent, while Microsoft's Internet Explorer would have the string "MSIE" and version number placed in the User-Agent field.

In addition to the GET request, a browser can issue several other types of requests. Thus, let's turn our attention to the structure of HTTP Request methods, including the format of such requests.

As previously noted, a Request message is transmitted from a client to a server. The first line of the message includes the request method to be applied to the resource, the identifier of the resource, and the protocol version in use. To provide backward compatibility with prior versions of HTTP, there are two valid formats for an HTTP request, both of which are indicated in Figure 2.3.

In examining the HTTP Request message formats shown in Figure 2.3, several items warrant discussion. First, if an HTTP/1.0 server receives a Simple-Request, it must respond with an HTTP/0.9 Simple-Response. An HTTP/1.0 client capable of receiving a Full-Response should never generate a Simple-Request. Secondly, the Request-line begins with a request-method token, followed by the Request-URL and the protocol version, ending with a carriage-return line feed (CRLF). Thus, for a Full-Request,

Request-line=Method SP Request-URL SP HTTP-Version CRLF

The Method token identifies the method to be performed on the resource identified by the Request-URL, where, under HTTP 1.0,

Method="GET"/"HEAD"/"POST"/extension method

and

extension-method=token

The "GET" token is used to retrieve information identified by the Request-URL. The "HEAD" token functions similar to the "GET"; however, the server does not return any Entity-Body (information) in the response, i.e., only HTTP headers are returned. The "POST" token provides a mechanism to annotate existing resources, post a message, or provide a block of data to a server, such as the submission of a form.

When the client transmits a Request, it usually sends several header fields. As previously noted, those fields include a field name, a colon, one or more space (SP) characters, and a value. After the Request-line and General-Header, one or more optional HTTP Request-Headers can follow that are used to pass additional information about the client and its request, or to add certain conditions to the request. The format of a header field line is as follows:

Field Name	Value
Content Type	text/html

Table 2.5 lists seven common HTTP request headers and provides a brief description of each.

One of the more interesting aspects of an HTTP Request is the Referrer header field. If you were browsing a Web page and clicked on an anchor, the Referrer header field informs the destination server

Table 2.5 Common HTTP Request Headers

HEADER	DESCRIPTION
HOST	Specifies the target hostname
Content-length	Specifies the length (in bytes) of the request content
Content-type	Specifies the media type of the request
Authentication	Specifies the username and password of the user
Refer	Specifies the URL that referred the user to the current resource
User-agent	Specifies the name, version, and platform of the client
Cookie	Returns a name/value pair set by the server on a previous response

```
Request=Simple Request/Full-Request
Simple-Request=[Entity-Body]
Full-Request=Request-Line
              *(General-Header
              | Request-Header
              | Entity-Header
              CRLF
              [Entity-Body]
```

Figure 2.4 HTTP response formats.

of the URL (i.e., the page being viewed) from where you invoked the anchor. Thus, this information can be used to determine indirect traffic flow as well as the effect of advertising.

2.2.3.2.2 Response Message After receiving and interpreting a Request message, a Web server replies with an HTTP Response message. The format of an HTTP Response message is shown in Figure 2.4.

Similar to a Request message, a Simple-Response should only be returned in response to an HTTP/0.9 Simple-Request. The Status-line is the first line of a Full-Response message and includes the protocol version, followed by a numeric status code and its associated textual phrase, with each element separated by SP (space) characters. Thus, the format of the Status-line is

Status-line=HTTP-Version SP Status-Code SP Reason-Phrase
    CRLF

Table 2.6 lists many currently defined status codes and their associated reason phrases.

The use of status codes can reflect multiple situations. For example, if a client went to a restricted Web server location, the server would reject the request with a "401" message. However, if the server wishes the client to authenticate its request, it would do so by first rejecting the request with a "401" message and indicate in the "www-Authenticate" field information about the authentication requirements so that the client can determine if it has authorization to authenticate. If it does, it would then include its User-ID and password in the subsequent request.

2.2.3.3 HTTP 1.1 The most popular version of HTTP is 1.1, which includes several improvements over prior versions of the protocol.

Table 2.6 Defined Response Status Codes and Reason Phrases

STATUS CODE	REASON PHRASE
100	Continue
101	Switching protocols
102	Processing
200	OK
201	Created
202	Accepted
204	No content
205	Reset content
206	Partial content
207	Multi-status
301	Moved permanently
302	Moved temporarily
304	Not modified
305	Use proxy services
306	Switch proxy
307	Temporary redirect
400	Bad request
401	Unauthorized
403	Forbidden
404	Not found
406	Not accepted
407	Proxy authorization required
408	Request timeout
409	Conflict
410	Gone (service)
415	Unsupported media type
500	Internal server error
501	Not implemented
502	Bad gateway
503	Service unavailable
504	Gateway timeout
505	HTTP version not supported
507	Insufficient storage

Some of those improvements include chunked data transfers; support for persistent connections, which reduces TCP overhead; byte ranges, which enable portions of a document to be requested; hostname identification, which allows virtual hosts; content negotiation, which permits multiple languages; and proxy support. While HTTP1.1 is more efficient than prior versions of the protocol, it is also more

Table 2.7   HTTP 1.1 Request Methods

METHOD	DESCRIPTION
GET	Asks the server for a given resource and no content
HEAD	Similar to GET, but only returns HTTP headers and no content
POST	Asks the server to modify information stored on the server
PUT	Asks the server to create or replace a resource on the server
DELETE	Asks the server to delete a resource on the server
CONNECT	Used to allow SSL (secure socket layer) connections to tunnel through HTTP connections
OPTIONS	Asks the server to list the request methods available for a given resource
TRACE	Asks the server to echo back the request headers as it receives them

complex. For example, the number of HTTP Request Methods is now increased to eight. Table 2.7 lists the expanded set of Request Methods supported by HTTP1.1 along with a brief description of each method.

2.2.3.4 State Maintenance   As previously discussed, the HTTP protocol is stateless. This means that an HTTP session only lasts from a browser request to the server response, after which any subsequent request is independent of the prior request. The stateless nature of HTTP represents a problem if you use the browser to perform activities where information needs to be maintained, such as selecting items from an e-commerce Web site to fill a shopping cart.

The solution to the stateless nature of HTTP occurs in two ways. The most common method used to overcome the stateless nature of HTTP sessions occurs through the use of cookies. A second method occurs by the use of a hidden field in an HTML form whose value is set by the server.

2.2.3.4.1 Cookies   A cookie is a short file that functions as an identifier. The cookie is created by a Web server accessed by the client as a mechanism for the server to store information about the client, such as its preferences when visiting the site or the items selected by the user for potential purchase.

Cookies are stored on the client for a predefined period of time. Each time a client transmits a request to a server, any cookie previously issued by the server is included in the client request and can be used by the server to restore the state of the client. From a security perspective, once a cookie is saved on a client, it can only be transmitted to the Web site that created the cookie.

If you're using Microsoft's Internet Explorer, you can view your browser's cookies by selecting Tools> Internet Options and then selecting the Settings button in the Temporary Internet Files area and the View Files button in the resulting Settings window. Figure 2.5 illustrates the three dialog boxes that are displayed. The initial box in the upper left is displayed once you select the Internet Options from the Tools menu. Selecting the Settings button results in the display of the dialog box labeled Temporary Internet Files and History Settings. Finally, selecting the View Files button results in the box in the foreground, showing some of the cookies stored on the author's computer. Note that the left portion of the dialog box in the foreground provides a description of the cookie, including its Internet address, when it expires, as well as when it was last checked, accessed, and modified.

2.2.3.4.1.1 Types of Cookies   There are two types of cookies, referred to as *persistent* and *temporary*. A persistent cookie is one stored as a file on your computer that remains stored when you close your browser. A persistent cookie can only be read by the Web site that created it when you subsequently access that site again. In comparison, a temporary cookie is only stored for your current browsing activity and is deleted when you close your browser. Through the browser settings, the user can choose to automatically accept or block all cookies, or be prompted to accept or block specific cookies; however, when cookies are blocked, certain activities, such as filling a shopping cart, may be difficult or impossible to achieve.

2.2.3.4.2 Hidden Fields   A second method that can be used to overcome the stateless nature of HTTP sessions occurs through the use of hidden fields in an HTML form. The hidden field, as its name implies, is hidden from view. The server can set a value in the hidden field of a form, which when submitted by the client is returned to the server. By placing state information in hidden fields, the server can restore the state of the client.

2.2.4 Browser Programs

The modern browser can be considered to represent a sophisticated mini-operating system that allows other programs, referred to as

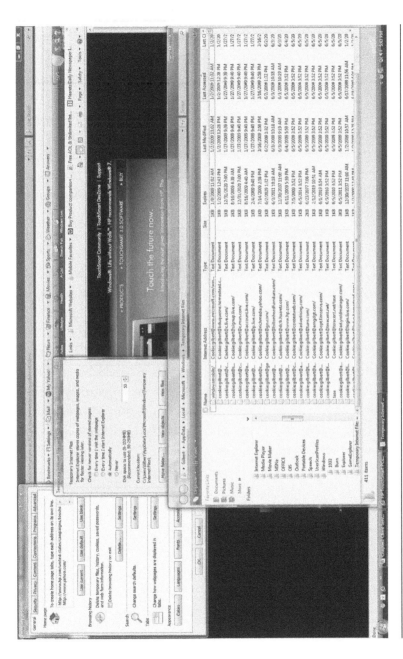

Figure 2.5 You can view cookies on your computer via Microsoft's Internet Explorer Tools menu.

plug-ins, to operate under its control. The browser can also include the ability to run interpreters that execute JavaScript and VBScript, both of which are commonly used for field validation of forms. Another interpreter that can be run within a browser is Java, which represents a high-level programming language that provides much more capability than JavaScript or VBScript. One additional type of program that is unique in a Windows environment is an ActiveX control. An ActiveX control represents a dynamic-link library (DLL). In the wonderful world of computers, a DLL represents a collection of small programs, any of which can be invoked when needed by a larger program that is running in a computer. Some DLLs enable the computer to communicate with a specific type of hardware, such as a printer or scanner, and are referred to as *device drivers.*

Because a DLL file is not loaded into random access memory (RAM) together with the main program, its use saves space in RAM. All DLL files have the file name suffix .dll, and they are dynamically linked with the program that uses them during program execution. Only when a DLL file is needed is it loaded into RAM and run.

2.2.4.1 Helpers Collectively, plug-ins, ActiveX, and Java applets are referred to as helpers. This name category is assigned because they handle documents on the client browser that the browser by itself is not capable of handling. Figure 2.6 provides a general overview of browser components. Note that while HTML decoding is built into each browser, other components are optional.

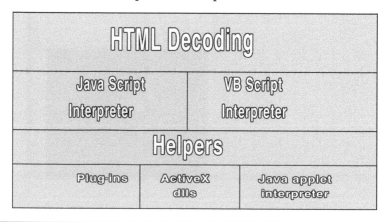

Figure 2.6   Browser components.

2.2.4.2 Plug-Ins   A plug-in is a computer program that functions as an extension of a browser, adding some specific functionality, such as displaying multimedia content inside a Web page. Some examples of plug-ins include Shockwave, RealPlayer, and QuickTime for multimedia as well as Net Zip and Neptune, which can be considered utility plug-in programs. NetZip permits the compression of data, while Neptune supports ActiveX for Netscape so that it operates similar to Microsoft's Internet Explorer.

Originally, Microsoft went to great lengths to make Internet Explorer compatible with Netscape. From JavaScript to HTML to plug-ins, Internet Explorer functioned similar to Netscape. In fact, early versions of Internet Explorer could even read the Netscape plug-in directory. Unfortunately, as Internet Explorer gained market share, its compatibility with Netscape diminished.

Figure 2.7 illustrates how you can view plug-ins on your Internet Explorer browser. In this example, you would first select Tools from the browser's menu bar and then click on the tab labeled "Programs." You would then select the "Manage add-ons" button, which would result in the display of a dialog box labeled "Manage add-ons." Note that the term *add-ons* is now used by many browsers, including Internet Explorer, to reference all programs that can be controlled via the browser and its associated plug-ins. In fact, if you carefully examine Figure 2.7, you will note (under the Sun Microsystem's heading) the entry of the Java plug-in.

2.2.4.3 Java   Java is a high-level programming language that is unusual in that it is both compiled and interpreted. Using a compiler, a Java program is first translated into an intermediate language called Java bytecodes, which represents platform-independent coding that is subsequently interpreted by the interpreter on the Java platform. The interpreter parses or divides the code into small components, so that each Java bytecode instruction is executed on the computer. Although Java program compilation only occurs once, interpretation occurs each time the program is executed.

2.2.4.3.1 Java Bytecodes   Java bytecodes can be viewed as machine-code instructions for what is referred to as a Java Virtual Machine (Java VM). Every Java interpreter included in a Web browser that

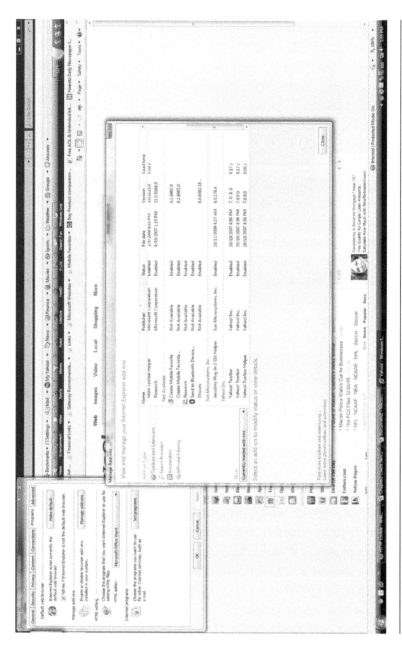

Figure 2.7 Viewing the programs controlled by Microsoft's Internet Explorer.

can run applets as well as a specialized development tool can be considered as an implementation of a Java VM. Thus, Java bytecodes permit a programmer to develop software that can operate on any Java VM, permitting platform independence as long as the platform includes a Java interpreter. Now that we have an appreciation for the Java VM, let's discuss another feature of Java that provides additional functionality. That feature is the Java API.

2.2.4.3.2 The Java API   The Java Application Programming Interface (Java API) represents a collection of predefined software components, which, when invoked, performs predefined functions. The Java API is grouped into libraries of related classes and interfaces, with each library referred to as a package.

2.2.4.3.3 Java Programs   The most common types of Java programs are applets and applications. Of the two, most readers are probably more familiar with Java applets, as they represent a program that executes within a Java-enabled browser. That is, an applet represents a program written in Java that can be included within an HTML Web page. When you use a Java-enabled browser to view a page that contains a Java applet, the applet's code is transferred from the server to the client, where it is executed by the browser's Java Virtual Machine. In comparison, an application represents a stand-alone program that executes directly on a Java-enabled computer platform.

There are several varieties of Java applications that warrant a brief discussion. First, a special type of Java application, known as a *server*, supports clients on a network. Examples of Java servers include Web servers, print servers, proxy servers, and other types of servers that transmit Java applications. Another type of Java program is a servlet, which can be viewed as an applet that runs on a server. Servlets are commonly used in constructing interactive Web applications in place of CGI scripts.

Another type of Java program that deserves mention is JavaScript. JavaScript represents a cross-platform object-based scripting language. JavaScript is a small, concise language designed for embedding in other products and applications, including Web browsers. Inside a browser, JavaScript can be connected to the objects of its environment, in effect providing program control over its environment.

JavaScript contains a core set of objects, such as Array, Date, and Math as well as a core set of operators, control structures, and statements referred to as *language elements*. This core JavaScript can be extended for client-side and server-side operations. In the client side, core JavaScript is extended by supplying objects that provide a degree of control over a browser, such as enabling a user to place elements into a form or navigate through a Web page. In comparison, server-side Java extends the core scripting language by providing elements necessary for running JavaScript on a server. One example of a server-side JavaScript extension would be an application that communicates with a back-end database.

The integration of a JavaScript program into a Web page is obtained through the use of the HTML <SCRIPT> tag. The following HTML coding indicates an example of the integration of a JavaScript program into an HTML Web page:

```
<HTML>
<HEAD>
<TITLE> JavaScript Example </TITLE>
<SCRIPT LANGUAGE = "JavaScript">
MsgBox "Welcome to popcorn.com."
</SCRIPT>
```

2.2.4.4 VBScript   Microsoft's Visual Basic Scripting (VBScript) can be viewed as a more powerful and potentially more dangerous extension to HTML than Java applets: A VBScript communicates with host applications using Windows Script. When using Windows Script, Microsoft's Internet Explorer and other host applications do not require special coding for each scripting component, enabling a computer to compile scripts, obtain and call entry points, and even create a standard language run time for scripting. In a client-server environment, a VBScript-enabled browser will receive scripts embedded within a Web page. The browser will parse and process the script.

Similar to the inclusion of JavaScript into a Web page, the integration of a VBScript is obtained through the use of the HTML <SCRIPT> tag. The following HTML code indicates an example of the integration of a VBScript into an HTML Web page:

```
<HTML>
<HEAD>
<TITLE> VBScript Example </TITLE>
<SCRIPT LANGUAGE = "VBScript">
MsgBox "Welcome to popcorn.com."
</SCRIPT>
```

Through the use of the SCRIPT LANGUAGE tag, the Web browser is informed how to interpret the code. While Netscape browsers and some versions of Microsoft's Internet Explorer support JavaScript, only the latter browser supports VBScript.

If a browser does not support a particular scripting language embedded into a Web page, it will normally either display the script as part of the Web page or hide the script from view. The latter situation occurs when the script is encased in comment tags (<! - - and - - >) and simply ignores the script. For example, returning to our prior script example, if we encase the script as follows, it will be ignored by a browser that does not support VBScript.

```
<HTML>
<HEAD>
<TITLE> VBScript Example </TITLE>
<SCRIPT LANGUAGE = "VBScript">
<!- -
MsgBox "Welcome to PopCorn.com!"
-- >
</SCRIPT>
</HEAD>
```

2.2.4.5 ActiveX   ActiveX represents a set of rules that defines how applications should share information. Developed by Microsoft, ActiveX has its roots in two Microsoft technologies referred to as Object Linking and Embedding (OLE) and Component Object Model (COM).

Programmers can develop ActiveX controls in a variety of programming languages, such as C, C++, Java, and Visual Basic. An ActiveX control can be viewed as being similar to a Java applet. However, unlike a Java applet that is limited in capability and cannot perform disk operations, ActiveX controls have full access to the Windows operating system. While this capability provides ActiveX controls with more capability than Java applets, it also entails a degree of security risk. To control this risk, Microsoft developed a registration system that enables browsers to identify and authenticate an ActiveX control prior to its download.

2.3 Server Operations

In the client-server model illustrated in Figure 2.1, we noted that the server layer can consist of one or more computers. While you can always expect a Web server in the client-server model, it's also possible that the Web server will communicate with an application server. The application server, in turn, can communicate with a database that either resides on the application server or on a separate device, such as a back-end database or a redundant array of independent disks (RAID). In this section, we will briefly examine Web-server operations, including the manner by which they interconnect to application servers and a database.

2.3.1 Evolution

The modern Web server can be viewed as a descendent of Web servers developed at the U.S. National Center for Supercomputing Applications (NCSA), where Mosaic, the browser that evolved into Netscape, was developed, and CERN, the European Organization for Nuclear Research. As work on client-browser and Web-server software progressed during the late 1990s at NCSA and CERN, commercial applications on the Internet rapidly expanded, resulting in software developers offering products for this rapidly expanding market. Although there are only a limited number of Web-server programs to choose from today, each operates in a similar manner. That is, all communications between Web clients and the server use HTTP, and the Web server commences operation by informing the operating system that it's ready to accept communications through a specific port. That port is 80 for HTTP, which is transported via TCP, and 443 when secure HTTP (https) is employed.

Table 2.8 Common Web Server Application Programs

PROGRAM	OPERATING ENVIRONMENT
Internet Information Server	Microsoft bundles this product with its Windows 2000/2003 Server
Apache	An open source, no-charge-for-use HTTP server that Operates under UNIX, Linux, and Windows
SunONE (renamed Java System)	Originally developed by Netscape jointly with Sun Microsystems, versions operate under Windows and UNIX
WebSTAR	A server suite from 4D, Inc., that operates on a Macintosh platform
Red Hat Content Accelerator	A kernel-based Web server that is limited to supporting static Web pages in a Linux environment

2.3.2 Common Web Server Programs

There are a number of Web server application programs that operate under different operating systems. Some Web server programs are bundled with general server software designed to operate under several versions of Windows on Intel Pentium and AMD platforms. Other Web server programs operate under UNIX and Linux operating systems. Table 2.8 lists some of the more popular Web server programs and a brief description of the operating environment of the program.

2.3.2.1 Server Characteristics In general, Web servers can be considered to have two separate types of directories. One directory structure is created by the operating system and commences at the beginning of the disk drive, which is considered to represent the root directory. The second directory commences from a location on the disk drive under which Web documents are normally stored. This Web directory also has a root, referred to as either the *document root* or the *Home Directory local path*.

The left-hand portion of Figure 2.8 illustrates the Microsoft Internet Information Server's Default Web Site Properties dialog box with its Home Directory tab selected. Note that the local path is shown as C:\inetpublwwwroot, which represents the default home directory from which server content flows in response to a client query. By clicking on the Browse button, the Browse for Folder window is opened, which is shown in the right-hand portion of Figure 2.8.

Let's assume that the computer URL or site name is www.popcorn.com and that you store a document named "welcome" in the wwwroot

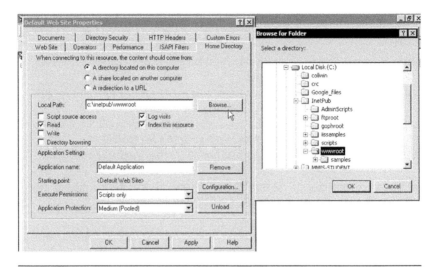

Figure 2.8   The root or home directory is specified with respect to the disk root.

directory. Then, C:\inetpub\wwwroot\welcome represents the welcome document directory address. Thus, the URL request of http://www. popcorn.com would elicit the return of the Welcome Web page from the path C:\inetpub\wwwroot\welcome.html. From the preceding, we can note that a Web server maps URL requests to a directory structure on the computer in terms of the Web home page or document root. In addition to being able to specify a local path or document root, the server operator can configure a Web server to generate content from a share on another computer or a redirection to a URL. The latter in effect permits redirection of requests from one directory to another location that could be on the same computer or on a different computer located thousands of miles away.

A modern Web server has several characteristics that deserve mentioning. Among those characteristics are the ability to support multiple sites on the same computer and the capability to provide clients with documents from the document roots or Internet directories on other servers. The first characteristic is referred to as *virtual hosting*, while the ability to provide documents from other servers turns the Web server into a *proxy server*. In addition to supporting Web-page delivery, modern Web servers include support for FTP, Gopher, News, e-mail, and database access. Web servers also commonly run CGI scripts as well as servlets, the latter representing a compiled Java class. Because

CGI scripts and servlets can significantly enhance client-server operations, let's focus our attention upon both.

2.3.2.1.1 CGI Scripts   The Common Gateway Interface (CGI) represents a standard for interfacing external applications with servers. To understand the need for CGI, you need to realize that a plain HTML-coded document is static and does not change. This means that if you need to vary the document, such as by placing an order or entering a request for an item that could range from the price of a stock to the weather in a zip code, you need a tool to output dynamic information. A CGI program provides that tool, as it is executed in real time, which enables it to output dynamic information.

The term *Common Gateway Interface* dates to the early development of the Web, when companies desired to connect various databases to their Web servers. The connection process required the development of a program that, when executed on a Web server, would transmit applicable information to the database program, receive the results of the database query, and return the results to the client. Because the connection process between the server and the database functioned as a gateway, the resulting standard acquired the name Common Gateway Interface.

A CGI program can be written in any language that can be executed on a particular computer. Thus, C, C++, Fortran, PERL, and Visual Basic represent some of the languages that can be used in a CGI program. In a UNIX environment, CGI programs are stored in the directory /cgi-bin. In a Microsoft Internet Information Server environment, CGI programs are located in C:\internetpub\wwwroot\scripts. That location holds CGI programs developed through the use of a scripting language such as PERL.

One of the most common uses for CGI scripts is for form submission, with a CGI script executing on the server processing the entries in the form transmitted by the client. CGI scripts can be invoked directly by specifying their URL directly within HTML or even embedded within another scripting language, such as JavaScript.

2.3.2.1.2 Servlets   A servlet represents a compiled Java class. Similar to CGI, servlets operate on a server and are called through HTML. When a Web server receives a request for a servlet, the request is passed to the servlet container. The container then loads the servlet. Once the servlet is completed, the container reinitializes itself and returns control to the server.

Although similar to CGI, servlets can be faster, as they run as a server process and have direct access to Java APIs. Because servlets are written in Java, they are platform independent.

In concluding our discussion of servlets, let's turn our attention to a related cousin, referred to as Java Server Pages (JSP). Java Server Pages are similar to servlets in that they provide processing and dynamic content to HTML documents. JSPs are normally used as a server-side scripting language and are translated by the JSP contained in servlets.

Prior to moving on to the application server, a few words are in order concerning the Microsoft server standard referred to as ISAPI.

2.3.2.1.3 ISAPI   Short for Internet Server API, ISAPI represents a Microsoft server-specific standard to load a DLL into the address space of a server to interpret a script. Although similar to CGI, the ISAPI is faster, as there is no need for a server to spawn a new executable as is the case when a CGI script is used. Instead, a DLL is loaded that provides the interpretation of the script.

2.3.3 Application Servers

If we briefly return our attention to Figure 2.1, we can note that the application server represents a tier-2 device along with a conventional Web server. In actuality, both a Web server and application server can reside on the same or on separate computers. The application server, also commonly referred to as an *appserver*, can range in scope from a program that handles application operations between a client and an organization's back-end databases to a computer that runs certain software applications. In this section, we will focus our attention upon several application server models and various popular software products that can be used between the application server and the tier-3 database layer.

2.3.3.1 Access   For many clients, access to an application server is transparent. The client will use a browser to access a Web server. The Web server, depending upon its coding, can provide several different ways to forward a request to an application server. Some of those ways include the use of CGI, Microsoft's Active Server Page, and the Java Server Page.

An Active Server Page (ASP) is an HTML page that includes one or more scripts processed by the Web server prior to the Web page being transmitted to the user. An ASP file is created by including a VBScript or JavaScript statement in an HTML file or by using an ActiveX Data Objects program statement in a file. In comparison, a Java Server Page uses servlets in a Web page to control the execution of a Java program on the server.

2.3.3.2 Java Application Servers Java application servers are based upon the Java 2 Platform, Enterprise Edition (J2EE). J2EE employs a multitier model that normally includes a client tier, middle tier, and an Enterprise Information Systems (EIS) tier, with the latter storing applications, files, and databases. In comparison, the middle tier can consist of a Web server and an EJB (Enterprise Java Bean) server.

The use of J2EE requires a database that can be accessed. When using J2EE, you can access a database through the use of JDBC (Java Database Connectivity), APIs (Application Program Interfaces), SQLJ (System Query Language-Java), or JDO (Java Data Objects).

JDBC represents an industry-standard API for database-independent connectivity between the Java programming language and a wide range of databases. SQLJ, which stands for SQL Java, represents a specification for using SQL with Java, while JDO represents an API standard Java model that makes Plain Old Java Objects (POJOs) persistent in any tier of an enterprise architecture. Figure 2.9 illustrates the relationship of the three tiers to one another when a J2EE platform is employed. In examining Figure 2.9, note that EJB (Enterprise Java Beans) represents a server-side component architecture for the Java 2 platform. EJB enables development of distributed, secure, and portable applications based upon Java.

There are two types of EJBs: Entity Beans and Session Beans, with the former representing an object with special properties. When a Java program terminates, any standard objects created by the program are lost, including any session beans. In comparison, an entity bean remains until it is explicitly deleted. Thus, an entity bean can be used by any program on a network as long as the program can locate it.

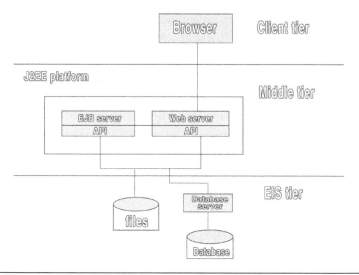

Figure 2.9   The three-tier relationship when a J2EE platform is used.

Because it's easy to locate data on permanent storage, entity beans are commonly stored within a database. This allows the entity bean to run on a server machine. When a program calls an entity bean, control is passed to the server, and the program thread stops executing. Upon completion, control is restored to the calling program, and the program resumes execution.

2.3.3.3 General Server Tools   In concluding our discussion concerning application servers, we need to briefly consider two general server tools—Cold Fusion and ODBC—as well as a specialized family of tools, Microsoft's .NET Framework.

Cold Fusion is a popular development tool set originally from Macromedia that is now sold by Adobe Systems. The initial use of Cold Fusion was to enable databases to be integrated with HTML Web pages. Cold Fusion Web pages include tags written in Cold Fusion Markup Language (CFML), which simplifies the integration with databases, eliminating the need for more complex languages, such as C++. For example, using Cold Fusion, you could create a Web page that asks users for their sex and age, information that would be used by a Web server to query a database for an insurance premium that would be presented in HTML code for display on the user's browser.

The second tool, ODBC (Open Data Base Connectivity), represents a standard database access method developed by the SQL Access group. By inserting a middle layer, called a *database driver*, between an application and the DBMS, it becomes possible to access data from any application, regardless of which DBMS is handling the data. The database driver in effect translated application data queries into commands that the DBMS understands, requiring that the application and the DBMS be ODBC compliant.

We conclude our discussion of the tools used in client-server operations by focusing on a specialized family of tools, Microsoft's .NET Framework.

2.3.3.4 Microsoft's .NET Framework   The Microsoft .NET Framework represents a software infrastructure for the firm's .NET platform, which provides a common environment for creating and operating Web services and applications. NET can also be considered to represent an Internet and Web strategy that employs a server-centric computing model.

NET is built upon a series of Internet standards, such as HTTP for communications between applications; XML (eXtensible Markup Language), which is a standard format for exchanging data between Internet applications; SOAP (Simple Object ACCESS Protocol), which represents a standard for requesting Web services; and UDDI (Universal Description, Discovery and Integration), which is a standard for searching and discovering Web services.

As you might expect, the .NET framework can be installed on computers running Microsoft's Windows operating system and functions as a mechanism for delivering software as Web services. NET includes a large library of coded solutions to common programming problems and a software module that functions as a virtual machine to manage the execution of programs written specifically for the framework.

Included in the .NET framework are such common class libraries as (a) ADO.NET, a set of computer software components that can be used by programmers to access data and data services similar to Java Persistence APIs and (b) ASP.NET, which enables Web services to link to applications, services, and devices via HTTP, HTML, XML, and SOAP. Through the use of the class library, programmers can develop applications with a wide range of features and even combine it with their own code to produce tailored applications.

A key function of the .NET framework is its Common Runtime Engine (CRE). The CRE represents the virtual-machine component of the .NET framework. To ensure that program operations occur within certain parameters with respect to memory management, security, and exception handling, all .NET programs execute under the supervision of the CRL.

The .NET framework can be considered as language neutral and theoretically independent. It currently supports C++, C#, Visual Basic, Microsoft's version of JavaScript called *Jscript*, COBOL, and many third-party languages.

Version 3.0 of the .NET Framework is included with Windows Server 2008 and Windows Vista. Version 3.5 of the framework was released during 2009 on Windows 7. The .NET Framework family also includes versions for mobile- or embedded-device use. A version of the framework referred to as .NET Compact Framework is available on Windows CE platforms, including Windows Mobile devices such as smartphones.

Since its announcement during 2000, .NET has been incorporated into a variety of Microsoft products. Such products include Visual Studio. NET and Visual Basic.NET as well as different versions of Windows, providing a building block for creating and operating Internet services.

Now that we have an appreciation for the tools used in client-server operations, we will conclude this chapter by examining the efficiency of the architecture as the distance between client and server layers increases.

2.4 Distance Relationship

In the three-tier client-server model, the first two tiers are usually separated from one another, while the third tier is normally located with the second tier. Thus, for the purpose of examining the distance relationship between tiers, we can view the three-tier model as being a two-tier one. That is, we can examine the effect upon client-server architecture as the distance between client and server increases. In doing so, we can use two popular TCP/IP tools. Those tools are the Ping and Traceroot programs contained in modern operating systems.

2.4.1 Using Ping

The Ping utility program, by default, generates four data packets that are transmitted to a defined destination. That destination can be specified either as a host address or as a dotted decimal address. The recipient

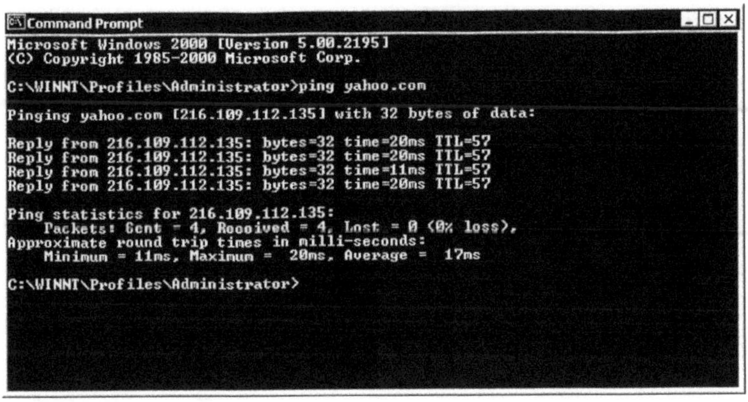

Figure 2.10 Using Ping to ascertain the round-trip delay to Yahoo.com.

of the packets echoes the packets back to the originator. Because the originator knows when it transmitted each packet, it becomes possible to compute the time in terms of round-trip delay. Ping is based upon the use of the Internet Control Message Protocol (ICMP). ICMP type 8 (Echo) messages are transmitted to an indicated destination, which responds with ICMP type 0 (Echo Reply) messages.

To illustrate the effect of distance upon client-server operations, let's examine the round-trip delays between this author's computer located in Macon, Georgia, and two servers, one located in the United States and the second located in Israel. Figure 2.10 illustrates the pinging of the Yahoo server. In examining the entries in the referenced illustration, you will note that four replies are listed from the IP address 216.109.112.135, which represents the IP address of the Yahoo server. The round-trip delay times are indicated by "time =" and have values of 20, 20, 11, and 20 milliseconds, respectively. Below the last reply line, the program generates a summary of statistics for pinging the destination. In the example shown for pinging Yahoo, the average round-trip delay was indicated to be 17 milliseconds.

For our second example, this author pinged the server logtel. com, a data-communications seminar organization located in Israel. Figure 2.11 illustrates the results associated with pinging that location. As you might expect, the round-trip delay has considerably increased due to the increased distance between client and server. However, what may not be apparent is the reason for the increase being approximately an order of magnitude, from an average of 17 ms for pinging Yahoo

```
Command Prompt                                                    _ □ X
Microsoft Windows 2000 [Version 5.00.2195]
(C) Copyright 1985-2000 Microsoft Corp.

C:\WINNT\Profiles\Administrator>tracert www.yahoo.com

Tracing route to www.yahoo.akadns.net [216.109.118.71]
over a maximum of 30 hops:

  1   <10 ms   <10 ms   <10 ms   205.131.176.1
  2   <10 ms    10 ms   <10 ms   s4-0-8.hsa1.atl1.bbnplanet.net [4.24.209.73]
  3   <10 ms    10 ms   <10 ms   ge-6-0-0.bbr1.atlanta1.level3.net [64.159.1.245]
  4    20 ms    20 ms    10 ms   as-2-0.bbr1.washington1.level3.net [64.159.1.2]
  5    20 ms    20 ms    10 ms   ge-1-1-53.car1.washington1.level3.net [4.68.121.69]
  6    20 ms    20 ms    10 ms   4.79.228.6
  7    20 ms    20 ms    10 ms   v132.bas1-m.dcn.yahoo.com [216.109.120.150]
  8    20 ms    20 ms    20 ms   p8.www.dcn.yahoo.com [216.109.118.71]

Trace complete.

C:\WINNT\Profiles\Administrator>_
```

Figure 2.11   Using Ping to determine the round-trip delay to a server located in Israel.

to an average of 223 ms when pinging the Logtel server. To obtain an appreciation of the key reason behind the increased round-trip delay, we need to turn to the second TCP/IP tool, Traceroot.

2.4.2 Using Traceroot

As its name implies, Traceroot is a program that traces the route from source to destination. Under Microsoft Windows, the name of the program was truncated to Tracert.

Tracert invokes a series of ICMP Echo messages that vary the time-to-live (TTL) field in the IP header. The first IP datagram that transports the ping has a TTL field value of 1. Thus, when the datagram reaches the first router along the path to the destination, the router decrements the TTL field value by 1, and the resulting value of zero throws the datagram into the great bit bucket in the sky and returns an ICMP message type 11 (Time Exceeded) to the originator. The ICMP message returned to the sender includes the router's IP address and may additionally include information about the router. The originator increments the TTL value by 1 and retransmits the ping, allowing it to flow through the first router on the path to the destination. The second router then returns an ICMP Type11 message, and the process continues until the Tracert program's ping reaches the destination or the default number of hops used by the program is reached.

Figure 2.12 illustrates the use of the Microsoft Tracert program to trace the path from the author's computer in Macon, Georgia, to the

```
Command Prompt                                                    _ □ ×

C:\WINNT\Profiles\Administrator>ping logtel.com

Pinging logtel.com [212.150.150.132] with 32 bytes of data:

Reply from 212.150.150.132: bytes=32 time=220ms TTL=114
Reply from 212.150.150.132: bytes=32 time=221ms TTL=114
Reply from 212.150.150.132: bytes=32 time=220ms TTL=114
Reply from 212.150.150.132: bytes=32 time=231ms TTL=114

Ping statistics for 212.150.150.132:
    Packets: Sent = 4, Received = 4, Lost = 0 (0% loss),
Approximate round trip times in milli-seconds:
    Minimum = 220ms, Maximum =  231ms, Average =   223ms

C:\WINNT\Profiles\Administrator>
```

Figure 2.12 Using Tracert to observe the path from the author's computer to the Yahoo server.

```
Command Prompt                                                    _ □ ×

Tracing route to www.logtel.com [212.150.150.132]
over a maximum of 30 hops:

  1    <10 ms    <10 ms    <10 ms  205.131.176.1
  2    <10 ms    <10 ms     10 ms  s4-0-8.hsa1.atl1.bbnplanet.net [4.24.209.73]
  3     10 ms    <10 ms    <10 ms  ge-6-1-0.bbr2.atlanta1.level3.net [64.159.3.17]
  4    <10 ms    <10 ms     10 ms  so-5-0-0.gar1.atlanta1.level3.net [4.68.96.22]
  5    <10 ms     10 ms    <10 ms  uunet-level3-oc12.atlanta1.level3.net [4.68.127.58]
  6    <10 ms    <10 ms     10 ms  0.so-2-1-0.x12.atl5.alter.net [152.63.84.154]
  7    <10 ms     10 ms    <10 ms  0.so-0-0-0.t12.atl5.alter.net [152.63.10.106]
  8     20 ms     31 ms     20 ms  0.so-6-0-0.t12.nyc9.alter.net [152.63.13.10]
  9     30 ms     20 ms     20 ms  0.so-1-2-0.x12.nyc4.alter.net [152.63.21.13]
 10     20 ms     20 ms     20 ms  pos7-0.ig5.nyc4.alter.net [152.63.35.37]
 11     90 ms    100 ms     90 ms  Barak-gw6.customer.alter.net [157.130.255.42]
 12    220 ms    211 ms    210 ms  bb3-2.ser1-0-0.barak.net.il [212.150.232.66]
 13    210 ms    210 ms    221 ms  212.150.234.78
 14    210 ms    210 ms    211 ms  212.29.206.198
 15    230 ms    210 ms    210 ms  barak-1-acc-3.barak.net.il [206.49.94.116]
 16    220 ms    210 ms    211 ms  62.90.17.98
 17      *       221 ms    220 ms  webnt1.barak.net.il [212.150.150.132]

Trace complete.

C:\WINNT\Profiles\Administrator>
```

Figure 2.13 Using Tracert to examine router hop delays to a server located in Israel.

Yahoo server. In comparison, Figure 2.13 illustrates the use of the Tracert program to trace the path to the Logtel server located in Israel.

In comparing the two uses of the Tracert program, we can note that there are 8 router hops to Yahoo.com, while there are 17 hops to the Logtel server. Because each router hop requires some processing time, we can attribute a portion of the delay to the number of router hops traversed from source to destination. However, as the radio commentator Paul Harvey is fond of saying, "That's only part of the story."

If you carefully examine the Tracert to Logtel.com shown in Figure 2.13, you will note that for the first 10 hops the delay was under 20 ms. It wasn't until hop 11 that the delay appreciably increased, going from 20 to either 90 or 100 ms, depending upon which of the three traces occurred. At hop 10, the router description indicates that it was in New York City, while at hop 11 the router appears to be a gateway that funnels traffic to Israel. At hop 12, the router description indicates that it is in Israel. Thus, approximately 70 to 80 ms of delay can be attributed to the router acting as a funnel for traffic to Israel at hop 11, while another 110 to 120 ms of delay can be attributed to the propagation delay between the New York gateway and Israel. Once the packets arrive in Israel, the delay from hop 12 to hop 17 is approximately 10 ms. Thus, the primary delays are the gateway funneling traffic from the East Coast to Israel and propagation delay.

If your organization was located in the United States and had customers in Israel, the results of the previously discussed Tracert would be reversed. That is, Israeli users would experience bottlenecks due to propagation delay and traffic being funneled through a peering point located in New York City. We can expand this situation to users in Western Europe, South America, Japan, China, and other locations around the globe who, when accessing servers located in the United States, would also experience bottlenecks from traffic flowing through peering points as well as propagation delays. To alleviate these delays, your organization can move servers storing duplicate information closer to the ultimate user, which is the key rationale for content delivery networking. However, because only the largest companies may be able to afford placing servers at distributed locations around the globe, most content delivery methods depend upon the use of a third party to provide this service.

3

Understanding TCP/IP

The ability to understand technical details associated with content delivery requires an understanding of the TCP/IP protocol suite. In this chapter we will briefly review the TCP/IP protocol suite, focusing our attention upon the fields that govern the identification of applications and the delivery of IP datagrams.

3.1 The TCP/IP Protocol Suite

The TCP/IP protocol suite dates to the work of the Advanced Research Projects Agency (ARPA) during the 1970s and early 1980s. During that time period, the quest to interconnect computers resulted in the development of a series of protocols that evolved into the modern TCP/IP protocol suite.

3.1.1 Protocol Suite Components

Figure 3.1 illustrates the major components of the TCP/IP protocol suite and their relationship to the International Standards Organization (ISO) Open System Interconnection (OSI) reference model. In examining Figure 3.1, note that the TCP/IP protocol suite does not specify a physical layer, nor does it specify a data-link layer. Instead, the protocol suite uses its Address Resolution Protocol (ARP) as a mechanism to enable the protocol suite to operate above any data-link layer that is capable of transporting and responding to ARP messages. This enables the TCP/IP protocol suite to interoperate with Ethernet, Fast Ethernet, Gigabit Ethernet, and Token-Ring local area networks.

In examining the relationship of the TCP/IP protocol suite to the OSI Reference Model shown in Figure 3.1, several additional items warrant mention. First, although applications are transported at Layer 5 in the protocol suite, they correspond to Layers 5, 6, and 7 of the OSI

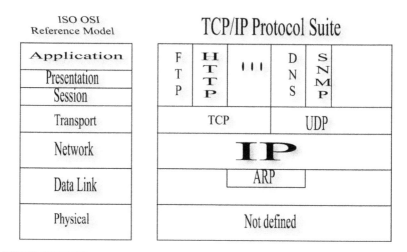

Figure 3.1   Major components of the TCP/IP protocol suite.

Reference Model. Secondly, applications are commonly carried by one of two transport protocols, TCP or UDP. As we will note later in this chapter, TCP provides a connection-oriented, reliable transport facility, while UDP provides a best-effort, nonreliable transport facility.

Applications transported by TCP and UDP are identified by Destination Port fields within each transport layer header. When TCP is used, the TCP header plus application data is referred to as a *TCP segment.* In comparison, when UDP is employed as the transport layer, the UDP header plus application data is referred to as a *UDP datagram.* An IP datagram is formed by the prefix of an IP header to either a TCP segment or UDP datagram. Because the IP header contains Source and Destination address fields, routing occurs through the examination of IP header fields. Different applications are identified via the use of port numbers within the TCP or UDP header, making it possible for a common destination, such as a corporate server, to provide Web, e-mail, and file transfer support. As we probe more deeply into the protocol suite, the use of IP addresses and TCP and UDP port numbers to define applications destined to specific devices will become more clear.

3.1.2 *Physical and Data-Link Layers*

As a review, the physical layer represents the electrical and mechanical components necessary to connect to the network. In comparison, the data-link layer uses a protocol to group information into data packets that flow on the network. Because the data link uses a Layer 2 protocol, source and destination addresses are indicated in terms of Media Access Control (MAC) addresses.

3.1.2.1 MAC Addressing MAC addresses are 48 bits or 6 bytes in length, subdivided into a vendor code and identifier that corresponds to the vendor code. The IEEE assigns vendor codes, and the vendor or manufacturer burns into each LAN adapter's Read Only Memory (ROM) a unique 48-bit address using the assigned vendor code but varying the identifier number in each adapter. If the vendor is successful at marketing its LAN adapters, it will request additional vendor codes from the IEEE and repeat the previously described process.

Although the use of MAC addresses ensures that there will be no duplicate addresses on a LAN, the absence of any network identification made it difficult to interconnect local area networks. That is, without a LAN identifier, it becomes difficult to note the destination local area network for a Layer 2 frame. In fact, the method of routing data between LANs was originally based on bridging, a Layer 2 technique in which the 48-bit MAC addresses were used to determine if a frame should flow across a bridge. Because early bridges interconnected LANs located in close proximity to one another, it was difficult to interconnect LANs located in different cities or even at different locations within the same city. To overcome these limitations, network protocols, such as TCP/IP, that operate at the network layer include the ability to assign unique network addresses to each network, making it possible to route data between networks based upon a destination network address contained in each packet. Prior to discussing the network layer in the TCP/IP protocol suite, we need to cover the use of ARP, which functions as a "bridge" between the network layer and the data-link layer and thus explains its location in Figure 3.1. However, prior to discussing ARP, a few words are in order concerning Layer 3 addressing in the TCP/IP protocol suite.

3.1.2.2 Layer 3 Addressing Today there are two versions of the Internet Protocol (IP) in use, referred to as IPv4 and IPv6. IPv4 uses 32-bit addressing, while IPv6 employs the use of 128-bit addresses. Because approximately 99% of organizations currently use IPv4, we

Class A	0			

Class B	01			

Class C	110			

Class D	111			

Class E	1111			

Figure 3.2 IP address classes.

will focus our attention in this section upon the 32-bit addressing scheme used by IPv4.

Under IPv4, there are five address classes, referred to as Class A through Class E. The first three address classes are subdivided into network and host portions, as indicated in Figure 3.2.

Class A addresses were assigned to very large organizations. If you examine Figure 3.2, you will note that one byte of the four 8-bit bytes in the address is used to denote the network, while the remaining three bytes in the 32-bit address are used to identify the host on the network. Although an 8-bit byte normally provides 256 unique addresses, under IPv4 the first bit in the address field is set to a binary 1 to identify a Class A address, reducing the number of unique bits in the address to seven. Thus, there can only be a maximum of 2^7 or 128 Class A addresses. Because one Class A address represents a loopback address, while the IP address of 0.0.0.0 is used for the default network, this reduces the number of available Class A addresses to 126 and explains why, many years ago, all Class A addresses were assigned. Because three bytes of the Class A network address are used to identify each host, this means that each Class A network can support $2^{24} - 2$, or 16,777,214, distinct hosts. The reason we subtract 2 from the total reflects the fact that a host address of all 0's is used to identify the network ("this network"), while a host address of all 1's represents the network broadcast address.

Returning our attention to Figure 3.2, we can note that a Class B address extends the number of bytes used to identify the network to two, resulting in two bytes being used to identify the host on the specified network. Because the first two bits in the 32-bit address are used to identify the address as a Class B address, this means that 14 bits are available to identify 2^{14} (16,384) unique networks. Thus, there are considerably more Class B addresses available for use than Class A addresses. Because each Class B network uses two bytes to define the host address on the network, this means there are $2^{16} - 2$, or 65,534, possible hosts on each Class B network. Class B addresses were typically issued to large organizations.

The third IPv4 address that is subdivided into network host portions is the Class C address. A Class C address uses three bytes to define the network portion of the address, while the remaining byte in the 32-bit address is used to identify the host on the network. A Class C address also uses the first three bits in the first byte in the address to identify the address as a Class C address. Thus, there are 2^{21} (2,097,152) unique Class C network addresses.

A Class C network address is the most popularly used IP address, commonly issued to small to mid-sized organizations. However, because only one byte is available to define the hosts on a network, a Class C address supports the least number of network hosts. The number of unique hosts on a Class C network is limited to $2^8 - 2$, or 254. The subtraction of two from the prior computation reflects the fact that, similar to Class A and Class B addresses, two Class C addresses have special meanings and are not used to identify a specific host on a network. Those addresses are 0 and 255. A host address of 0 is used to indicate "this network," while a host address of 255 represents the broadcast address of the network. Thus, the inability to use those two addresses as host addresses results in 254 hosts being capable of having unique addresses on a Class C network.

Although Class A, B, and C are the most commonly used IPv4 addresses, two additional class addresses warrant a brief mention: Class D and Class E. Class D addresses are used for multicast operations, while Class E addresses are reserved for experimentation.

Now that we have an appreciation for the five types of IPv4 addresses, let's turn our attention to the manner by which network addresses are translated into MAC addresses. That translation, as we previously noted, is accomplished through the use of the Address Resolution Protocol (ARP).

3.1.2.3 ARP   When a router receives an IPv4 packet addressed to a specific network and host on that network, the destination address is specified as a 32-bit address. However, data delivery on the local area network is based upon Layer 2 MAC addresses. This means that the 32-bit Layer 3 IP address received by a router must be translated into a 48-bit MAC address in order for the packet to be delivered by the Layer 2 protocol.

When a router receives a Layer 3 packet, it first checks its cache memory to determine if a previous address translation occurred. If so, it forms a Layer 2 frame to deliver the Layer 3 packet, using the previously learned Layer 2 MAC address as the destination address in the frame. If no previous address translation occurred, the router will use ARP as a mechanism to determine the Layer 2 address associated with the Layer 3 destination address. In doing so, the router forms an ARP packet, indicating the IP address it needs to learn. The ARP packet is transported as a Layer 2 broadcast to all hosts on the network. The host that is configured with the indicated IP address responds to the broadcast with its MAC address. Thus, the router uses ARP to learn the MAC address required to deliver Layer 3 addressed packets to their correct destination on a Layer 2 network, where data delivery occurs using MAC addresses. Now that we have an appreciation for the use of ARP to enable Layer 3 addressed packets to be delivered on Layer 2 networks, we can turn our attention to the higher layers of the TCP/IP protocol suite.

3.1.3 The Network Layer

The Internet Protocol (IP) represents a network layer protocol that enables IP datagrams to be routed between source and destination networks.

Figure 3.3 illustrates the formation of an IP datagram, showing the relationship of the IP header to the two transport layer headers commonly used in the TCP/IP protocol suite: TCP and UDP. Note that the application data is first prefixed with either a TCP or UDP header prior to being prefixed with an IP header.

The IP header consists of 20 bytes of information that is subdivided into specific fields. An option exists within the IP header that enables the header to be extended through the addition of optional bytes; however, this extension is rarely employed.

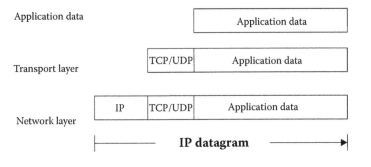

Figure 3.3 Forming an IP datagram.

3.1.3.1 IP Header The top portion of Figure 3.4 illustrates the fields within the IPv4 header. The lower portion of that figure provides a brief description of each of the IPv4 header fields. For the purpose of content delivery, the key fields of interest are the TTL and Protocol fields as well as the 32-bit source IP address and 32-bit destination IP address fields.

3.1.3.1.1 TTL Field The Time to Live (TTL) field indicates the number of hops the IP packet can traverse prior to being discarded. The purpose of this field is to ensure that packets do not continuously flow through the Internet if the destination is not located. To prevent endless wandering, routers decrement the TTL field value and, if the result is zero, discard the packet. In a content delivery networking environment, the movement of Web server data closer to the requester commonly ensures that the decrement of the TTL field value never reaches zero, which would require a packet to be sent to the great bit bucket in the sky.

3.1.3.1.2 Protocol Field The Protocol field is 8 bits in length and indicates the type of transport packet carried in the IP datagram. Because the Protocol field is 8 bits in length, up to 256 protocols can be defined. Some of the more popular protocols are the Internet Control Message Protocol (decimal 1); the Transmission Control Protocol (TCP), which is defined by decimal 6 in the IP Protocol field; and the User Datagram Protocol (UDP), which is defined by decimal 17 in the IPv4 header's Protocol field. Thus, the IPv4 Protocol field value defines the upper-layer protocol used to transport data. Later in this chapter, we will note that both TCP and UDP headers include Port fields whose values define the application carried at the transport layer.

Ver	IHL	ToS	Size
Identification		FLAGS	Fragment offset
TTL	Protocol		Checksum
32-bit Source Address			
32-bit Destination Address			
Options (if any)			

Legend:

VER	VERSION NUMBER
IHL	IP Header Length (number of 32-bit words in the header)
ToS	Type of Service byte, now known as the Differentiated Services Code Point (DSCP)
Size	Size of the datagram in bytes (header plus data)
Identification	16-bit number that, together with the source address, uniquely identifies the packet
FLAGS	Used to control if a router can fragment a packet
Fragment offset	A byte count from the start of the original packet set by the router that performs fragmentation
TTL	Time to Live or the number of hops a packet can be routed over
Protocol	Indicates the type of packet carried
Checksum	Used to detect errors in the header
Source address	The IP address of the packet originator
Destination address	The IP address of the final destination of the packet

Figure 3.4   The IPv4 header.

3.1.3.1.3 Source and Destination Addresses Fields   The remaining two fields in the IPv4 header of interest with respect to content delivery are the Source and Destination IP addresses. Each address is 32 bits in length, with the Source address indicating the originator of the packet, while the Destination address indicates the ultimate recipient of the packet.

As explained earlier in this chapter, under IPv4 there are five address classes, labeled A through E. The vast majority of data traffic on the Internet occurs through the use of address classes A, B, and C, while address D is used for multicast transmission and address class E is reserved for experimental operations. Concerning address classes A, B, and C, the Destination addresses for each are subdivided into a network portion and a host portion. Thus, the use of those addresses conveys both the network where the packet is headed as well as the host on that network.

Now that we have a general appreciation for the manner by which Source and Destination IPv4 addresses are used to convey information, let's literally move up the protocol suite and examine how TCP and UDP are able to denote the application being transported. In doing so we will also examine the key differences between each transport-layer protocol.

3.1.4 The Transport Layer

In the TCP/IP protocol suite, the transport layer is equivalent to Layer 4 in the ISO Reference Model. While the Protocol field in the IPv4 header enables up to 256 higher layer protocols to be defined, the two transport layer protocols commonly used in the protocol suite are the Transmission Control Protocol (TCP) and the User Datagram Protocol (UDP).

3.1.4.1 TCP The Transmission Control Protocol (TCP) represents a reliable, connection-oriented protocol. It obtains reliability due to the fact that the protocol includes an error-detection and -correction capability. The protocol is connection-oriented, as it supports a three-way handshaking method under which the recipient must make its presence known prior to the actual exchange of data occurring.

Figure 3.5 illustrates the format of the TCP header. From the viewpoint of content delivery, the Source and Destination ports are of key concern, since their values identify the application being transported.

Both Source and Destination Port fields are 16 bits in length. Prior to discussing the use of these ports, a few words are in order concerning the other fields in the TCP header. Thus, let's quickly review a few of those fields to obtain an appreciation for why TCP is considered to represent a reliable, connection-oriented Layer 4 protocol.

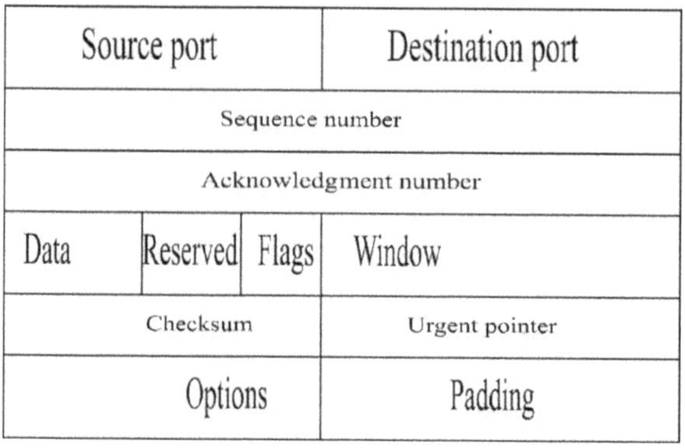

Source port			Destination port	
Sequence number				
Acknowledgment number				
Data	Reserved	Flags	Window	
Checksum			Urgent pointer	
Options			Padding	

Figure 3.5   The TCP header.

3.1.4.1.1 Sequence Number   The Sequence Number field is 32 bits in length. This field contains the sequence number of the first byte in the TCP segment, unless the SYN bit (located in the flag field) is set. If the SYN bit is set, the sequence number becomes the initial sequence number (ISN), and the first data byte is ISN + 1.

3.1.4.1.2 Acknowledgment Number Field   The Acknowledgment Number field is 32-bits in length. If the ACK control bit (located in the Flag field) is set, the Acknowledgment Number field contains the value of the next sequence number the sender of the TCP segment is expecting to receive. Once a connection is established, the next sequence number is always present in the Acknowledgment Number field. Thus, the Sequence Number and Acknowledgment Number fields not only provide a method for ensuring the correct order of segments at a receiver, but in addition provide a mechanism to note if a segment is lost.

3.1.4.1.3 Window Field   The Window field is 16 bits in length. This field contains the number of data bytes beginning with the one indicated in the Acknowledgment field that the sender of the segment is willing to accept. Thus, you can view the entry in the Window field as a flow-control mechanism, since a small entry reduces the transmission of data per segment, while a larger entry increases the amount of data transmitted per segment.

3.1.4.1.4 Checksum Field   The Checksum field is similar to the Window field with respect to field length, since it is also 16 bits. The Checksum field contains the 1's complement of the 1's complement sum of all 16-bit words in the TCP header and text. If a TCP segment contains an odd number of bytes, an additional padded byte of zeros is added to form a 16-bit word for checksum purposes; however, the padded byte is not transmitted as part of the TCP segment.

The Checksum also covers a 96-bit pseudo header that is conceptually prefixed to the TCP header. The pseudo header consists of the Source and Destination Address fields, the Protocol field, and the TCP length field. The purpose of the Checksum covering those fields is to provide protection against misrouted segments, thereby enhancing the reliability of this transport protocol.

Now that we have a general appreciation for TCP let's turn our attention to the second popular transport protocol in the TCP/IP protocol suite: the User Datagram Protocol (UDP).

3.1.4.2 UDP The User Datagram Protocol (UDP) represents a best-effort, nonreliable transport protocol. Unlike TCP, which requires the establishment of a connection prior to the transfer of data, when using UDP, data transfer occurs prior to knowing if a receiver is present. Thus, UDP relies on the application to determine whether, after a period of no response, the session should terminate.

Figure 3.6 illustrates the fields in the UDP header. Although both the TCP and UDP headers include 16-bit Source and Destination ports, the UDP header is streamlined in comparison to the TCP header. The UDP header has no flow-control capability and, as we will shortly note, has a very limited error-detection capability.

3.1.4.2.1 Length Field In examining the UDP header shown in Figure 3.6, the Length field consists of 16 bits that indicate the length in bytes of the UDP datagram to include its header and data.

3.1.4.2.2 Checksum Field The Checksum is a 16-bit 1's complement of the 1's complement sum of a pseudo header of information from

Source port	Destination port
Length	Checksum

Figure 3.6   The UDP header.

the prefixed IP header, the UDP header, and the data (padded with zeroed bytes, if necessary) to ensure that a multiple of two bytes occurs. Similar to the TCP header Checksum, the UDP header Checksum provides protection against misrouted datagrams. However, unlike TCP, there is no method within UDP for error detection of transmitted data, requiring the application to take charge of any required error detection and correction operation.

3.1.4.3 Port Meanings In our prior examination of TCP and UDP headers, we noted that both Layer 4 protocols have 16-bit Source and Destination fields. Because those fields function in the same manner for each protocol, we will discuss their operation as an entity.

3.1.4.3.1 Destination Port The Destination Port indicates the type of logical connection provided by the originator of the IP datagram. Here the term *logical connection* more specifically refers to the application or service transported by the TCP segment, which is identified by a port number in the Destination Port field.

3.1.4.3.2 Source Port The Source Port is normally set to a value of zero by the originator. However, when meaningful, the assignment of a nonzero value indicates the port of the sending process, which will then indicate the port to which a reply should be addressed. Because the values of each field are port numbers, this author would be remiss if he did not discuss their ranges.

3.1.4.3.3 Port Numbers Ranges Each 16-bit Destination Port and Source Port field is capable of transporting a number from 0 through 65,535, for a total of 65,536 unique port numbers. Port numbers are divided into three ranges, referred to as Well-Known Ports, Registered Ports, and Dynamic and/or Private Ports. Well-Known Ports are those port numbers from 0 through 1,023, or the first 1,024 port numbers. Registered Ports are those port numbers from 1,024 through 49,151, while Dynamic and/or Private Ports are those port numbers from 49,152 through 65,535.

Well-Known Port numbers are assigned by the Internet Assigned Numbers Authority (IANA) and are used by system processes or by programs to identify applications or services. Table 3.1 lists some

Table 3.1 Common Well-Known Port Numbers

PORT NUMBER	DESCRIPTION
17	Quote of the Day
20	File Transfer Protocol—Data
21	File Transfer Protocol—Control
23	Telnet
25	Simple Mail Transfer Protocol
43	Whois
53	Domain Name Server

of the more common Well-Known Port numbers. Although port numbers listed in Table 3.1 are applicable to both TCP and UDP, port numbers are commonly used with only one protocol.

For example, FTP (File Transfer Protocol) is transported as a reliable, connection-oriented process that occurs through the use of TCP. In comparison, SNMP (Simple Network Management Protocol) is transported on a best-effort basis by UDP. However, some applications, such as Voice over IP, use a combination of TCP and UDP. For example, when dialing a telephone number, the dialed digits are transported by TCP, which is a reliable protocol. However, once a connection is established to the dialed party, digitized voice is transported via UDP. The reason for the latter results from the fact that real-time voice cannot be retransmitted if a bit error occurs. Thus, the application would either drop an errored packet or ignore the error when it reconstructs a short segment of voice transported via a UDP packet.

Now that we have an appreciation for the operation and utilization of the TCP/IP Transport Layer, we will conclude this chapter by turning our attention to the Domain Name System (DNS). In doing so, we will review how the DNS operates, not only to obtain an appreciation of how name resolution occurs, but also to obtain the knowledge necessary to appreciate how DNS can be used as a mechanism to support load balancing, a topic we will discuss in more detail later in this book.

3.2 The Domain Name System

When you enter a URL into your Web browser or send an e-mail message, you more than likely use a domain name. For example, the URL http://www.popcorn.com contains the domain name popcorn.com. Similarly, the email address beverly@popcorn.com contains the same domain name.

3.2.1 Need for Address Resolution

While domain names are easy to remember, they are not used by routers, gateways, and computers for addressing. Instead, computational devices are configured using dotted decimal digits to represent their IPv4 addresses.

Dotted decimal addresses are then converted into binary equivalents, which represent the true addresses of computational devices. Although many books reference IPv4 addresses as being assigned to computational devices, in actuality those addresses are assigned to device interfaces. This explains how routers and network servers with multiple network connections can have packets transmitted from each interface with a distinct source address as well as receive packets with an explicit destination address that corresponds to a particular interface. Because IPv4 Class A, B, and C addresses indicate both a network and host address, such addresses identify both a network for routing purposes as well as a particular device on a network.

The use of IPv4 addressing by computational devices means that a translation device that resolves the domain name into an IP address is required to provide routers with the information necessary to deliver packets to their intended destination. That translation or resolution service is referred to as the Domain Name Service and is the focus of this section.

3.2.2 Domain Name Servers

Computers that are used to translate domain names to IP addresses are referred to as *domain name servers*. There are a series of domain name servers that maintain databases of IP addresses and domain names, enabling a domain name to be resolved or translated into an IP address. Some companies operate a domain name server on their local area network, while other organizations depend upon the DNS operated by their Internet Service Provider.

If a browser user enters a URL for which no previous IPv4 address was found, the local DNS on the organization's LAN will query the ISP's

Table 3.2 Top-Level Domains

.aero	Aviation
.biz	Business organizations
.com	Commercial
.coop	Cooperative organizations
.edu	Educational
.gov	Government
.info	Information
.int	International organizations
.mil	U.S. Department of Defense
.museum	Museums
.name	Personal
.net	Networks
.org	Organizations

DNS to determine if a resolution occurred at a higher level. Similarly, if the organization uses the services of the ISP's DNS and a query does not result in a resolution, then that DNS will forward the query to a higher authority. The highest authority is referred to as the top-level domain.

3.2.3 Top-Level Domain

Each domain name consists of a series of character strings separated by dots (.). The leftmost string references the host, such as www or ftp. The rightmost string in the domain name references the top-level domain, such as gov or com.

When the Internet was initially established, there were only a handful of top-level domains. Those top-level domains included .com (commercial), .edu (educational), .gov (government), .mil (U.S. Department of Defense), .net (networks), and .org (organization). Since then, domain name registries have expanded considerably, as has the number of top-level domain name servers. Table 3.2 lists presently defined domain name registries other than those defined for countries. Concerning the latter, there are presently over 100 two-letter domain registries for countries, such as .ar (Argentina), .il (Israel), and .uk (United Kingdom). The IANA is responsible for defining domain name suffixes.

Within each top-level domain, there can be literally tens of thousands to millions of second-level domains. For example, in the .com first-level domain, you have

Microsoft
Google
Yahoo

as well as millions of other entries. Although every .com top-level domain must be unique, there can be duplication across domains. For example, lexus.com and lexus.biz represent two different domains. By prefixing a word to the domain, such as ftp.popcorn.com or www.popcorn.com, you obtain the name of a specific host computer in a domain. That computer has an IP address that is determined through the use of the Domain Name Service.

3.2.4 DNS Operation

When you enter a URL into your browser in the form of a domain name, that name must be converted into an IP address. That address will then be used by the browser to request a Web page from the computer whose interface is assigned that address. To obtain that address, the browser must use the facilities of a domain name server. Thus, the browser must know where to look to access the name server.

3.2.5 Configuring Your Computer

When you install your computer's TCP/IP software, one of the first functions you need to perform is to configure your network settings. When you do so, you will set your computer's IP address, its subnet mask, default gateway, and the address of the name server your computer should use when it needs to convert domain names to IP addresses.

Figure 3.7 illustrates the Microsoft Windows 2000 Internet Protocol (TCP/IP) Properties dialog box. Note that if you select the button "Use the following IP addresses," you are able to specify the IP address, subnet mask, default gateway, and up to two DNS server addresses. However, if your organization uses the Dynamic Host Configuration Protocol (DHCP), you would then select the button labeled "Obtain an IP address automatically," which would result in the DNS addresses being transmitted to the host from a DHCP server along with its IP address, subnet mask, and gateway address when the host connects to the network. If you're working in a

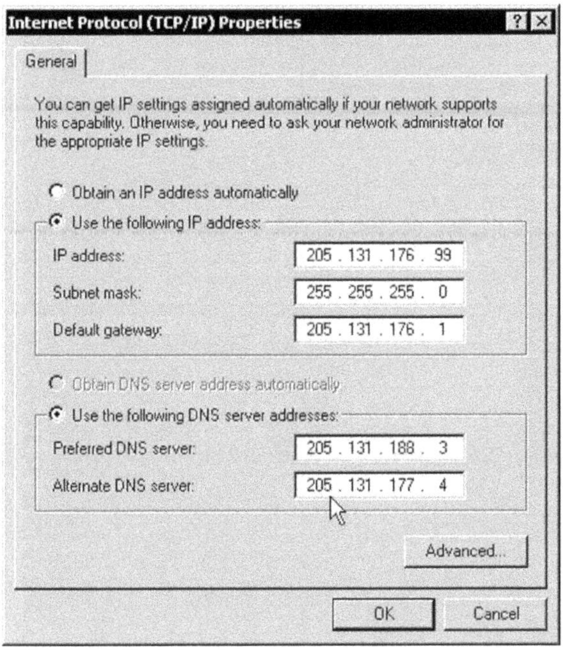

Figure 3.7   Using the Windows 2000 Internet Protocol (TCP/IP) Properties dialog box.

Windows environment, there are several tools you can consider using to obtain DNS and other addressing information. If you're using an older version of Windows, such as WIN95 or WIN98, you can view current IP address assignments through the use of Winipfg.exe. If you're using Windows 2000 or Windows XP, you can use IPConfig from the command prompt.

The top portion of Figure 3.8 illustrates the use of the IPConfig program without any options. When used in this manner, the program returns the connection-specific DNS suffix, IP address, subnet mask, and default gateway address. Next, the IPConfig program was executed a second time; however, this time the "all" option was included in the command line. Note that the use of the "all" option provides additional information about the configuration of the computer, including the DHCP and DNS server addresses as well as DHCP leasing information.

Once a computer knows the IP address of its domain name server, it can request the server to convert a domain name into an IP address. If the name server received a prior request to obtain an IP address for a host with a particular domain name, such as www.popcorn.com,

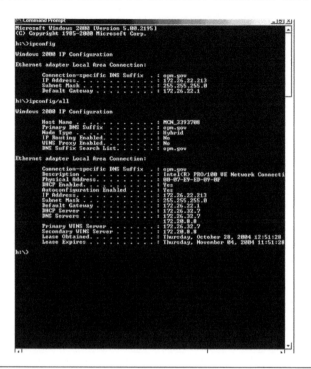

Figure 3.8 Using IPConfig to obtain information about the network settings associated with a computer.

the server merely needs to access its memory to return the IP address associated with the request previously stored in cache memory to the computer making the resolution request. If the name server did not have prior knowledge of the resolution, it would then initiate contact with one of the root name servers.

3.2.6 Root Name Servers

Currently there are 13 root name servers in existence, with most of them located in the United States, while several servers are located in Japan and London. Each root server functions in a similar manner, responding to a DNS query with the address of a name server for the top-level domain for a particular query. That is, each root server knows the IP address for all of the name servers that support a particular top-level domain. Thus, if your browser was pointed to the URL www.popcorn.com and the local name server had not previously resolved the IP address for that host and domain address, the local name server would contact one of the root name servers. Assuming the root name server had not previously resolved the host and domain name, the root server would respond with the IP address of the domain, which in our example is the name server for the .com domain, enabling your name server to access that server.

Root servers are labeled A through M, with each name server having a file that contains information in the form of special records that contain the name and IP address of each root server. Each root server in turn is configured with the IP addresses of the name servers responsible for supporting the various top-level domains. Thus, a resolution request that cannot be serviced by the local domain server is passed to an applicable root server, which in turn returns the IP address of the top-level domain to the local DNS. That name server then transmits a query to the top-level name server, such as a COM, EDU, or GOV name server, requesting the IP address for the name server for the domain in which the host that requires address resolution resides. Because the top-level domain name server has entries for all domain servers for its domain, it responds with the IP address of the name server that handles the domain in question. The local name server uses that IP address to directly contact the name server for the host and domain name it needs to resolve, such as www.popcorn.com. That name server returns the IP address to the local name server, which then returns it to the browser. The browser then uses that IP address to contact the server for www.popcorn.com to retrieve a Web page.

3.2.7 The NSLookup Tool

If you're using a version of Microsoft Windows that has the TCP/IP protocol suite installed, you can use the NSLookup diagnostic tool to obtain information from domain name servers. NSLookup operates in two modes, referred to as *interactive* and *noninteractive*. The noninteractive mode is normally used when you need to obtain a single piece of data, while the interactive or program mode provides you with the ability to issue a series of queries.

The top portion of Figure 3.9 illustrates the use of NSLookup in its noninteractive mode of operation. In this example, NSLookup was used to obtain the IP address of the Web server www.eds.com. In the second example, NSLookup was entered by itself to place the

```
Command Prompt - nslookup                                    _ □ X
C:\>nslookup www.eds.com
Server:  ns3.opm.gov
Address:  205.131.188.3

Non-authoritative answer:
Name:     eagle-ldir.xweb.eds.net
Address:  207.37.253.223
Aliases:  www.eds.com


C:\>nslookup
Default Server:  ns3.opm.gov
Address:  205.131.188.3

> set all
Default Server:  ns3.opm.gov
Address:  205.131.188.3

Set options:
   nodebug
   defname
   search
   recurse
   nod2
   novc
   noignoretc
   port=53
   type=A
   class=IN
   timeout=2
   retry=1
   root=A.ROOT-SERVERS.NET.
   domain=
   MSxfr
   IXFRversion=1
   srchlist=

> server a.root-servers.net
Default Server:  a.root-servers.net
Address:  198.41.0.4

>
```

Figure 3.9   Using Microsoft's NSLookup in noninteractive and interactive query mode.

program into its interactive mode of operation. The program responds by indicating the name server and its IP address, and then displaying the ">" character as a prompt for user input. At this point in time, you can enter an NSLookup command. In the interactive example, the "set all" command was entered to obtain a list of set options. Note that one option is the root server, with its current value set to A.ROOT-SERVERS.NET. This represents the root server that the local DNS server uses by default. Next, the server command was used to set the root server as the default name server. Note that this action returned the IP address of the root server.

3.2.8 Expediting the Name Resolution Process

The name resolution process is expedited by name servers using caching. When a name server resolves a request, it caches the IP address associated with the name resolution process. The next time the name server receives a request for a previously resolved domain, it knows the IP address for the name server handling the domain. Thus, the name server does not have to query the root server, since it previously learned the required information and can simply retrieve it from cache memory. While caching can be very effective, it has two limitations. First, not all requests are duplicates of prior requests. Secondly, cache memory is finite. Thus, when a name server receives an IP address, it also receives a Time to Live (TTL) value associated with the address. The name server will cache the address until the TTL period expires, after which the address is purged to make room for new entries.

3.2.9 DNS Resource Records

The key to the operation of name servers is the resource records. Resource records define data types in the domain name system. DNS records are coded in ASCII and translated into a binary representation for internal use by a DNS application.

The DNS system defines a number of Resource Records (RRs). The text representations of RRs are stored in what are referred to as *zone files* that can be considered to represent the domain name database.

3.2.9.1 SOA Resource Record At the top of each zone file is a Start of Authority (SOA) record. This record identifies the zone name, an e-mail contact, and various time and refresh values applicable to the zone. The top portion of Figure 3.10 illustrates the RFC 1537–defined format for the SOA record, while the lower portion of that illustration shows an example of the SOA record for the fictional popcorn.com domain.

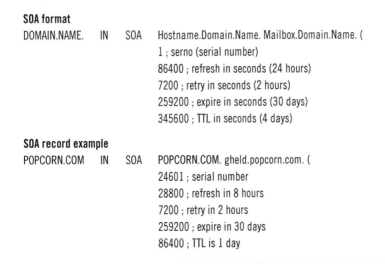

SOA format

```
DOMAIN.NAME.    IN    SOA    Hostname.Domain.Name. Mailbox.Domain.Name. (
                              1 ; serno (serial number)
                              86400 ; refresh in seconds (24 hours)
                              7200 ; retry in seconds (2 hours)
                              259200 ; expire in seconds (30 days)
                              345600 ; TTL in seconds (4 days)
```

SOA record example

```
POPCORN.COM    IN    SOA    POPCORN.COM. gheld.popcorn.com. (
                            24601 ; serial number
                            28800 ; refresh in 8 hours
                            7200 ; retry in 2 hours
                            259200 ; expire in 30 days
                            86400 ; TTL is 1 day
```

Figure 3.10   The SOA record format and an example of its use.

In examining the format of the SOA record shown in Figure 3.10, the trailing dot (.) after the domain name signifies that no suffix is to be appended to the name. The class of the DNS record is shown as IN, which stands for "Internet," while SOA indicates the type of DNS record, which is Start of Authority. The mailbox is that of the individual responsible for maintaining DNS for the domain. The serial number (serno) indicates the current version of the DNS database for the domain and provides the mechanism whereby other name servers can note that the database was updated. The serial number commences at 1 and is increased by 1 each time the database changes.

The Refresh entry tells the secondary name server how often to poll the primary for changes. The Retry entry defines the interval in seconds at which the secondary name server tries to reconnect to the primary in the event it failed to connect at the Refresh interval.

The Expire entry defines how long the secondary server should use its current entry if it is unable to perform a refresh, while the TTL value applies to all records in the DNS database on a name server.

3.2.9.2 Name Server (NS) Records   There is only one SOA record per domain. However, because there can be multiple name servers, there can also be multiple NS records. Name servers use NS records to locate one another, and there must be at least two NS records in every DNS entry. The format of an NS record is shown as follows:

DOMAIN.NAME.   IN NS Hostname.Domain.Name.

3.2.9.3 Address (A) records   The purpose of the Address (A) record is to map the host name of a computer to its numeric IP address. The format of an Address record is indicated as follows:

Host.domain.name.   IN A www.xxx.yyy.zzz

3.2.9.4 Host Information (HINFO) Record   A Host Information (HINFO) record is optional. When used, it can be employed to provide hardware operating-system information about each host. The format of an HINFO record is shown as follows:

Host.domain.name.   IN HINFO "cputype" "OS"

3.2.9.5 Mail Exchange (MX) Records   The purpose of a Mail Exchange (MX) record is to allow mail for a domain to be routed to a specific host. A host name can have one or more MX records, since large domains will have backup mail servers. The format of an MX record is shown as follows:

```
Host.domain.name.    IN MX MM otherhost.domain.name.
                     IN MX MM otherhost2.domain.name.
```

The preference numbers (NN) signify the order in which mailers will select MX records when attempting mail delivery to the host. The lower the number, the higher the host is in priority.

To illustrate the use of the MX record, assume that your organization's mail server had the address mail.popcorn.com. Further assume that, for convenience, you wanted your e-mail addresses to be user@popcorn.com. rather than user@mail.popcorn.com. To accomplish this, your MX record would be coded as follows:

```
popcorn.com.    IN MX 10 mail.popcorn.com.
```

3.2.9.6 Canonical Name (CNAME) Records   The Canonical Name (CNAME) record enables a computer to be referred to by an alias host name. The CNAME record format is shown as follows:

```
Alias.domain.name.    IN CNAME otherhost.domain.name.
```

It's important to note that there must be an A record for the host prior to adding an alias. The host name in the A record is known as the canonical or official name of the host.

3.2.9.7 Other Records   In addition to the previously mentioned DNS records, there are many other resource records. Those records range in scope from Pointer (PTR) records that provide an exact inverse of an A record (allowing a host to be recognized by its IP address) to an A6 resource record, which is used for an IPv6 address for a host. A full list of DNS record types can be obtained from IANA DNS parameter listings. Readers are encouraged to use a search tool such as Bing or Google to research IANA DNS parameters.

4

THE CDN MODEL

Until now, we have only briefly covered the major reasons for having a content delivery system and a few of the methods that could facilitate the operation of a content delivery network (CDN). In this chapter we will probe more deeply into the content delivery model, examining so-called edge operations that move the content of customers to the edges of the Internet. In actuality, the term *edge*, while appropriate, can mean different things to different persons with respect to their physical location. However, prior to discussing edge operations, we will first build upon information previously presented in this book to obtain a better appreciation for the rationale for CDN. In doing so, we will view the Internet as a large transmission facility that has a series of critical links. Such a view will allow us to better understand bottlenecks and how a distributed content delivery network can overcome such bottlenecks. Because this author believes that both sides of a coin need to be shown, as we discuss edge operations we will also examine some of the limitations associated with the distribution of content across the Internet.

4.1 Why Performance Matters

Earlier in this book, we looked at the interconnection of communication carrier networks at peering points and how those locations could adversely affect the flow of data. In addition, we looked at the flow of traffic from users distributed across the globe accessing a common Web server and noted that some users would have their traffic flow over a large number of router hops to reach the server. Since router hops and the crossing of traffic at peering points correspond to transmission delays, as the distance between the user of the server and the server increases, so too will the delays. Those delays can affect the ability of potential customers of Web sites to interact with the site, to view videos, send e-mails, or perform other operations. Due to such factors, we can state that there is literally a price associated with a degraded level of performance, as some users may point their browsers elsewhere. Thus, the resulting economics associated with poor performance is worth noting.

4.1.1 Economics of Poor Performance

To understand the economics associated with poor performance, let's assume that your organization's Web site sells discount airline seats. Now let's assume that a potential customer of the Web site enters his or her dates of travel and travel locations in order to request a discount price. However, in doing so, the potential customer may then wish to alter the travel dates and check the rates to one or more alternate but nearby locations, since airlines are notorious for having many travel restrictions as well as having rates between cities that enable considerable savings by flying either from or to a closely located airport instead of from the intended point of origination or destination. Because of the previously described travel discrepancies, the typical potential customer may need to enter data on a series of Web pages as well as flip through a series of page responses.

If a potential customer is comparing prices of several travel sites, she is typically pressed for time. Thus, potential customers who experience page access and display delays associated with router hop and peering points may in effect bail out from further accessing the Web site for which they are experiencing delays and proceed to another site. For example, suppose a person is viewing airline flights from New York to Los Angeles. That person might start her investigation of flights by searching the Web site for the cost of an economy coach ticket on the day she wishes to depart and return. Depending upon the availability and price of the ticket, she may modify the search using different travel dates and/or a different cabin. Thus, there are more than likely several searches a person would perform prior to making a decision. If the Web site being accessed is sluggish, there is a high probability that the person doing the searching might enter the URL of a competitor into her Web browser.

In the wonderful world of marketing, we are probably familiar with the adage, "Time is money." We can equate this adage to the use of the Internet by noting that every bailout of a potential customer results in the potential loss of revenue. However, when customers are driven away due to what they perceive to be a poorly performing Web site—but which in reality are the delays resulting from the path by which data flows between the potential customer and the Web site—a lasting impression of poor site performance can occur. This means that the Web site operator not only loses the possibility of a current sale but, in addition, may lose the opportunity for future sales, since the potential customer now has a negative view of the Web site.

4.1.2 Predictability

Another problem that potential customers encounter when accessing a Web server across many router hops and peering points is predictability. A centrally hosted infrastructure results in potential customers at locations from Andorra to Zambia accessing a common location. Some routes may require the traversal of a large number of router hops and peering points, while other routes may require the traversal of a lesser number of router hops and perhaps a few or even no peering points. As you can imagine, depending upon the geographic location of the potential customer and Web server being accessed, different potential customers can be expected to encounter different delays, making the access and retrieval of Web pages anything but predictable. Delays, while slightly annoying when a Web page consists of text, can rise to a level of frustration when images and video can be selected by the viewer. For example, when viewing a video that is transmitted from a single server via both a long distance and through several peering points, the cumulative random delays can result in a high level of buffering occurring. This, in turn, more than likely results in a high level of viewer dissatisfaction, since every few moments the video will pause while the buffer on the viewer's computer is refilled. Then, as the buffer allows a few seconds of "smooth" video to be viewed, the random delays result in the buffer being emptied and then refilled, causing the video to stop playing and typically displaying the word "buffering" at the bottom of the area in which the video is being viewed. In addition to the problems associated with the distance and number of peering points between viewer and server, the geographic distribution of potential customers also needs to be considered as well as the time of day when Web access occurs.

Data flow on the Internet has peaks and valleys that partially correspond to the typical workday. That is, for Monday through Friday, activity increases from a relatively low level prior to the 8 a.m. to noon period as workers arrive and perform both job-related and personal activities that requires Internet access. From approximately noon until 2 p.m., activity tapers off as workers go to lunch and run errands. In the afternoon, activity peaks between 4 p.m. and 5 p.m. and then tapers off as people leave work. However, as workers arrive at home, some persons begin to use the Internet to perform a variety of activities that may not be possible or are restricted at work, ranging from checking personal e-mail to retrieving stock market quotations. Thus, there are several activity peaks during the late afternoon and evening. In addition, on weekends, when there is minimal access of the Internet from work, tens of millions of persons located around the globe access the Internet from home or from libraries and colleges and universities, creating variable traffic peaks and valleys through-out the weekend. To further compound a challenging situation, the distribution of activity varies by time zone, with, for example, users in Los Angeles and New York who access a server located in Chicago having a distribution of activity that is two hours behind (Los Angeles) and one hour ahead (New York) of Chicago users.

When traffic loads are considered along with the geographic loca-tion of potential customers, it becomes apparent that the potential customers of a centrally located computer infrastructure consisting of a Web server and back-end database servers will have different expe-riences with respect to Web-server access and page-retrieval opera-tions each time they point their browsers to a particular Web site. Once again, this unpredictability can result in the loss of potential customers who decide to perform their search for products they desire on other Web sites, resulting in an additional effect upon the bottom line of the Web site operator.

4.1.3 Customer Loyalty

During the initial Internet boom from 1997 through 2000, many market research organizations viewed the popularity of sites only with respect to page clicks. In the euphoria of that period, the fact that few clicks were converted into purchases was irrelevant. Fortunately, the burst of the so-called Internet bubble resulted in a return to rational market research where the bottom line truly matters.

When potential customers cannot predictably access an organization's Web site, they normally make a rational decision to go elsewhere. This decision can occur via the entry of a new URL to the use of a search engine to locate another site providing a similar product. Over time, potential customers may even remove the current site from their browser's Favorites list. Regardless of the action performed, the result will be similar in that, instead of acquiring a loyal customer who could be the source of repeated business, the potential customer is, in effect, driven away.

4.1.4 Scalability

Another problem associated with the centralized Web site model is scalability. The centralized model requires the Web site operator to add more equipment to one location to satisfy access increases that can occur from locations scattered over the globe.

In a distributed model where content delivery is moved to the literal edges of the Internet, an increase in Web access is distributed over many servers. As a result of this action, it may not be necessary to upgrade any Web server. In addition, if the organization is using the facilities of a content delivery network provider, the responsibilities associated with computer upgrades become the responsibility of the service provider. This means that if your organization enters into a contract with a service provider that includes a detailed service-level agreement, the service provider will upgrade its equipment at one or more locations when service becomes an issue. This upgrade, at most, should only temporarily affect one of many locations and thus should not be compared to a central site upgrade that can affect all customers on a global basis. Thus, the scalability issue also includes the effect upon potential customers, with a centralized model providing a high likelihood of a complete outage occurring during an equipment upgrade process, while a distributed model upgrade only affects potential customers whose traffic flows through a particular edge server.

4.1.5 Flexibility

As indicated in our prior discussion concerning scalability, the centralized approach can result in a complete outage during a hardware upgrade. Thus, a distributed approach, where content is moved forward to edge servers, provides more flexibility with respect to hardware upgrades. First, moving content onto many servers can forgo the need for a centralized hardware upgrade. Even if a centralized server is necessary to coordinate the distribution of data to edge servers, the upgrade of the central server can be planned to minimize its effect on the distribution of information to the edge servers. Thus, if a hardware upgrade becomes necessary and you plan correctly, it only at most affects one of many edge servers at a time and allows your organization to better plan for partial outages. Thus, the use of a content delivery network can provide a more flexible solution to your Web site data access requirements.

4.1.6 Company Perception

There is the well known adage, "You are what you eat." In the wonderful world of the Internet, the performance of your company's Web site can have a significant influence upon how actual and potential customers view your organization and your organization's brand perception. If users attempting to access your corporate Web site encounter significant delays, not only will this result in a number of users pointing their browsers elsewhere, but, in addition, it will result in a negative view of your organization. From a personal perspective, there are several Web sites that I prefer to avoid during the holiday season, as the specific vendors (whom I prefer not to name) have for several years apparently failed to upgrade their sites. Consequently, efforts to purchase an item becomes a major waste of time as customers stare at their Internet browsers waiting for a response to their requests. Unfortunately, such vendors fail to appreciate that the heavy investment in commercial advertising can come to naught if customers and potential customers decide to abandon their organization's Web site. Thus, the performance of your organization's Web site in precluding access delays can have a direct impact upon brand perception and customer loyalty.

4.1.7 Summary

Based upon information presented in this section, it's obvious that Web performance matters. Because customers and potential customers consider access delays to represent Web server performance, the centralized server model has many limitations. As we previously noted, those limitations include a lack of predictability, the potential loss of customer loyalty, difficulty in scaling a centralized server to accommodate traffic growth, an impairment of organizational flexibility, and the possibility that the operation of a centralized site will provide delays that negatively impact the perception of your organization. Because these limitations can result in the loss of customer revenue, there is an economic penalty associated with them. That economic penalty can vary considerably, based upon the severity of one or more of the noted limitations as well as the type of merchandise or service sold by the Web site.

Prior to examining how moving content to edge servers can reduce latency and enhance server access, let's obtain a more detailed view of the factors associated with Web server access delays. In doing so, we turn our attention to examining Internet bottlenecks in an effort to obtain a better understanding behind the rationale for moving content toward actual and potential users.

4.2 Examining Internet Bottlenecks

Previously in this book, we noted that the distance between the user and a Web site in terms of the number of router hops and peering points significantly contributes to site access delays. In this section, we will probe more deeply into Internet bottlenecks and examine data flow from source to destination, noting the effect of a series of potential and actual bottlenecks upon Web server access.

4.2.1 Entry and Egress Considerations

Two of the often overlooked Internet bottlenecks are the entry and egress transport facilities used by a customer or potential customer to access a particular Web server.

The entry transport facility refers to the type of access the user employs to log on to the Internet and the activity over that transport facility. While the egress transport facility refers to the communications link from the Internet to a particular Web server, it also represents a reverse connection. That is, the egress transport facility with respect to a user becomes the access transport facility of the server. Similarly, the entry transport facility of the user can be viewed as the egress transport facility of the server. To eliminate possible confusion, we can note that the typical browser user sends requests in the form of URLs to a Web site to retrieve a Web page. The Web server responds with a Web page whose size in bytes is normally several orders of magnitude greater than the packet sent by the browser user that contains a URL request. Thus, instead of focusing our attention upon the transmission of the URL to the server, we can focus our attention upon the Web server's response. In doing so, we can note that the user's access method to the Internet results in a delay in the delivery of a server page based upon the operating rate of the access line. Similarly, the user's egress transport facility can be viewed as a delay mechanism with respect to the server delivering a Web page to the Internet. Now that we have an appreciation for the manner by which we can focus our attention upon Web page delays with respect to the browser user's view of access and egress, let's take a closer look.

4.2.2 Access Delays

Previously, we noted that the access line connecting a browser user to the Internet represents the egress delay associated with delivering a Web page to the user. Because there are several types of transport facilities a browser user can employ to access the Internet, we need to consider each method when computing the effect of the access transport facility upon Web page egress delays. For example, a user might access the Internet via dial-up connection using the public switched telephone network at 56 kilobits per second (Kbps), over a DSL modem connection at 1.5 megabits per second (Mbps), a cable modem connection operating at 6 Mbps, or a corporate T1 connection operating at 1.544 Mbps. While the first two connection methods provide dedicated access to the Internet, the cable modem and corporate T1 connection both represent a shared access method, with achievable throughput based upon the number of users accessing the Internet and their activity. For example, the cable modem access to the Internet occurs via a shared Ethernet LAN (local area network); thus the number of users receiving data when a user requests a Web page will govern the overall response. Similarly, the number of corporate users communicating on a T1 transmission facility will govern the response they receive when requesting a Web page. We can obtain an average throughput per user from the use of elementary mathematics. For example, assuming each corporate user is performing a similar activity and 10 users are accessing the Internet, then the average throughput of each user becomes 1.544 Mbps/10 or 154,400 bps.

In actuality, a T1 line that operates at 1.544 Mbps uses 8,000 bits per second for framing. Thus, the actual data rate available to transport data over a T1 connection becomes 1.544 Mbps minus 8,000 bps or 1.536 Mbps. For most organizations estimating T1 performance, the variability of an estimate within a margin of error of 10% to 20% allows computations to occur using a data rate of 1.544 Mbps. However, as noted, a better measurement occurs when the data transport capacity of 1.536 Mbps is used for a T1 line.

As previously discussed, most Internet entry actions consist of transmitting a short URL to access a server page. Thus, throughput delays associated with requesting a Web page do not significantly vary among the previously mentioned access methods. However, the opposite is not true. That is, there can be significant differences in Web page display delays based upon the method a user employs to access the Internet. For example, consider Table 4.1, which shows the delay or latency associated with delivering a Web page varying in size from 10,000 bytes to 300,000 bytes in increments of 10,000 bytes based upon four data rates.

In examining the entries in Table 4.1, let's start with the leftmost column, which shows the Web page size. Most Web pages contain a mixture of text and graphics, with the latter primarily in the JPEG format that permits a high degree of image compression. Even so, it's common for a typical Web page to consist of between 150,000 and 175,000 bytes. One notable exception to this average Web page size is the Google home page, which is shown in Figure 4.1. Note that the Google home page is streamlined, with only one graphic image on the page. This action facilitates the delivery of that home page to users regardless of the data transport mechanism they are using to access the Internet.

Table 4.1   Web Page Delays Based upon Page Size and the Speed of the Access Line Connection

WEB PAGE SIZE (BYTES)	WEB PAGE DELAY (S)			
	56,000-BPS DATA-RATE DELAY	150,000-BPS DATA-RATE DELAY	1.554-MBPS DATA-RATE DELAY	6-MBPS DATA-RATE DELAY
10,000	1.42857	0.53333	0.05208	0.01333
20,000	2.85714	1.06667	0.10417	0.02667
30,000	4.28571	1.60000	0.15625	0.04000
40,000	5.71429	2.13333	0.20833	0.05333
50,000	7.14286	2.66667	0.26042	0.06667
60,000	8.57143	3.20000	0.31250	0.08000
70,000	10.00000	3.73333	0.36458	0.09333
80,000	11.42857	4.26667	0.41667	0.10667
90,000	12.85714	4.80000	0.46875	0.12000
100,000	14.28571	5.33333	0.52083	0.13333
110,000	15.71429	5.86667	0.57292	0.14667
120,000	17.14286	6.40000	0.62500	0.16000
130,000	18.57143	6.93333	0.67708	0.17333
140,000	20.00000	7.46667	0.72917	0.18667
150,000	21.42857	8.00000	0.78125	0.20000
160,000	22.85714	8.53333	0.83333	0.21333
170,000	24.28571	9.06667	0.88542	0.22667
180,000	25.71429	9.60000	0.93750	0.24000
190,000	27.14286	10.13333	0.98958	0.25333
200,000	28.57143	10.66667	1.04167	0.26667
210,000	30.00000	11.20000	1.09375	0.28000
220,000	31.42857	11.73333	1.14583	0.29333
230,000	32.85714	12.26667	1.19792	0.30667
240,000	34.28571	12.80000	1.25000	0.32000
250,000	35.71429	13.33333	1.30208	0.33333
260,000	37.14286	13.86667	1.35417	0.34667
270,000	38.57143	14.40000	1.40625	0.36000
280,000	40.00000	14.93333	1.45833	0.37333
290,000	41.42857	15.46667	1.51042	0.38667
300,000	42.85714	16.00000	1.56250	0.40000

At the opposite end of Web page design with respect to graphic images are the home pages of the major television networks, such as ABC.com, CBS.com, FOX.com, and NBC.com, as well as portals such as Yahoo.com and MSNBC.com. In addition, many newspapers' on-line Web sites, such as NYTimes.com and JPost.com, are packed with a large number of small graphic images that cumulatively

Figure 4.1   The Google home page is optimized for delivery to a Web browser user.

results in a Web page that can easily exceed 150,000 bytes of data. For example, consider Figure 4.2, which shows the home page for Yahoo. com viewed on January 5, 2010, on a wide-screen HP TouchSmart all-in-one computer. If you focus your attentions on Figure 4.2, you will note a series of small images or icons under the column labeled "My Favorites." If you examine the four small pictures under the main picture, they function as a selector for the story and images that will be displayed as you move your cursor over each. Because the images and stories are downloaded, they add to the size of the Web page and cumulatively add up to produce a rather large download that would be poorly handled by a data rate less than a broadband speed.

You can obtain an appreciation for the size of graphic images by moving your cursor over an image and performing a right click operation. From the resulting pop-up menu, select "Properties," which will display the size of the image in bytes as well as other information about the image.

Figure 4.3 illustrates an example of the display of the Properties box associated with the main image of Casey Johnson located to the right

Figure 4.2   The home page of Yahoo.com contains graphics scattered on the page that cumulatively result in a large download of bytes of data.

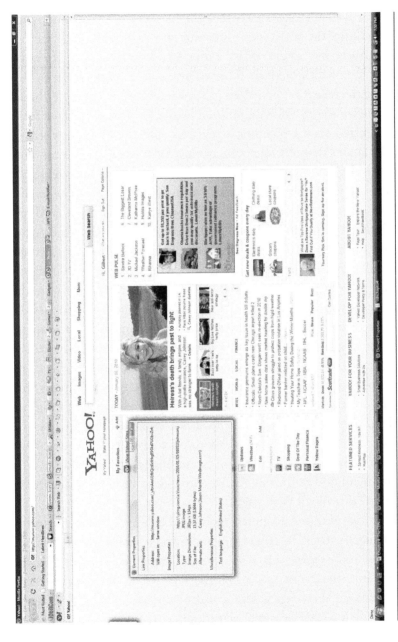

Figure 4.3 Viewing the Properties box associated with one of four images downloaded when accessing the home page of Yahoo.com.

of the box. Note that this image, which is one of four images on the typical home page of Yahoo.com for any day of the week, consists of almost 16,000 bytes. Thus, when you add up the number of bytes for the series of small images and other graphics on the typical home page of Yahoo.com, the amount of data easily approaches 150,000 bytes.

Returning our attention to Table 4.1, let's focus our attention upon columns 2 through 5. Those columns indicate the delay in seconds for the reception of a Web page of indicated size in bytes based upon the transport facility employed by the browser user. If we focus our attention on the columns associated with the Web page size of 150,000 bytes that represents an average Web page size, we can note that the page exit delay or latency will range from approximately 21 seconds when the user employs a 56-Kbps dial-up modem to a fifth of a second when using a cable modem operating at 6 Mbps. Similarly, at a Web page size of 200,000 bytes, the Web page delays range from approximately 28.6 seconds at 56 Kbps to 0.266 seconds at a cable modem operating rate of 6 Mbps. Thus, as you might expect, Web page delays associated with exiting the Internet via the browser user's access line increase as the Web page size increases. In addition, the delay is proportional to the operating rate of the access line. Thus, both the page size in bytes returned to the user as well as the Internet connection method play an important role in the overall delay. This information also indicates why most Web pages that include a variety of images are not suitable for viewing with a dial-up modem. Although it's possible to avoid downloading images and replace them with text labels to speed up a download, the old adage that a picture is worth a thousand words applies in the modern Web environment and reinforces the importance of having the capability to rapidly download Web pages.

Now that we have an appreciation for the delays attributable to the type of access to the Internet employed by browser users, let's turn our attention to the egress delays. In actuality, we are referring to the connection from the Internet to a particular Web server. As previously mentioned, since a Web page is several orders of magnitude larger in terms of bytes than a URL request, we can ignore the delay associated with the packet containing the URL flowing to the Web server. However, it's important to note that a server has a fixed maximum capability with respect to the number of simultaneous users it can service. In actuality, this author is referring to the maximum number of open TCP/IP connections a server can support, which is usually limited to fewer than 2,000. Because the connections are open, we usually refer to them as the number of simultaneous open connections. One of the most common hacker methods to disrupt service is to transmit a sequence of connection requests while cycling through a list of IP addresses that are used as source addresses in each TCP/IP connection. Because the server responds to each request and sets a timer so that the connection will eventually time out, by loading the server with phony connection requests, the hacker makes it difficult, if not impossible, for legitimate users to access the server. Because, for practical purposes, we can ignore the delay associated with egress operations consisting of short URLs transported to a server, we can continue to focus our attention on the flow of Web pages toward the user.

4.2.3 Egress Delays

Previously, we noted that a user's browser connection to the Internet has a bearing on latency. Similarly, so does the connection of a Web site to the Internet. Because input delays are based upon the size of the data packet, the small amount of data in the form of a URL request means that we can ignore input delays without being significantly in error. Thus, similar to our investigation of user access delays, the primary egress transport facility delay involves the flow of a Web page over the transport facility that connects a Web site to the Internet. This allows us to simplify our analysis while being more correct than most bureaucrats.

Most Web sites are connected to the Internet by T1 or T3 lines, with the latter operating at approximately 45 Mbps. However, unlike our prior computations for the Internet access line that is normally not shared, the egress connection is shared by many users. Thus, we need to consider the average number of users accessing a Web server, as each user request results in the return of a Web page. While it's true that different users will be requesting different Web pages that are formed from different text and graphic images, for simplicity we can consider that each Web page has a similar composition in bytes. In effect, we are looking for an average Web page size, with some users requesting a larger page size while other users are requesting a smaller Web page

Table 4.2 Time Delays in Seconds for Delivering a Web Page from a Server to the Internet

WEB PAGE SIZE (BYTES)	150,000-BPS DATA RATE			W45-MBPS DATA RATE		
	1-USER DELAY	10-USER DELAY	100-USER DELAY	1-USER DELAY	10-USER DELAY	100-USER DELAY
10,000	0.05333	0.53333	5.33333	0.00178	0.01778	0.17778
20,000	0.10667	1.06667	10.66667	0.00356	0.03556	0.35556
30,000	0.16000	1.60000	16.00000	0.00533	0.05333	0.53333
40,000	0.21333	2.13333	21.33333	0.00711	0.07111	0.71111
50,000	0.26667	2.66667	26.66667	0.00889	0.08889	0.88889
60,000	0.32000	3.20000	32.00000	0.01067	0.10667	1.06667
70,000	0.37333	3.73333	37.33333	0.01244	0.12444	1.24444
80,000	0.42667	4.26667	42.66667	0.01422	0.14222	1.42222
90,000	0.48000	4.80000	48.00000	0.01600	0.16000	1.60000
100,000	0.53333	5.33333	53.33333	0.01778	0.17778	1.77778
110,000	0.58667	5.86667	58.66667	0.01956	0.19556	1.95556
120,000	0.64000	6.40000	64.00000	0.02133	0.21333	2.13333
130,000	0.69333	6.93333	69.33333	0.02311	0.23111	2.31111
140,000	0.74667	7.46667	74.66667	0.02489	0.24889	2.48889
150,000	0.80000	8.00000	80.00000	0.02667	0.26667	2.66667
160,000	0.85333	8.53333	85.33333	0.02844	0.28444	2.84444
170,000	0.90667	9.06667	90.66667	0.03022	0.30222	3.02222
180,000	0.96000	9.60000	96.00000	0.03200	0.32000	3.20000
190,000	1.01333	10.13333	101.33333	0.03378	0.33778	3.37778
200,000	1.06667	10.66667	106.66667	0.03556	0.35556	3.55556
210,000	1.12000	11.20000	112.00000	0.03733	0.37333	3.73333
220,000	1.17333	11.73333	117.33333	0.03911	0.39111	3.91111
230,000	1.22667	12.26667	122.66667	0.04089	0.40889	4.08889
240,000	1.28000	12.80000	128.00000	0.04267	0.42667	4.26667
250,000	1.33333	13.33333	133.33333	0.04444	0.44444	4.44444
260,000	1.38667	13.86667	138.66667	0.04622	0.46222	4.62222
270,000	1.44000	14.40000	144.00000	0.04800	0.48000	4.80000
280,000	1.49333	14.93333	149.33333	0.04978	0.49778	4.97778
290,000	1.54667	15.46667	154.66667	0.05156	0.51556	5.15556
300,000	1.60000	16.00000	160.00000	0.05333	0.53333	5.33333

size. Again, when we discuss the size of a Web page, we are referring to the number of bytes of data contained on the page and not its
length. Thus, we can modify our previous computations performed in
Table 4.1 to reflect the activity of additional users at a Web site.

Table 4.2 provides a summary of the use of an Excel spreadsheet
model to project the time delays in seconds associated with a Web
page delivery. Similar to Table 4.1, the first column indicates varying

Web page sizes in bytes, ranging from 10,000 bytes to 300,000 bytes in increments of 10,000 bytes. Columns 2, 3, and 4 indicate the delays associated with 1, 10, and 100 users querying a server and sharing a 1.5-Mbps T1 transport facility connecting the server to the Internet. Similarly, columns 5, 6, and 7 indicate the delays associated with 1, 10, and 100 users accessing a common Web server and sharing a T3 transport facility operating at approximately 45 Mbps that connects the server to the Internet.

In examining the entries in Table 4.2, note that the delay in delivering a Web page from a server onto the Internet is primarily a function of three factors. Those factors include the Web page size in bytes, the transport facility operating rate, and the number of users requesting the delivery of Web pages over the common connection between the server and the Internet.

A careful examination of the data presented in Table 4.2 indicates that a popular Web site that has a T1 connection to the Internet can encounter significant Web page delivery delays when even 10 users are actively requesting Web pages. For example, at a Web page size of 150,000 bytes, the delay in placing one Web page onto the Internet is 8 seconds, which in the modern world of Internet usage may appear to be an eternity to many persons. When the number of users requesting Web pages increases to 100, the delay increases to 80 seconds, which is obviously such a significant amount of time that most persons accessing the Web site more than likely believe that the system is down, and they have either pointed their browsers elsewhere or begun a search for another site that will satisfy their requirements.

To reduce delay times, many organizations have upgraded their facilities by installing T3 connections to the Internet that operate at approximately 45 Mbps. If you examine the row in Table 4.2 associated with a Web page size of 150,000 bytes and move to the rightmost column, you will note that the use of a T3 transmission facility when there are 100 users results in a Web page delay of approximately 2.67 seconds. While this is significantly less than the 80 seconds associated with the use of a T1 line shared by 100 users, it still represents a large delay if a user needs to scroll through a series of Web pages. In addition, we need to note that the access and egress transport facilities are cumulative, further adding to the delays experienced by a browser user accessing a Web server.

Because of the previously mentioned egress delays, large organizations that wish to operate a centralized service may opt to upgrade their transport facility to an Optical Carrier (OC), typically installing an OC-3 or OC-12 transport facility. An OC-3 facility operates at 155 Mbps and, in effect, can be considered to represent the capacity of 100 T1 facilities or approximately 3.5 T3 facilities. In comparison, an OC-12 facility operates at 622 Mbps. As you might expect, at higher data rates, the monthly cost of service dramatically increases. Although the cost of a leased facility varies by distance, to provide a general reference for readers, where a T1 line might cost $500 per month, an OC-12 might be over $15,000 per month. Thus, selecting an Optical Carrier transport facility is usually associated with large organizations. What they obtain in addition to a higher data rate is the ability—for some additional cost—to install concentric rings that provide a near-instantaneous ability to reroute data in the event of a failure on the primary ring. Because many large organizations, such as an airline or rental car agency, could lose a significant amount of revenue due to a communications failure, the use of Optical Carrier transport facilities with dual rings is gaining advocates. However, if your organization is looking for a different approach to minimizing egress delays, one potential solution is to consider the use of edge servers.

4.2.4 Benefits of Edge Servers

The distribution of Web server content onto edge servers can significantly reduce many of the delays computed in Table 4.2. This is because fewer browser users can be expected to access distributed Web sites in comparison to the number of users that can be expected to access a centralized site. Unfortunately, the distribution of server content onto edge servers will have no bearing on the delays associated with a user's access line. This is because the user's access line remains fixed unless the user was previously accessing a Web site from work and then went home and accessed the same site via a different access line. While this is certainly possible, for the vast majority of Web users, their access line can be considered as fixed along with the transmission delays associated with their access line. Thus, there are certain limitations associated with the distribution of server content that will not significantly improve operations over the use of a centralized Web site. Now that we have an appreciation for Internet entry and egress delays due to the transport facility operating rate and potential user sharing of the facility, let's turn our attention to several additional bottlenecks. One bottleneck that we previously covered and that deserves a more detailed examination involves peering points and their effect upon Web servers responding to a browser user's request.

4.2.5 Peering Points

The Internet represents a collection of networks that are interconnected in order to permit the flow of data from a computer located on one network to a computer connected to another network. Those networks that are interconnected can range in size from a local area network with a handful of attached computers to the LAN to networks operated by an Internet Service Provider (ISP) that can consist of hundreds of thousands of DSL or cable modem users or even large ISPs, such as America Online, that at one time supported approximately 20 million users but more recently had about 5 million users as former dial-up subscribers gravitated to DSL and cable modem connections.

4.2.5.1 Rationale Because of the global nature of the Internet, most networks are not directly connected to one another. Instead, networks were originally interconnected via the use of the transmission facilities of one or more third-party networks. An example of this interconnection via the use of third-party networks is illustrated in Figure 4.4. In this example, for data transmitted from a computer user located on network A to arrive at a computer located on network E, the transmission facilities of two other networks, such as networks B and C or networks B and D, must be employed to provide an interconnection to the destination network. Similarly, a computer user on network B that requires access to a computer located on network E would need to use the transmission facilities of either network C or network D. Because routers require time to examine the destination address in the IP header of a packet, check its routing table, and route the packet from the interface it was received on to another interface for transmission toward its ultimate destination, there is a delay or latency associated with each router through which a packet traverses. As a packet crosses more networks, it also

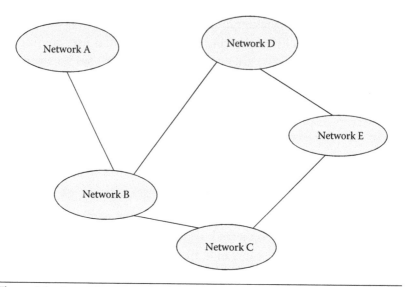

Figure 4.4 A computer user on network A needs to use the transmission facilities of third-party networks to reach a computer located on networks C, D, or E.

passes through additional routers, which cumulatively adds to the delay or latency encountered. In addition, as additional networks are traversed, the potential of encountering a network failure increases. Thus, as the number of networks traversed increases, so too does the delay as well as the probability that the data packet will not arrive at its intended destination.

4.2.5.2 Peering and Transit Operations Although the term *peering point* will be used in this book, it is important to note that the alternate name of *exchange point* is also commonly used to reference the point where two or more networks interconnect. In fact, some Web sites that provide a listing of interconnections on the Internet satisfy this quirk in terminology by using both terms. Figure 4.5 illustrates the Web site home page at http://www.bgp4.as/internet-exchanges, which lists Internet exchange points around the globe. This site depends upon viewers sending e-mails to the Webmaster to notify the site of additions and updates. Because the site has links to each exchange point or peering point, you can use this site to view peering points on a global basis. However, when this author used this site, he discovered a few bad links that can result in a bit of frustration and might be due to the failure of one or more persons to periodically double-check links.

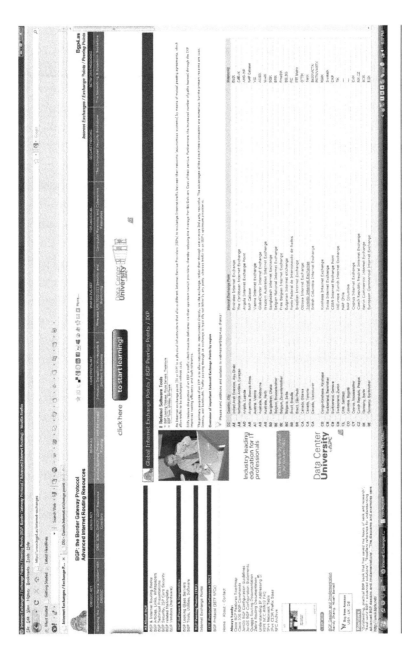

Figure 4.5 The Web site www.bgp4.as provides a link to numerous peering points around the globe.

To obtain an appreciation for the wealth of information that can be obtained from a site that lists peering points, this author scrolled down the screen shown in Figure 4.5 until he reached the entry for the Danish Internet Exchange Point. By clicking on that entry, his browser was directed to DIX, a facility operated by UNIC at its Network Operations Center located in Lyngby, which is north of Copenhagen, Denmark. The site's home page, which is shown in Figure 4.6, provides a brief history of DIX and includes three graphs that indicate the traffic load over the past 24 hours, for one week, and for one year.

If you focus your attention upon the first graph shown at the top of Figure 4.6, you will note that traffic peaks at approximately between 9:30 and 10 p.m. Because the actual printout of the Web page shows a light graph that is not very visible in the screen capture, this author was able to view the maximum traffic load at about 12 Gbps, with the maximum capacity being 13 Gbps according to the x-axis legend in the graph. Thus, DIX is reaching capacity during the evening, and routers are more than likely dropping packets, which results in some delays.

While Figure 4.6 provides three graphs that illustrate the daily, monthly, and yearly traffic, you actually need to do some analysis to determine the effect of traffic delays. If you click on the entry "Service Information" displayed in the left column of Figure 4.6, you will see a Web page that will provide you with such information as how networks can be connected to DIX and the fact that they use a Cisco 6509 switch that has both 1-Gbps and 10-Gbps ports. While the information is interesting, it does not provide the viewer with any latency information, which could be extremely valuable when attempting to determine the value of using edge servers. While you can make some educated guesses based upon the occupancy of data on the exchange, especially in the evening, they at best are educated guesses.

One of the more interesting peering or exchange points is the British Columbia Internet Exchange, whose Web address is http://www.bc.net. At this site you can select a transit exchange server and run either a bandwidth test or a diagnostic test, or both. The bandwidth test performs two TCP (transmission-control protocol) throughput tests between your desktop computer, which can be located anywhere on the Internet, and the specified NDT (network diagnostic tool) server. First, data is streamed for 10 seconds from your

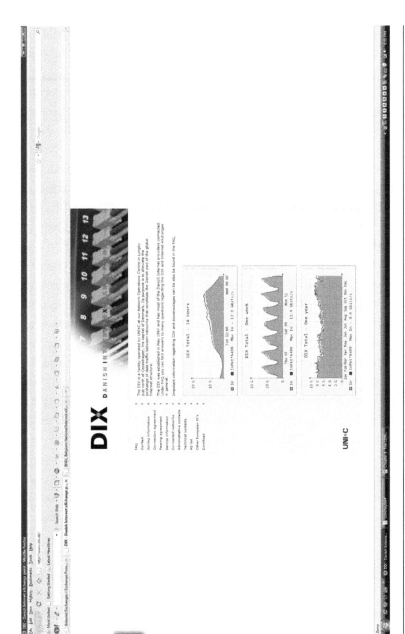

Figure 4.6 The home page of the Danish Internet Exchange Point.

desktop to the server, and then a second 10-second test is performed in the opposite direction. In comparison, the diagnostic test, which is more formally referred to as NPAD (Network Path and Application Diagnosis), is designed to diagnose network performance problems in your end-system on which your browser is running or the network between it and the specified NPAD server.

To illustrate the capability of BCIE, this author ran the bandwidth test from his computer located in Georgia to the Vancouver server. Figure 4.7 illustrates the display of the test results, with the BCNET page shown in the background, while the foreground shows the test results and the display of detailed statistics. While the test was performed at a bit after 2 p.m. on a Tuesday, not exactly a period of anticipated heavy traffic, the test results illustrate how finding the correct test can provide you with the ability to determine both the bandwidth available for accessing a distant location and the round-trip delay. Note that in the Detailed Statistics box, it even informs you that no network congestion was observed. Thus, by using a Web browser from several locations to a site that offers a similar capability, you can determine the anticipated latency during such peak times as an early Friday afternoon or a Monday morning before lunch.

As an alternative to using the facilities of an exchange or peering point, you can use a test tool built into Windows and other operating systems. Two tools that are readily available are Ping and Traceroute, the latter called Tracert in Windows. Ping can be used to both verify that a distant site is reachable and the round-trip delay to the site. In comparison, Tracert can be considered as Ping on steroids, as it displays the path to the destination as well as route information and the round-trip delay to each route on the path, which can be used to determine where potential bottlenecks reside. Later in this chapter, we will discuss the use of Tracert as well as illustrate its use.

4.2.5.3 Transit and Peering Operations   Returning to our discussion of peering or data exchange between networks, let's probe a bit more into this topic. When two network operators interconnect their facilities to exchange data, they need to decide upon the type of data exchange they are willing to support. If a network operator is willing to accept traffic from the other network that is destined for a different network, then the network operator is providing a transit facility to the other network.

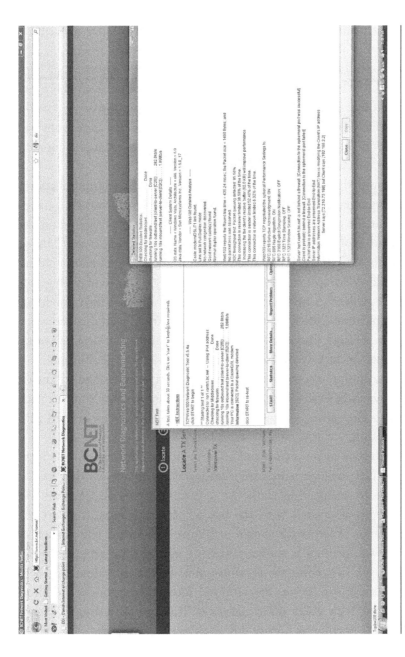

Figure 4.7 Using the BCNET transmit exchange test facility.

That is, the network operator in effect has agreed to receive traffic from the other network and pass it through its network onto the Internet regardless of its destination. Because Internet traffic is bidirectional, this means that the network operator also agrees to receive traffic from the Internet and pass such traffic through its network.

If, instead of agreeing to accept any traffic, let's assume that both network operators are only willing to accept traffic from the other network that is destined for them. In this situation, the two networks are peering with one another. That is, as long as the data from one network is destined to the other, it can pass through the peering connection, while all other traffic will be blocked.

Because there is no free lunch in the field of communications, most organizations will charge a fee for providing a transit capability. That fee can vary, ranging from a fee structure based upon the bandwidth of the connection to an amount per megabyte (Mb) or gigabyte (Gb) of data that flows through one network from another network. A no-cost transit agreement usually occurs when a big network provider has interconnections to other similar-sized providers. In comparison, a for-fee transit agreement is usually established when smaller network providers are only connected to one or a few other networks. In fact, if you point your browser at any peering point or exchange point, you will more than likely find an entry labeled similar to "Services & Prices," which when clicked upon takes you to a page that lists the various connection options and the cost associated with each option.

In contrast to transit operations, a peering point represents a location where many networks are interconnected to one another for the purpose of exchanging traffic on a peering basis. To illustrate the advantages associated with the use of peering points, consider the two groups of networks shown in Figure 4.8. In the left portion of Figure 4.8, peering is shown occurring among four networks without the use of a common peering point. In this situation, $(n - 1)/2$ communications circuits are required for each network to be interconnected with every other network. Thus, in the example shown in the left portion of Figure 4.8, each network requires $(4 - 1)/2$ or $3/2$ links. Because there are four networks to be interconnected, a total of $(4 \times 3)/2$ or 6 communications circuits are required to interconnect each network to every other network.

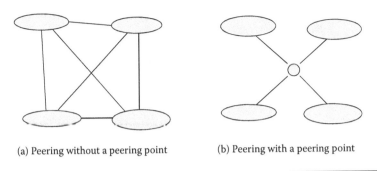

(a) Peering without a peering point   (b) Peering with a peering point

Figure 4.8   Understanding the value of a peering point.

In the right-hand portion of Figure 4.8, the use of a peering point is shown. In this example, the four networks are interconnected at a common location. Thus, each network only requires one communications circuit for the interconnection, or a total of four circuits for the four networks.

The advantages associated with the use of peering points involve both the simplicity of interconnections as well as economics. For example, if the collection of four networks previously shown in Figure 4.8 were increased by just one, then the total number of communications circuits required to interconnect every network to each other without peering points would be $5 \times (5 - 1)/2$ or 10. Similarly, an increase in the number of networks to be interconnected to six would result in the need for $6 \times (6 - 1)/2$ or 15 communications circuits. In comparison, the use of a peering point would only require each network to have one communications connection to the peering point, or a total of six communications connections in order to provide an interconnection capability for all six networks. Table 4.3 indicates the number of communications circuits that would be required to interconnect two or more networks with and without the use of a peering point.

From an examination of the entries in Table 4.3, it is apparent that the use of a peering point can provide a significant reduction in communications links, especially as the number of networks to be interconnected increases. Because each communications link requires the use of a router port and routers can only support a finite number of serial ports, another router is required after the maximum support level is reached. Both routers and router ports represent costs that need to be considered. In addition, when peering occurs without the use of a peering point, the result can be a mesh network structure

Table 4.3 Communications Circuits Required to Provide Network Interconnections

NUMBER OF NETWORKS TO BE INTERCONNECTED	WITHOUT USING A PEERING POINT	USING A PEERING POINT
2	2	2
3	3	3
4	6	4
5	10	5
6	15	6
7	21	7
8	28	8
9	36	9
10	45	10

employed to interconnect networks to one another. Under this situation, configuring routers becomes more complex than when a peering point is employed, since the latter only requires the routing of data over a single communications path for one network to obtain connectivity with all other networks. Another factor that needs to be considered is latency or delay time. In a mesh network structure, the individual communications links normally operate at a fraction of the data rate of a peering point network. In addition, in the mesh structure, many routes are possible, so the router has to make more computations than a router at a peering point. This, in turn, reduces the latency or delay associated with the use of a peering point. Thus, the cost of equipment, personnel time and effort, delays from packet transits, and the complexity of connecting networks without the use of a peering point have resulted in most network connectivity now occurring via peering points.

4.2.5.4 Global Structure of Peering Points The concept associated with peering points has now been adopted on a global basis, with locations throughout the United States, Europe, South America, Asia, and Australia. Sometimes the term *metropolitan area exchange* (MAE) is used, while other terms employed as synonyms include *network access point* (NAP) and *Internet exchange* (IX). Regardless of the term used, peering points are now the primary method by which ISPs interconnect their separate networks to enable traffic to flow throughout the Internet.

4.2.5.5 Representative Peering Points Previously in this book, we looked at the statistics provided by one peering point in Denmark and observed the use of the BCNET transmit-exchange test facility. In addition, we briefly discussed how peering points can now be encountered on a global basis, and we looked at one Web site that provided links to exchange points on a global basis. To obtain a better appreciation for the global nature of peering points, we will describe the European Internet Exchange (Euro-IX) and several European exchange points as well as examine the use of a Windows tool for determining the latency or delay associated with transmitting data from one location to another.

4.2.5.5.1 Euro-IX The European Internet Exchange (Euro-IX) was set up by the operators of European Internet Exchange points. The goal of Euro-IX is to assist ISPs looking to peer at a European exchange point.

Table 4.4 lists a majority of the European Internet Exchange points by country as of early 2010. The number of European Internet Exchange points had grown to 123 by early 2010 from approximately 90 when the first edition of this book was written in 2005. To obtain an appreciation of the use of a European Internet Exchange point, we will briefly examine three members of Euro-IX: the Vienna Internet exchange (VIX), the Belgium National exchange (BNIX), and the London Internet exchange (LNX).

4.2.5.5.2 The Vienna Internet Exchange The Vienna Internet exchange (VIX) was originally located at the Vienna University computer center. Since beginning operations in 1996, it has expanded to a second location within Vienna at Interxion, Austria, which is located in the 21st district in the north of the city. VIX provides a peering point in the geographic center of Europe. Both locations use the same state-of-the-art Ethernet switching technology based upon the use of Foundry Networks BigIron RX-16 nonblocking high-performance switches. The BigIron RX series of switches was the first hardware to provide support for 2.2-billion packet-per-second switching and can be considered to represent an extremely fast Layer 2 and 3 Ethernet switch. Redundancy is supported at both locations through the use of redundant switch-fabrics through redundant power supplies and

Table 4.4 Members of the Euro-IX by Country

Austria
   Grazer Internet eXchange
   VIX: Vienna Internet eXchange
Belgium
   BNIX: Belgium National Internet eXchange
   FREEBIX: Free Belgium Internet eXchange
Bulgaria
   SIX: Balkan Internet eXchange (Sofia)
Croatia
   CIX: Croatian Internet eXchange
Czech Republic
   Neutral Internet eXchange
   Commercial Brno Internet eXchange (Brno)
Cyprus
   CYIX: Cyprus Internet eXchange
Denmark
   DIX: Danish Internet eXchange
Estonia
   TIX: Tallinn Internet eXchange
   TLLIX: Tallinn Internet eXchange (Tallinn)
Finland
   FICIX-Espoo Finnish Communication and Internet eXchange (Espoo)
   FICIX-Oulu Finnish Communication and Internet eXchange (Oulu)
   TREX: Tampere Region Internet eXchange
France
   Equinix Paris Equinix Paris eXchange (Paris)
   EuroGix: A peering point
   FNIX6: eXchange in Paris
   FreeIX: A Free French eXchange
   GEIX: Gigabit European Internet eXchange (Paris)
   GNI: Grenoble Network Initiative
   LYONIX: Lyon Internet eXchange
   MAE: Metropolitan Area Exchange (Paris)
   MAIX: Marseille Internet eXchange
   MIXT: Mix Internet eXchange and Transit
   PaNAP: Paris Network Access Point (Paris)
   PARIX: A Paris Internet eXchange
   PIES: Paris Internet eXchange Service
   PIX: Paris Internet eXchange
   POUIX: Paris Operators for Universal Internet eXchange
   SFINX: Service for French Internet eXchange

Table 4.4 (continued)   Members of the Euro-IX by Country

Germany
  ALP-IX: Alpen Internet eXchange (Munich)
  BECIX: Berlin Internet eXchange
  BCIX: Berlin Commercial Internet eXchange
  DE-CIX: Deutsche Commercial Internet eXchange
  ECIX: European Commercial Internet eXchange (formerly BLNX) (Berlin)
  ECIX: European Commercial Internet eXchange (Dusseldorf)
  ECIX: Hamburg European Commercial Internet Exchange (Hamburg)
  INXS: Internet Exchange Service (Munich and Hamburg)
  Franap: Frankfurt Network Access Point
  MAE: Metropolitan Area Exchange (Frankfurt)
  KleyRex: Kleyer Rebstcker Internet eXchange (Frankfurt)
  MANDA: Metropolitan Area Network Darmstadt
  M-CIX: Munich Commercial Internet eXchange
  N-IX: Nurnberger Internet eXchange
  Stuttgarter Internet eXchange (Stuttgart)
  Work-IX Peering Point (Hamburg)
  Xchangepoint, multinational
Greece
  AIX: Athens Internet eXchange
  GR-IX: Greek Internet eXchange (Athens)
  GR-IX-(b): Greek Internet eXchange (Athens)
Holland
  R-IX: Rotterdam Internet eXchange (Rotterdam)
Hungary
  BIX: Budapest Internet eXchange
Iceland
  RIX: Reykjavik Internet eXchange
Ireland
  CNIX: Cork Neutral Internet eXchange (Cork)
  ExWest eXchange West (Galway)
  INEX: Internet Neutral eXchange Association
Italy
  MIX: Milan Internet eXchange (Milan)
  NaMeX: Nautilus Mediterranean eXchange Point (Rome)
  TOP-IX: Torino Piemonte eXchange Point (Torino)
  NaMeX: Nautilus Mediterranean eXchange Point (Rome)
  TIX: Tuscany Internet eXchange
  MiNAP: Milan Neutral Access Point (Milan)
  VSIX: VSIX Nap del Nord Est Padova
  FVG-IX: Friuli Venezia Giulia Internet eXchange (Udine)

continued

Table 4.4 (continued)   Members of the Euro-IX by Country

Kazakhstan
   KAZ-IX: Kazakhstan Traffic eXchange (Almaty)
Latvia
   LIX: Latvia Latvian Internet eXchange (Riga)
   SMILE: Santa Monica Internet Local eXchange (Riga)
Luxembourg
   LIX: Luxembourg Internet eXchange
   LU-CIX: Luxembourg Commercial Internet eXchange (Luxembourg)
Malta
   MIX: Malta Internet eXchange
Netherlands
   AMS-IX: Amsterdam Internet eXchange
   GN-IX: Groningen Internet eXchange
   NDIX: Dutch German Internet eXchange
   NL-IX: NL Internet eXchange
   GN-IX: Groningen Internet eXchange (Groningen)
   FR-IX: Friese Internet eXchange (Leeuwarden)
Norway
   BIX: Bergen Internet eXchange (Bergen)
   FIXO: Free Internet eXchange Oslo (Oslo)
   NIX: Norwegian Internet eXchange (Oslo)
   NIX2: Norwegian Internet eXchange (Oslo)
   SIX: Stavanger Internet eXchange (Stavanger)
   TIX: Tromsø Internet eXchange (Tromsø)
   TRDIX: Trondheim Internet eXchange (Trondheim)
Poland
   LIX: Poland Lodz Internet eXchange (Lodz)
   PIX: Poznan Internet eXchange (Poznan)
   PLIX: Polish Internet eXchange (Warsaw)
   WIX: Warsaw Internet eXchange
Portugal
   GIGAPIX: Gigabit Portuguese Internet eXchange (Lisbon)
Romania
   BUHIX: Bucharest Internet eXchange
   Ronix: Romanian Network for Internet eXchange
   InterLAN: Internet Exchange Bucharest, Cluj-Napoca, Constanta, Timisoara
Russia
   CHEL-PP: Chelyabinsk Peering Point (Chelyabinsk)
   EKT-IX: Ekaterinburg Internet eXchange (Ekaterinburg)
   IX-NN: IX of Nizhny Novgorod Nizhny (Novgorod)
   KRS-IX: Krasnoyarsk Internet eXchange (Krasnoyarsk)

Table 4.4 (continued)   Members of the Euro-IX by Country

    MSK-IX: Moscow Internet eXchange (Moscow)
    NSK-IX: Novosibirsk Internet eXchange (Novosibirsk)
    PERM-IX: Perm Internet eXchange (Perm)
    RND-IX: RND-IX Rostov on Don
    SPB-IX: St.-Petersburg Internet eXchange (St. Petersburg)
    SMR-IX: SAMARA-IX (Samara)
    ULN-IX: Ulyanovsk Internet eXchange (Ulyanovsk)
    Ural-IX: Ural-IX (Ekaterinburg)
    VLV-IX: Vladivostok Internet eXchange (Vladivostok)
Scotland
    World.IX: European Commercial IX (Edinburgh)
    ScotIX: Scottish Internet eXchange
Republic of Slovenia
    SIX: Slovenian Internet eXchange (Ljubljana)
    SIX: Slovak Internet eXchange (Bratislava)
    SIX: Kosice Slovak Internet eXchange (Kosice)
    Sitelix: Sitel Internet eXchange (Bratislava)
Spain
    CATNIX: Catalonia Internet eXchange (Barcelona)
    ESPANIX: Spain Internet eXchange
    GALNIX: Galicia Internet eXchange
    MAD-IX: Madrid Internet eXchange
    EuskoNIX: Punto neutro Vasco de Internet Bilbao
Sweden
    GIX: Gothenburg Internet eXchange (Gothenburg)
    IXOR: Internet eXchange point of the Oresund Region (Malmoe)
    Linkoping Municiple eXchange
    LIX: Lule Internet eXchange
    NETNOD: Internet eXchange (Stockholm)
    Netnod: Gothenburg Netnod (Gothenburg)
    Netnod: Malmoe Netnod (Malmoe)
    Netnod: Sundsvall Netnod (Sundsvall)
    Netnod: Lulea Netnod (Lulea)
    NorrNod: NorrNod Umea
    RIX-GH: Gaveleborg Regional Internet eXchange
    STHIX: Stockholm Internet eXchange (Stockholm)
Switzerland
    CIXP: CERN eXchange for Central Europe
    SWISSIX: Swiss Internet eXchange
    TIX: Telehouse's Zurich eXchange
    Equinix: Zurich

continued

Table 4.4 (continued)   Members of the Euro-IX by Country

Ukraine

  Crimea-IX: Crimea Internet eXchange (Simferopol)

  DTEL-IX: Digital Telecom Internet eXchange (Kiev)

  UA-IX: Ukrainian Internet eXchange (Kiev)

  KH-IX: Kharkov Internet eXchange (Kharkov)

  Od-IX: Odessa Internet eXchange (Odessa)

  UTC-IX: Ukrtelecom Internet eXchange

United Kingdom

  LINX: London Internet eXchange (London)

  MaNAP: Manchester Network Access Point (Manchester)

  LIPEX: London Internet Providers eXchange (London)

  LONAP: London Network Access Point (London)

  MCIX: Manchester Commercial Internet eXchange (Manchester)

  RBIEX: Redbus Interhouse Internet eXchange (London)

  PacketExchange: Distributed over 19 cities across the EU, North America, and Asia Pacific; based in London

  MerieX: Meridian Gate Internet eXchange (London)

---

power feeds. To provide redundancy for communications, each location includes diversity-routed optical-fiber cable transmission facilities. Both IPv4 and IPv6 peering is supported on the same peering LAN using Border Gateway Protocol, Version 4 (BGP4) routing protocols.

A VIX member is required to be an ISP with its own Internet connectivity. Each VIX member is required to have its own autonomous system (AS) number with already-established global Internet connectivity. A VIX member must also provide Internet access to its customers at the IP level. Thus, a content provider would not qualify for VIX membership. Participants have the choice of connecting to VIX at either of the two locations currently established, while the redundant VIX infrastructure at both sites is provided and operated by the University of Vienna. Participants are expected to use their VIX connection as a complementary tool for optimization of regional Internet traffic flows. The only routing protocol that can be used across the VIX infrastructure is BGP4. Although the preferred method of connecting to VIX is via the installation of a BGP4 peering router at one or both of the VIX locations and to directly connect the peering router port to the local VIX switch as an alternative, customers can also connect to VIX through the use of a fiber-optic cable or Layer 2/Ethernet carrier link (DWDM, EoMPLS, VLAN) from the BGP4 peering router abroad to one of the VIX locations.

Table 4.5 Vienna Internet Exchange Tariffs

	2005	2010
Service	Fee in Euros	Fee in Euros
Setup	100/month	1000 per contract
VIX switch port		
10 Mbps (10 Base T)	100/month	
100 Mbps (100 Base T)	300/month	200/month
1 Gbps (1000 Base SX)	1000/month	600/month
10 Gbps (10 GigBaseSR, 10 GigBaseLR)		2000/month
Housing for shelf in 19-inch rack		
Up to 3 height units	225/month	150/month
4 to 5 height units	375/month	50/month per additional
6 to 9 height units	675/month	

4.2.5.5.2.1 Membership Costs   VIX services are provided on a not-for-profit basis. This means that its tariffs are set to recover the cost of operation and do not include any profit. Table 4.5 indicates the VIX tariff in effect during 2005, when the first edition of this book was written, as well as in 2010, when the second edition was written. Thus this table provides an interesting example of the cost of peering over a five-year period. Note that some services were replaced by other services in the five-year period, such as the elimination of low-speed 10-Mbps switch ports. Also note that the pricing is shown in Euros. In early 2005, a Euro was worth approximately $1.40, while in 2010 the Euro was approximately $1.45, so readers can multiply Euro entries in the table by 40%–45% to obtain an approximate charge.

In addition to the tariffs listed in Table 4.5 during 2005, there was a supplemental charge of 150 Euros/month that was only applicable to the University of Vienna. This charge was for an ATM/OC-3 multimode port on a LS1010 switch. The ATM switches were eventually replaced by BigIron switches, and the additional fee has disappeared. Thus, when you compare fees over the past five years, it is obvious that they have decreased. Today, users of VIX have three fees to consider: a setup fee, a VIX switch-port fee, and a fee for housing equipment. The VIX switch-port fee is based upon the speed of the interconnection, while the housing fee is based upon the amount of shelf space required for equipment located at the Vienna Internet exchange.

4.2.5.5.3 Belgian National Internet Exchange   Moving northwest from Vienna, Austria, we turn our attention to the Belgian National

Internet exchange (BNIX). BNIX was established in 1995 by the Belgian National Research Network (BELNET) and represents a peering point where ISPs, content providers, and other business users can exchange traffic with each other in Belgium. In 2010, BNIX had two different locations. One location is at Interxion, an organization with headquarters in Amsterdam that designs and operates carrier-neutral Internet exchange centers across Europe. Interxion operates exchange points in many European cities, including Brussels. The second BNIX location is operated by Level (3), a global communications and information services company perhaps best known in some quarters for the large international fiber-optic network it constructed that interconnects 62 North American and 16 European locations. Local (3) opened its Brussels gateway in March, 2000, in a 5700-m² building in a state-of-the-art facility.

When this second edition was prepared during 2010, there were over 40 members that were connected to the BNIX network, which supports the exchange of IP multicast traffic as well as IPv4 and IPv6 traffic. From the BNIX Web site, you can obtain a listing of the members of the Internet eXchange to include their IPv4 addresses and, if used, their IPv6 addresses.

In 2005, BNIX was constructed based upon a distributed Layer-2-switched medium consisting of Fast Ethernet (100 Mbps) and Gigabit Ethernet (1000 Mbps) switches connected to one another using 10-gigabit Ethernet technology. According to BNIX, this interconnection method provides a high-speed, congestion-free interconnection facility that enables participating ISPs to exchange data without experiencing any significant bottlenecks. By 2010, BNIX had introduced the use of 10-Gbps Ethernet technology, which provided members with high-speed, congestion-free interconnections between members of the network.

4.2.5.5.4 London Internet Exchange, Ltd. In concluding our brief tour of representative European exchange points, we now focus our attention upon the London Internet Exchange, Ltd. (LINX). LINX represents the largest exchange point in Europe and is a founding member of Euro-IX.

LINX was founded in 1994 by a group of Internet service providers and has grown rapidly. In early 2010, LINX had 352 members and had accepted three new applications for membership in January. The Internet eXchange Point had 693 connected member ports and supported over 567 Gbps of peak traffic. Currently, LINX operates two physically separate networks based upon different architectures and equipment obtained from different communications vendors. One manufacturer is Extreme Networks, while the second vendor is Brocade Communications, formerly known as FOUNDRY Networks. The two networks are deployed over 10 locations around London and interconnected through the use of multiple 10-Gbps Ethernet via fiber-optic networks.

LINX represents a not-for-profit partnership between ISPs, providing a physical interconnection for its members to exchange Internet traffic through cooperative peering agreements. Candidates for becoming a LINX member must have an Autonomous System Number (ASN) and use the BGP4+ protocol for peering.

4.2.5.5.4.1 Membership Costs   Although the LINX tariff has some similarities to the previously discussed VIX tariffs, there are also some significant differences between the two fee schedules. Table 4.6 provides a summary of the LINX tariff in effect during early 2005. In examining Table 4.6, note that in addition to a setup or joining fee, LINX was charging members a quarterly membership fee. While LINX was billing subscribers similar to VIX for port and rack space, LINX, unlike VIX, also had a traffic charge, which for large data exchanges could significantly add up to a considerable expense.

While LINX was similar to VIX in 2005—in that both operate as not-for-profit entities—LINX at that time provided interconnections

Table 4.6   The London Internet Exchange Price list in 2005

SERVICE	PAYMENT SCHEDULE	GBP	EURO
Joining fee	Once	1000	1500
Membership fee	Quarterly	625	938
Port fees			
100 Mbps	Monthly	175	263
1 Gbps	Monthly	644	966
10 Gbps	Monthly	2415	3625
Traffic charge			
Per Mbyte	Monthly	0.60	0.86
Rack space			
Per unit	Monthly	50	75

Table 4.7   LINX Monthly Port Charges Effective January 2010

PORT SIZE	PORTS ON BROCADE LAN	PORTS ON EXTREME LAN
100-M ports	£160	£160
1-G ports	£446	£335
10-G ports	£1665	£1250

at up to 10 Gbps, which was a considerably higher peering rate than the operating rate provided by the Vienna Internet eXchange. Since 2005, both LINX and VIX have reduced their fees. In fact, effective 1 January 2010, the LINX membership fee was reduced to 1500 pounds per year, with 1-Gbps Ethernet and 10-Gbps Ethernet port fees also reduced. Concerning port fees, they now vary based upon the type of LAN you connect with, Brocade or Extreme, and the port operating rate. Table 4.7 illustrates the monthly LINX port cost as of January 2010.

Although a 10-Gbps interconnection should minimize bottlenecks, in actuality potential bottlenecks depend upon the traffic exchanged at a particular point in time. Thus, in concluding our discussion of peering points, we will return to the use of the Traceroute program to examine peering point delays.

4.2.5.6 Peering Point Delays   In concluding our discussion of peering points, we will return to the use of the Microsoft Tracert program included in different versions of the Windows operating system. To use Tracert, you need to open an MS-DOS window in older versions of Windows, or what is now referred to as the Command Prompt window when using more modern versions of the Windows operating system, such as Windows 2000, Windows XP, Windows Vista, and the newly released Windows 7. When using a more modern version of the Windows operating system, you can locate the Command Prompt menu entry by selecting Start > Programs > Accessories > Command Prompt.

4.2.5.6.1 Using Tracert   The use of Tracert can provide you with the ability to determine where bottlenecks are occurring when you encounter delays in accessing a server. Although most persons have the inclination to cite the server as the contributing factor when experiencing slow response time, it's quite possible that the delay resides in the Internet.

To determine if the network represents most of the delay you are experiencing when accessing a server, you could first use the Ping program built into Windows. As previously mentioned in this book, Ping provides you with the round-trip delay in milliseconds (ms) to a defined IP address or host name. If the round-trip network delay appears to be reasonable, then the delay can be attributable to the server. In comparison, if the round-trip delay provided through the use of the Ping program is relatively lengthy, then the response time delay you are experiencing has a significant network component. When this situation arises, you can then use the Tracert program to determine where the delays in the network are occurring.

To illustrate the use of Tracert, let's assume you are accessing www.londontown.com, a Web site that provides a variety of tourist services for persons visiting London, England. Figure 4.9 illustrates the home page of www.londontown.com. Note that from this site you can search for a hotel or bed-and-breakfast, arrange for airport transfers, book sightseeing tours, and even reserve theater tickets to the best shows in London. Because London is one of the most popular tourist destinations in the world, www.londontown.com represents a popular Web site.

Because the response to page requests to Londontown.com can be relatively long during an approaching holiday, let's use the Tracert program to examine the delays associated with the route to that Web site. Figure 4.10 illustrates the use of the Tracert program. In this example, this author traced the route to Londontown.com while accessing the Internet from his workplace located in Macon, Georgia.

In examining the entries shown in response to the use of the Tracert program, note that each line of output corresponds to a "hop" that the data has to go through to reach its destination. The first hop represents the delay associated with the author's connection to the Internet. Because all three tries have a latency under 10 ms, we can assume that the access line is not congested. Part of the reason for the lack of congestion can be traced to the time period when the Tracert program was used, which was in the early morning prior to a buildup in local access traffic.

The second hop results in the flow of data to a router located in Atlanta. The third hop also represents a router located in Atlanta. If you carefully read the router descriptions for the routers associated

Figure 4.9 The home page of Londontown.com.

Figure 4.10 Using Tracert to observe the delays in reaching www.Londontown.com.

with hops 2 and 3, you will note that the router located at hop 2 is associated with bbnplanet, while the router at hop 3 is associated with "level 3 communications," a wholesale telecom carrier that has rapidly expanded and operates many Internet eXchange or peering points. Thus, between hops 2 and 3, data flows from one carrier to another due to a peering arrangement. Because both hops 2 and 3 are located in Atlanta, propagation delay is minimal, and by hop 3, two out of three computed delays are shown to be under 10 ms, while the third delay is shown to be 10 ms. For all three times, the delay is minimal.

For hops 3 through 5, traffic remains on the level 3 network, where data is routed to Washington, D.C. Between hops 6 and 7, traffic exits the level 3 network and enters AboveNet. The latter represent an all-optical network backbone that interconnects data centers in the United States and Europe, including locations in Northern Virginia in the United States and London in the United Kingdom. Thus, hops 7 through 9 correspond to the routing of data on the AboveNet network in the United States. Note that by hop 9 for two out of three time measurements, the delay is 20 ms, with the third delay time shown as 10 ms. Again, these are reasonable delays.

4.2.5.6.2 Propagation Delay From hop 9 to hop 10, data flows from the AboveNet router located in the United States to that vendor's router located in the United Kingdom. Note that the time delay significantly increases from 10 to 20 ms at hop 9 to 90 ms at hop 10. This delay results from placing data onto a trans-Atlantic fiber cable and includes the propagation delay associated with data crossing the Atlantic Ocean.

Once data arrives in England at hop 10, the delay associated with reaching the Londontown.com Web site is negligible. This is more likely due to the use of relatively fast switches that override congestion due to the fact that it is +6 hours later in London, where users are more actively surfing the Internet. Thus, the primary delay in this situation results from an approximate 70-ms time required for data from a router located in the United States to reach a router located in the United Kingdom. This propagation delay represents 70/90 or approximately 78% of the total delay and could be avoided if the Web site operator established an agreement with a content delivery provider that resulted in the distribution of their server content onto a computer located in the United States. While the peering point delay shown in this example was vastly exceeded by the propagation delay, this is not always true. As indicated in this section, through the use of the Tracert program, you can determine the location where network delays occur, in effect obtaining a visual indication of network performance.

4.3 Edge Operations

From our examination of Internet bottlenecks, it's apparent that the centralized model of server-based content can result in several delays. Those delays include the bandwidth limitations associated with the access lines connecting the browser user and server to the Internet, peering point interconnection data rates and traffic, router hops traversed from the browser user to the server, and propagation delays based upon the distance between the two. By moving content from a centralized location to servers distributed geographically to areas that better match access requirements, many of the previously mentioned delays are minimized. For example, let's assume that a multinational Japanese organization has its server content distributed to edge servers located in Europe, Africa, the United States, Australia, and China from a single server residing in Tokyo.

Without the distribution of server contents, all user requests would have to traverse several networks, multiple router hops, and more than likely pass through multiple peering points. However, with content now distributed onto servers located around the globe, browser users avoid most, if not all, of the previously mentioned bottlenecks. Thus, moving content closer to groups of potential browser users represents a method to eliminate potential peering point bottlenecks, reduces the number of router hops data must traverse, minimizes propagation delays, and may even allow data flow to remain on one ISP network. In addition, because a centralized server acquires browser user requests similar to a funnel with a single entry point in the form of a Web server's access line, moving content to distributed edge servers removes a centralized Web site's network access constraint. Now that we have a basic appreciation for the advantages associated with moving Internet content onto distributed servers, commonly referred to as *edge servers*, let's turn our attention to how edge server operations are performed.

4.3.1 CDN Operation

There are several commercially available Content Delivery Network operators, each employing a slightly different method of operation. Because Akamai Technologies can be considered to represent the leader in the field of CDN providers, we will focus our attention upon the CDN operation of this vendor. In doing so, we will first note their support for an emerging standard in the form of a markup language provides the ability to easily distribute content onto edge servers. Once this is accomplished, we will discuss their relatively new support for the distribution of high-definition video, which is rapidly growing in importance for many Web site operators.

4.3.2 The Akamai Network

Akamai traces its roots back to the emergence of the World Wide Web (WWW) in 1995, when MIT Professor of Applied Mathematics Tom Leighton, who literally worked in close proximity to the developer of the browser, Tim Berners-Lee, was intrigued by the need to better deliver Web content by moving the content onto distributed servers. Working with the assistance of then graduate student Danny Lewin and others, the result was the launching of a commercial service in April 1999, with Yahoo! being a charter customer.

The Akamai network in 2005 had grown to approximately 15,000 servers. By early 2010, the vendor's server population had further increased to over 56,000. Those servers are distributed across the globe and are connected by approximately 1000 networks in more than 70 countries. Today Akamai provides a content delivery network facility that is used by over 1200 of the world's leading electronic commerce organizations to provide content delivery services. In fact, according to the company's Web site, Akamai delivers between 15% and 20% of all Web traffic. Its extensive customer base includes such organizations as Best Buy, the U.S. Department of Defense, FedEx Corporation, General Motors, IBM Corporation, QVC, Sony Entertainment Group, Toyota, Victoria's Secret, and Yahoo!

4.3.2.1 Type of Content Support Through the year 2000, most content delivery network providers focused their efforts upon delivering static content. While the delivery of such content was satisfactory for many organizations, the growth in electronic commerce and development of tools to enhance Web pages with varying content increased the need to support both dynamic and personalized content. In addition, the recent growth in the past few years in the use of a variety of gadgets, ranging from smart cell phones to netbooks to view television and high-definition video, has had a tremendous effect upon the ability of many Web servers to support the growth in demand. Today, several content delivery network providers, including Akamai Technologies, are capable of distributing the entire contents of customers' Web sites, including static and dynamic pages with high-definition video as well as various embedded objects. To obtain an appreciation for the manner by which content delivery operates, let's first examine how browser requests are commonly fulfilled by a centralized electronic-commerce Web site.

4.3.2.2 Centralized Web Site Access Let's assume that a browser user wishes to purchase the latest release of a movie on DVD. That person might access an electronic commerce site and search for a particular DVD, such as the *Star Wars Trilogy* DVD or the more recently released *Avatar*. When the browser user fills in a search line and clicks on a button, his or her search entry is forwarded from the Web server to

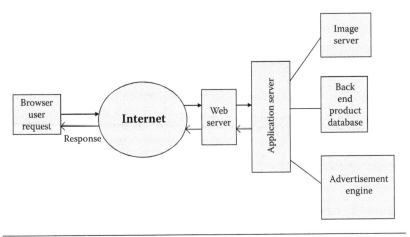

Figure 4.11   Centralized-site electronic commerce operation.

an application server, as illustrated in the right portion of Figure 4.11. The application server uses the newly furnished string query to perform a database query. The application server then assembles a page based upon information provided by the database server as well as such common page components as the site's logos, a navigation menu, and perhaps even selected advertising based upon the type of product queries. The browser user then receives the assembled page that allows him or her to add the DVD or DVDs to a digital shopping cart, select a suggested title generated by the application server, or perform another action such as "checkout."

If we assume that another browser user makes the same request, some of the same series of steps will have to be performed again. That is, the browser user's request will flow to the Web site, which in turn will pass the search query to an application server. That server might then check its cache memory to determine if the requested page can be rapidly delivered. If a copy of the page is not in memory, the application server will have to re-create the page. Although retrieval of the page from cache memory can slightly enhance response time, pages must still flow from the centralized site back to different browser users, resulting in a variable delay based upon the number of router hops and peering points that must be traversed, as well as traffic activity on the Internet, for a page to reach the requester.

4.3.2.3 Edge Server Model   In comparison to the centralized Web site model, when Akamai edge servers are used, all initial Web

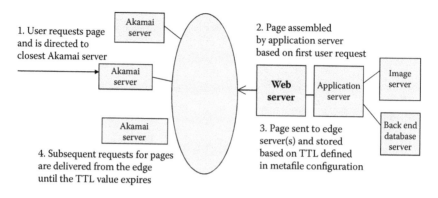

Figure 4.12 Data flow using Akamai edge servers.

page queries for a site that has contracted with the vendor flow to the vendor, while subsequent requests flow to an Akamai edge server. The edge server checks its internal cache to determine if the requested page was previously requested by another browser user and still resides in memory. Concerning cacheability of content, Akamai provides each Web site it supports with a metadata configuration file. The Web site manager uses that file to define how often specific pages can change.

For our previous DVD example, let's assume that the electronic commerce site operator only changes the DVD pricing at most once per day. Then, the Web site manager would assign the DVD page a time-to-live (TTL) value of one day. Thus, the first time a browser user requests the page, it will be assembled by the Web site application server as previously illustrated in Figure 4.11. Because the page has a TTL value of one day, this page will be stored on Akamai edge servers for the same period of time, enabling subsequent requests for that page to be directly served to a browser user closer to the user than a centralized Web site. Figure 4.12 illustrates the data flow associated with the use of Akamai edge servers.

In examining the data flow shown in Figure 4.12, note that although the Web page was created dynamically at the centralized Web site, the entire page can be stored on the Akamai network. This results from the fact that, although the page was assembled for an individual user, there are no user-specific components, such as the personalization of a page via the use of cookies, that could prohibit the caching of the page.

4.3.2.4 Limitations The key limitation associated with the distribution of Web server content onto edge servers concerns the use of cookies and agents for page personalization. Such sites as Yahoo, MSN, and other portals use cookies to create a dynamic and personalized user experience. For example, consider Figures 4.13 and 4.14. Figure 4.13 illustrates the Yahoo home page in early 2010 on the day of the Massachusetts senatorial election prior to this author signing into Yahoo to access his mail. In comparison, Figure 4.14 illustrates the Yahoo home page after this author signed into Yahoo. Note that in Figure 4.14, the page is slightly personalized, with "Hi, Gilbert" shown in bold under the right portion of the search bar. In addition, if this author were to click on the down arrow to the right of his name, he could then view his profile and his contacts, obtain a variety of account information, and see that he is now signed into Yahoo under a specific identifier. By using a cookie to create a dynamic and personalized experience, Yahoo also remembers that this author is signed in as he moves about the portal to check other features in addition to e-mail.

Although the use of cookies enables Web page personalization, sites using cookies are normally considered to be noncacheable. This means that the centralized Web site must maintain persistent connections to Akamai edge servers. Although the edge servers must then communicate with the centralized Web site, the original site only needs to have a finite number of connections to edge servers instead of tens of thousands or more connections to individual browser users. Despite the inability to cache dynamic pages, the serving of uncacheable content via edge servers offers several advantages. Those advantages include the ability of offloading CPU and memory from a centralized server to the ability of edge servers that can respond faster to browser users than serving requests from a central site. In addition, due to the fact that edge servers are located around the globe, reliability of browser user access is increased.

4.3.3 Edge Side Includes

Akamai Technologies, in collaboration with application server and content management organizations, including IBM and Oracle among others, developed a new markup language known as Edge

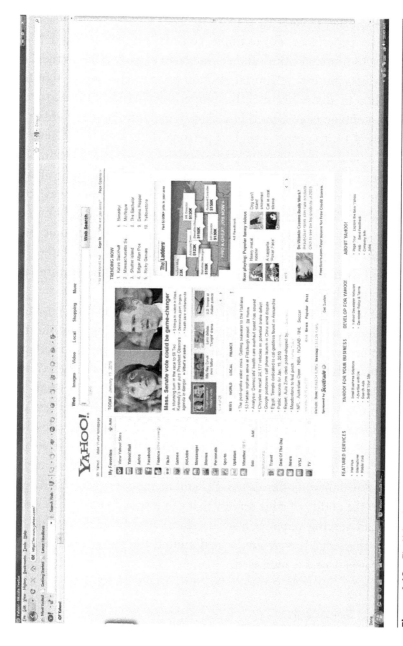

Figure 4.13 The Yahoo home page prior to sign-in.

Figure 4.14   The Yahoo home page after the author signed in.

Side Includes (ESI). Edge Side Includes represents a simple markup language used to define Web page fragments for dynamic assembly at the edge of the Internet, enabling an organization with a single server to have its contents easily distributed around the globe via a service agreement with a content delivery network provider. Through the use of ESI, files can be retrieved that can be used to dynamically construct a Web page in response to browser user requests. Each file can be controlled with its own TTL value, which defines the time it will reside in cache memory, enabling only small portions of a page to be retrieved from a central Web site to build a full page for delivery to a browser user. Thus, cookies could be retrieved from the central Web site, while static portions of a page might be stored in cache memory on edge servers. This action enables an Akamai edge server to assemble a Web page instead of the application server connected to a centralized Web site. Because pages are assembled closer to the browser user, the pages can be delivered faster. In addition, because more requests are serviced on edge servers, this action reduces traffic to the centralized Web server.

4.3.3.1 ESI Support   The key to the ability to move dynamic content onto edge servers is the use of ESI. Both the application server and Akamai edge servers must support the ESI language to enable the applications that must be deployed if browser users are to obtain edge server support. The development of content using ESI begins at the centralized Web site with the development of templates and creation of fragments. This is followed by the local assembly of pages and their placement in cache memory at the central Web site and their distribution to Akamai edge servers for remote assembly and page caching. Thus, when a browser user request is directed to the central site, they can first retrieve information from cache at the central Web site, a location referred to as the edge of the data center. Subsequent browser user requests are directed to an edge server for processing. Because the ESI language represents the mechanism by which application servers and edge servers communicate, let's obtain an overview of its capabilities.

ESI represents a simple markup language used to define Web page components for dynamic assembly and delivery of Web applications onto edge servers. ESI represents an open-standard specification that is being coauthored by application server and content management vendors. At the time this book was prepared, vendors supporting the ESI effort included Akamai Technologies, ATG, BEA Systems, Circadence, Digital Island, IBM, Interwoven, Oracle, Sun, and Vignette.

The primary benefit of ESI is that its use accelerates the delivery of dynamic Web-based applications. The use of this markup language enables both cacheable and noncacheable Web page fragments to be assembled and delivered at the edge of the Internet. To provide this capability, ESI not only represents a markup language but, in addition, specifies a protocol for transparent content management delivery. By providing the capability to assemble dynamic pages from fragments, it becomes possible to limit the retrieval of data from a centralized Web site to noncacheable or expired fragments. This capability reduces the load on the centralized Web site, thereby reducing potential congestion as well as enhancing delivery of data to browser users.

The ESI markup language represents an XML-based markup language, which was designed to improve end-user performance while reducing the processing requirements on servers. ESI includes four key features. Those features are inclusion, conditional inclusion, environmental variables, and exception and error handling.

4.3.3.2 Inclusion and Conditional Inclusion   Inclusion provides the ability to retrieve and include files to construct a Web page, with up to three levels of recursion currently supported by the markup language. Each file can have its own configuration, including a specified time-to-live value, thereby enabling Web pages to be tailored to site operator requirements. In comparison, conditional inclusion provides the ability to add files based upon Boolean comparisons.

4.3.3.3 Environmental Variables   A subset of standard Common Gateway Interface (CGI) environmental variables is currently supported by ESI. Those variables can be used both inside of ESI statements and outside of ESI blocks.

4.3.3.4 Exception and Error Handling   Similar to HTML, ESI provides the ability to specify alternative pages to be displayed in the event a central-site Web page or document is not available. Thus, under ESI, users could display a default page when certain events occur. In

Table 4.8 ESI Tags

ESI TAG	FUNCTION
<esi: include>	Include a separate cacheable fragment
<esi: choose>	Conditional execution under which a choice is made based on several alternatives, such as a cookie value or URL; every "choose" must contain at least one "when" element and can optionally include only one "otherwise" element
<esi: try>	Permits alternative processing to be specified in the event a request fails; valid children of "try" are "attempt" and "except"
<esi: vars>	Allows variable substitution for environmental variables
<esi: remove>	Specifies alternative content to be removed by ESI but displayed by the browser if ESI processing is not performed
<esi... - ->	Specifies content to be processed by ESI but hidden from the browser
<esi: inline>	Specifies a separate cacheable fragment's body to be included in a template

addition, ESI includes an explicit exception-handling statement set that enables different types of errors to generate different activities.

4.3.3.5 Language Tags Similar to HTML, the ESI specification defines a number of tags. Table 4.8 summarizes the functions of seven key ESI tags.

4.3.3.6 The ESI Template The basic structure that a content provider uses to create dynamic content in ESI is referred to as a template page. That page, which is illustrated in Figure 4.15, contains one or more HTML fragments that are assembled to construct the page. As indicated in Figure 4.15, the template is formed through the use of

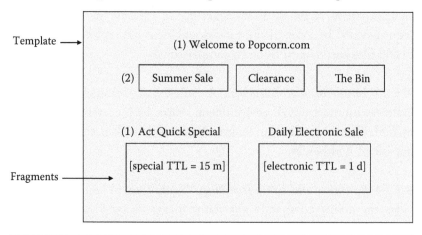

Figure 4.15 A sample ESI template page.

such common elements as a vendor logo, navigation bars, and similar "canned" static elements plus dynamic fragments. The formed template represents a file that is associated with the URL that a browser user requests. The file consists of HTML code that is marked up with ESI tags that informs the cache server or delivery network to retrieve and include pre-defined HTML fragments, with the file constructed by combining HTML and ESI tags. In examining the ESI template page shown in Figure 4.15, note that the Welcome logo (1) and text (2) represent static content that can be permanently cached. The targeted advertisements (3 and 4) represent fragments that can only be stored in cache until their time to live values expire, after which edge servers must retrieve new fragments.

If we examine the sample ESI template shown in Figure 4.15, we can obtain an appreciation for how the use of ESI considerably facilitates the flow of data. In this example, the Web page consists of static boilerplate in the form of a vendor logo and page headings and navigation bars that can be continuously cached on an edge server. The two fragments have TTL values of 15 minutes and 1 day, respectively. Thus, one fragment must be retrieved four times an hour from the central Web site; however, once retrieved the fragment can be cached until the TTL value expires. Thus, the edge server only has to periodically update the contents of this fragment throughout the day. In comparison, the second fragment is only updated on a daily basis. Thus, an edge server only needs to retrieve one fragment every 15 minutes and the other fragment on a daily basis in order to keep the Web page up to date.

4.3.4 Edge Side Includes for Java

In addition to ESI for HTML, an extension to ESI provides support for Java. Referred to as Edge Side Include for Java (JESI), its use makes it easy to program Java Server Pages (JSPs) using ESI. As a refresher, JSPs represent server-side software modules that are used to generate a user interface by linking dynamic content and static HTML through tags. Thus, through the use of JESI, you can facilitate the use of ESI tags within a JSP application. Table 4.9 provides a summary of JESI tags and their functions.

Table 4.9 JESI Tags

JESI TAG	FUNCTION
<jesi: include>	Used in a template to indicate to the ESI processor the manner by which fragments are assembled to form a page
<jesi: control>	Used to assign an attribute to templates and fragments
<jesi: template>	Used to contain the entire contents of a JSP container page within its body
<jesi: fragment>	Used to encapsulate individual container fragments within a JSP page
<jesi: codeblock>	Used to specify that a piece of code should be executed before any other fragments being executed
<jesi: invalidate>	Used to remove and/or execute selected objects cached in an ESI processor
<jesi: personalize>	Used to insert personalized content into a Web page where the content is placed in cookies that the ESI processor uses to insert into a page

4.3.5 Statistics

One of the major advantages associated with the use of edge servers is the intelligence provided by some vendors in the form of statistical reports. For example, Akamai Site Wise reports provide information about which site pages are viewed, how long visitors remain on a site, the amount of time visitors spend on different pages, and similar information. Table 4.10 lists some of the Web site statistics provided by Akamai Site Wise reports as well as the potential utilization of such reports.

As indicated in Table 4.10, such reports provide a tool for tailoring marketing and advertising resources as well as providing organizations

Table 4.10 Akamai Sitewise Statistics and Potential Utilization

STATISTIC	POTENTIAL UTILIZATION
Most requested page	Move popular content to home page
	Eliminate minimally used content
	Leverage popularity of content
Routes from entry	Identify points of entry to target advertising
Popular routes	Determine if page organization is properly constructed for visitor access
Transactions by product	Determine online revenue drivers
	Test price changes and compare product sales
Shopping-cart summary	Track fulfillment versus abandonment by product
	Contact customers that abandoned items with a special offer
Search-engine summary	Determine which search engines refer customers to target advertising
First time vs. returning customers	Determine value of different marketing programs
	Tailor content for repeat visitors
	Examine purchase patterns

with a window into the use of their Web content. Information about the access and use of Web pages can be a valuable resource for tailoring content to reflect the price sensitivity and product requirements of browser users, which can turn page hits into shopping-cart fulfillments. This in turn can result in increased revenues.

4.3.6 Summary

As indicated by our brief tour of ESI, this markup language represents the key to making edge operations practical. By providing the ability to subdivide Web pages into fragments, it becomes possible to cache dynamic portions of Web pages on a periodic basis, thereby reducing the amount of traffic that has to flow between browser users and a centralized Web site.

4.4 The Akamai HD Network

In concluding our discussion of Akamai, we will focus our attention upon the efforts of this content delivery network provider to support the rapidly evolving requirements for high-definition (HD) video. Referred to as the Akamai HD Network, this company's edge servers are being used to support adaptive bit-rate streaming video as well as digital video recorder technology for high definition based on Adobe's Flash, Microsoft's Silverlight, and Apple's iPhone. Because the streaming of high-definition video is both storage and bandwidth intensive, most Web servers typically used VGA 640 × 400 graphics. However, beginning in 2007, several Web sites recognized the demand for better-quality video and began to offer high-definition video. Because the use of high-definition video can result in rather long buffering delays, slow start-up times, and periodic and annoying delays, it made sense to add high-definition video to edge servers on many content delivery networks. Akamai, among other providers, has responded by marketing its HD Network technology as a mechanism to move HD content closer to the browser user.

To obtain an appreciation for how the Akamai HD network operates, let's turn our attention to the manner by which a Web site would use the Akamai network to support dynamic streaming for Flash over HTTP.

4.4.1 Using the HD Network with Flash

When using Flash over HTTP, each video file will have to be encoded at several different bit rates or quality settings to support multibit-rate outputs. Similarly, if desired, audio files can be encoded at separate bit rates. The Flash player on each client controls the viewing process based upon heuristics built into the player that are customizable by the client, although most clients simply use default settings. As an example of customization, clients can program their player to commence operations at a low bit rate, which enables immediate viewing. As viewing continues, the player's buffer fills, and the player can switch its operating mode to a higher bit rate. By monitoring the buffer occupancy level, bandwidth, and frame loss, the player can then determine if it should change its operational mode to support a different bit rate.

When the Flash player switches its bit rate and goes through the Akamai HD network, it sends a request to an edge server. The server then switches the bit rate at the next keyframe for video or next audio sample, or a combination of the two. Here, the term *keyframe* defines the starting and ending points of any smooth transition. They are called *frames* because their position in time is measured in frames on a strip of film, which in the digital world represents a sequence of frames displayed on a monitor. A sequence of keyframes defines which movement a viewer will see, whereas the position of the keyframes on a video defines the timing of the movement. Because only two or three keyframes over the span of a second or two do not create the illusion of movement, the remaining frames are filled with in-between frames. The idea is to create more than one keyframe, and then to set the desired effect values at each keyframe. For example, Adobe Premiere will create a gradual change in values between keyframes, which is referred to as interpolation. As an example of the use of keyframes, you could create a keyframe where the volume is –20 dB and another keyframe 5 seconds later where the volume is 0 dB. Then, Adobe Premiere will interpolate this to create a smooth 5-second volume increase.

You can view and work with keyframes when using Adobe Premiere by using either the Timeline or the Effect Controls window. When using Timeline, keyframes can be displayed in the timeline when a video track is expanded. When using the Effect Controls window, the right-hand side of the window represents a miniature timeline for the selected clip, which shows keyframes as diamond icons. This view allows you to view keyframes while providing you with the ability to manage their control. Returning our attention to the edge server in the content delivery network, as the edge server switches its delivery bit rate, the client player will temporarily use the data in its buffer. This action enables the bit-rate change to appear to be seamless to the client.

4.4.1.1 Selecting the Client Population   One of the keys to success is to carefully determine your potential audience and adjust your streaming accordingly. For example, if your organization is in the business of providing movies for air travelers that will be downloaded onto portable gadgets with screens less than 12 inches in diameter, it will not be advantageous to offer 1080p video, since both storage and transmission time would be extensive. Similarly, if your Web site offers downloads to be viewed on flat-screen TVs as well as portable gadgets, you would more than likely offer multiple versions of video based upon a mix of parameters that can be user selected.

4.4.1.2 Selecting Bit Rates   Adobe offers readers a calculator for determining encoding bit rates for a given frame size. That calculator can be viewed at http://www.adobe.com/devnet/flash/apps/flv_bitrate_ calculator/index.html. You can either use the calculator or determine an approximation by using the following formula:

Baseline bit rate (kbps) = (frame height × frame width × frame rate)

/motion factor/1024

where the motion factor is

7 for high-motion, high-scene changes
15 for standard motion
20 for low motion, such as a talking head, where movement
   is limited

4.4.1.3 Selecting Frame Sizes   When using Flash in your development effort, it's important to recognize that the encoder operates by dividing the viewing window into multiple 16 × 16-pixel macroblocks. Those macroblocks are compared to one another for compression purposes.

Table 4.11 Frame Sizes Divisible by 16

1152 × 768
1280 × 720
1024 × 576
768 × 512
768 × 432
720 × 480
640 × 480
576 × 432
512 × 384
528 × 352
512 × 288
480 × 320
448 × 336
384 × 288
320 × 240
256 × 192
256 × 144
240 × 160
192 × 144
128 × 96

Thus, when selecting the frame size, you should attempt to use widths and heights that are divisible by 16. If this is not possible, the next best divisor would be 8, followed by 4, which is preferable to anything else. Thus, Table 4.11 lists five popular frame sizes that are divisible by 16. If the frame sizes listed in Table 4.11 do not meet your requirements, you can then select a frame size divisible by 8, such as 1152 × 648 down to 128 × 72, or a frame size divisible by 4, such as 1216 × 684 down to 192 × 108. If you require a customized size, you can then select a frame size whose width and height are not divisible by a multiple of 4; however, this will result in some processing delay based upon the manner by which the encoder uses multiple blocks of 16 pixels.

4.4.1.4 Profiles A profile defines the technique used by the encoder and decoder. Flash supports three profiles referred to as Baseline, Medium, and High. The baseline profile requires the least amount of processing power, while the high profile requires the most. If your potential audience will be using Intel Atom or similar processors, you would probably consider using a baseline profile.

4.4.1.5 Levels The level defines the maximum resolution and bit rate. When working with personal computers with Flash, you can more than likely ignore the levels, since you can set the resolution independently, which in effect sets the level.

4.4.1.6 Keyframes One of the limitations of Flash is that it can only change bit rates at keyframe intervals. This means that you need to carefully consider the intervals at which keyframes appear in your video. For example, if you place keyframes too far apart, your video will react rather slowly to changes. In comparison, if you space keyframes closer than two seconds apart, your video will react more quickly to bit-rate changes. In general, you should consider keeping keyframes spaced at 2-second intervals or less for high-bit-rate applications. For lower bit-rate applications, keyframe rates up to one per 3 or 4 seconds can be considered.

5

CACHING AND LOAD BALANCING

In previous chapters in this book, our primary focus was upon understanding the benefits of content delivery; reviewing the relationships between Web servers, application servers, and back-end database servers; and examining how a content delivery provider, such as Akamai, structures its network and uses a markup language to facilitate data delivery. While our prior explanation of content delivery network (CDN) operations was of sufficient detail to provide readers with a firm understanding of such operations, two key content delivery functions were glossed over. Those functions are caching and load balancing, both of which will be covered in more detail in this chapter.

The rationale for caching and load balancing being presented in this fifth chapter is based upon the structure of this book. The first three chapters provided a solid review of the rationale for content delivery and the interrelationship of Web requests and server responses, while Chapter 4 was focused upon the use of a CDN service provider. If you use a CDN service provider, that provider will more than likely perform caching and load balancing transparently. However, if your organization has more than one Web server or if your organization decides that the enterprise should perform content delivery, then caching and load balancing needs to be considered. In this chapter, we will focus our attention upon both topics, examining how caching and load balancing operate as well as the advantages and disadvantages associated with each technology.

5.1 Caching

Caching represents a technique in which information that was previously retrieved is held in some type of storage to facilitate a subsequent request for the same information. There are two primary reasons behind the use of caching in a client–server environment on the Internet. First, caching will reduce delay or latency, as a request for data is satisfied from a cache that is located at or closer to the client than the server the client is accessing. Secondly, caching reduces network traffic. This reduction in network traffic occurs because data that is cached flows from the cache to the client instead of flowing from the server, reducing the length as well as the duration of the data flow.

Cache storage can include random access memory (RAM), flash memory, disk, or even a combination of different types of memory. There are several types of caches where data can be temporarily stored, ranging from a user's browser to the server as well as other devices along the request/response path. To obtain an appreciation of caching, let's turn our attention to the different types of caches that can be used to expedite the delivery of data, commencing with the browser cache.

5.1.1 Browser Cache

Earlier in this book, when we discussed the operation of browsers, we noted that a browser cache resulted in previously retrieved Web pages being stored on disk. Depending upon the settings in effect for your Web browser, your browser could check for a newer version of stored Web pages on every page-retrieval request, every time you start Microsoft's Internet Explorer, automatically, or never. Here the selection of "every page" results in the browser checking whether a copy of the page to be viewed is cached, while "every time you start Microsoft's Internet Explorer" means that the browser checks to see if a copy of the page to be viewed was put in cache on the current day. If you configure Internet Explorer for one of the first three options, a request for a Web page will result in the browser comparing the parameters of the Web page, such as its created and modified dates and file size to any previously stored page in cache. If the properties of the requested and stored page do not match, the browser will then retrieve a new copy of the page. Obviously, if you selected the "never" option, the browsers would not check the properties of the requested page. Instead, it would display the cached version of the page.

The primary purpose of a browser cache is to provide a more efficient method for retrieving Web pages. That is, instead of having to retrieve a previously retrieved Web page from the Internet, the page can be displayed from cache. This is not only more efficient, but in addition minimizes latency or delay while reducing traffic flow on the Internet.

You can appreciate the usefulness of a browser cache when you click on the browser's "back" button or on a link to view a page you recently looked at. In such situations, the use of the browser cache results in the near instantaneous display of a Web page. In comparison, if cache is not used, the delay to display a page can be as long as 20 or more seconds when the page contains a lot of images and is retrieved via dialup. Even if you are connected to the Internet via DSL or cable modem, delays can be relatively annoying when you flip through a series of screens if your browser is configured to disable caching.

Figure 5.1 illustrates the use of two dialog boxes from the Firefox Web browser. Both dialog boxes result from the selection of the Option entry in the Tools menu. The left dialog box labeled Options shows the selection of the Network tab, illustrating that by default the version of Firefox used by this author allocated up to 50 Mb of disk space for the cache. By clicking on the button labeled "Settings," the dialog box on the right labeled "Connection Settings" is displayed. Through the use of this dialog box, you could configure your browser to access a proxy server, which more than likely will have its own cache and which we will shortly discuss.

5.1.2 Other Types of Web Caches

In addition to browser caches, there are several other types of caches whose operation directly affects the delivery of Web content. Those additional caches include proxy caches, gateway caches, and server caches.

5.1.2.1 Proxy Caches
Web proxy caches operate very similar to browser caches; however, instead of providing support for a single computer, they are designed to support hundreds to thousands of computers. Thus, you can view a proxy as a large-scale browser with respect to its cache operation.

A proxy server typically resides on the edge of an organization's network, usually behind the router that provides connectivity to the Internet. The proxy cache can operate as a stand-alone device, or its functionality can be incorporated into another device, such as a router or firewall.

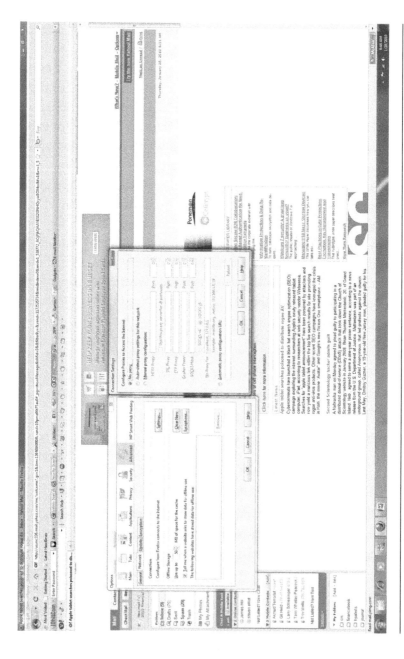

Figure 5.1   Through the use of the Tools menu, you can configure the amount of storage for cache as well as the use of various proxies.

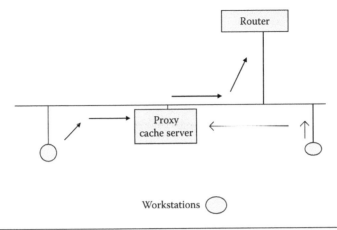

Figure 5.2   A proxy cache server supports a number of browser users.

Figure 5.2 illustrates the relationship between browser users, a stand-alone cache, and a router connected to the Internet. In order for browser users to effectively use the services of a proxy cache, they need to access the cache. To do so, browser user requests have to be routed to the proxy. One way to accomplish this is to use your browser's proxy settings to tell the browser what services should be routed to the proxy. If you are using Internet Explorer, you would go to Tools> Internet Options > Connections and select the button labeled LAN Settings. This action will result in the Local Area Network (LAN) Settings dialog box being displayed, as illustrated in the left portion of Figure 5.3. If you click on the Proxy Server box, you would then be able to enter the address and port number of the proxy. As an alternative, you could click on the button labeled Advanced if your organization operates multiple proxy servers or if you wish to define exceptions to the use of a proxy server. The right portion of Figure 5.3 illustrates the Proxy Settings dialog box, which enables you to define multiple proxy servers as well as exceptions to the use of a proxy server.

In comparing browser caches to proxy caches, you can view the proxy cache as a type of shared browser cache, since a large number of browser users are served by the proxy. Similar to a browser cache, the use of a proxy cache reduces both delay or latency and network traffic. Because the proxy cache stores Web pages requested by many browser users, they are more efficient than individual or even a series of individual browser caches. This is because the proxy cache stores pages previously accessed by a large group of users. This allows one user to

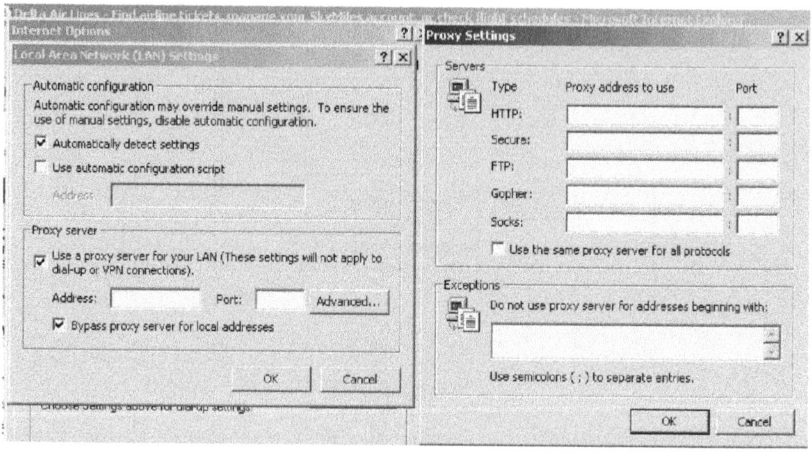

Figure 5.3 Internet Explorer as well as other browsers support the use of proxy servers for one or more Web applications.

be able to have his or her request for a Web page fulfilled by transmitting a Web page previously cached due to the activity of another user who visited the location now requested by the subsequent user. For example, assume several employees of an organization wish to access their Yahoo mail accounts during the day. As they point their browser to Yahoo.com, they would more than likely obtain the initial Yahoo! page from a proxy cache, which would expedite their initial access.

5.1.2.2 Gateway Caches   A gateway cache can be considered to represent a reverse proxy cache. This is because a gateway cache is typically installed by a Webmaster to make the Web site more scaleable. In comparison, a proxy cache is commonly installed by a network manager to conserve bandwidth. In addition, from a network perspective, the proxy cache resides in front of a network used by a group of browser users, while the gateway cache resides in front of a Web server used by distributed browser users whose access requests can originate from different networks.

While a gateway cache is commonly installed at a Web site, this device can also be distributed to other locations, with a load balancer used to route requests from a Web server to an individual gateway cache. When gateway caches are distributed across the Internet, in effect you obtain a content delivery network (CDN) capability. Thus, among the primary operators of a gateway cache are CDN operators, such as Akamai.

5.1.2.3 Server Caches Server cache is a function of the operating system used, the hardware platform, and the application program that provides a Web-site capability. The operating system typically stores in RAM previously accessed files, with the number of files stored a function of available memory as well as the size of each file. In comparison, the application program that provides a Web-server capability may allow you to cache a number of popularly requested Web pages in RAM, such as the home page that is retrieved when a browser user accesses your site.

5.1.3 Application Caching

One example of application caching occurs through the use of ASP.net, a Microsoft server-side Web technology used to create Web pages. Essentially, ASP.net treats every element in an ASP.net page as an object, compiling the page into an intermediate language. Then, a just-in-time (JIT) compiler converts the intermediate code into native machine code that is then executed on the host. Because the code is directly executed by the host, pages load faster than conventional ASP pages, where embedded VB Script or Jscript had to be continuously interpreted.

Under ASP.net, frequently accessed pages can be cached via the use of directives located at the top of each ASPX file. Page developers can declare a specific ASPX page for caching by including the Output Cache directive at the top of the file. The following example illustrates the format of the Output Cache directive.

```
<%@Output Cache
    Duration="of seconds"
    Location="Any|Client|Downstream|Server|None"
    VaryByCustom="browser|customstring"
    VaryByHeader="headers"
    VaryByParam="parametername" %>
```

The above coding is an example of enabling caching for a page declaratively. You can also enable caching programmatically in a page's code by manipulating the HttpCachePolicy object. Both methods work the same way for basic caching.

The first attribute, Duration, specifies how long in seconds to cache a Web page. Once a page is generated, ASP.net will place it into cache. Then, until the duration is reached, subsequent requests for the same page will be served from cache. Once the specified duration is reached, the page is discarded. However, the next request for the page results in its generation and placement into cache, starting the process over again.

The second attribute, Location, enables you to specify where the cached Web page resides. The default setting of Location="Any" caches the page on the client that originated the request, on the Web server that receives the request, or on any proxy servers located between the client and server that support HTTP1.1 caching. The remaining location attributes permit caching to occur at specific areas. For example, Location="Client" forces the page to be cached in the browser; Location="Server" results in the page being stored in the Web server cache; Location="Server And Client" uses the Web server or browser cache; and Location="Downstream" results in the page being stored anywhere other than the client browser.

The VaryBy attributes can be used to cache different versions of the same page. Differences in Web pages can result from different client browsers, the use of different query strings or form-content parameters, and different HTTP header values. For example, if your Web site provides several popular products whose descriptions are displayed via clients returning ProductId 27 and 54, if you specify VaryByParam="ProductId", ASP.net processes the page and caches it twice, once for ProductID=27 and once for ProductID=54. In comparison, without the use of this attribute, only one version of the page would be cached. As indicated by this brief tour of ASP. net caching, it provides a valuable technique to reuse previously performed processing that was used to create Web pages and apply it in subsequent requests for the same data. Now that we have an appreciation for the four common types of Web page caches, let's turn our attention to how caches operate.

5.1.4 Cache Operation

Regardless of the type of cache, each cache operates according to a set of rules that defines when the cache services a Web page request. Some of the rules are set by an administrator, such as the browser operator or the proxy administrator. Other rules are set by the protocol, such as

Table 5.1   Common Cache Rules

Examine response headers to determine if data should be cached. If the header indicates data
  should not be cached, it is not cached.
If the response does not include a validator such as a last-modified header, consider data to
  be uncacheable.
If the request is secure or authenticated, do not cache data.
Consider cached data to be fresh if
    Its age is within the fresh period
    A browser cache previously viewed the data and has been set to check once per session
    A proxy cache recently viewed the data and it was modified a relatively long time ago
If data is stale, the origin server will be asked to validate it or inform the cache if the copy is still valid.

HTTP 1.0 and HTTP 1.1. In general, a cache examines traffic flow content and creates a cache entry based upon the rules it follows. Table 5.1 lists some of the more common rules followed by a cache. As we review HTML META tags and HTTP headers, we will note how the rules listed in Table 5.1 can be applied to traffic that the cache examines.

In examining the entries in Table 5.1, note that the term *fresh* means that data is available immediately from cache. In addition, an age-controlling header or a timer provides the mechanism to determine if data is within the fresh period.

5.1.5 Cache Control Methods

The most common methods used to control the manner by which caching operates is through the use of HTML META tags and HTTP headers. As a review for some readers, META tags are HTML tags that provide information describing the content of a Web page. However, unlike HTML tags that display information, data within a META tag is not displayed, a term referred to as *nonrendered*.

5.1.5.1 META Tags   META tags are optional, and many Web page developers do not use such tags. However, because the META tags are used by search engines to enable them to more accurately list information about a site in their indexes, the use of this type of HTML tag has grown in popularity.

5.1.5.1.1 Types of META Tags   There are two basic types of META tags: HTTP-EQUIV tags and META tags that have a NAME attribute. META HTTP-EQUIV tags are optional and are the

equivalent of HTTP headers. Similar to normal headers, META HTTP-EQUIV tags can be used to control or direct the actions of Web browsers in a manner similar to normal headers. In fact, some servers automatically translate META HTTP-EQUIV tags into HTTP headers to enable Web browsers to view the tags as normal headers. Other Web-server application programs employ a separate text file that contains META data.

The second type of META tag, which is also the more popular type of tag, is a META tag with a NAME attribute. META tags with a NAME attribute are used for META types that do not correspond to normal HTTP headers, enabling specialized information to be incorporated into a Web page.

5.1.5.1.2 Style and Format   META tags must appear in the HEAD of an HTML document and are normally inserted at the top of a document, usually after the <TITLE> element. The format of a META tag is shown as follows:

<META name = "string1" content = "string2">

In examining the META tag format, note that you do not need to have a </META> at the end of the tag. Table 5.2 provides an alphabetically ordered list of some of the major types of META tags and a brief description of their potential utilization. To obtain a better appreciation for the use of META tags, let's examine a few examples. Suppose the content of a Web page should expire on July 19, 2012, at 2 p.m. in the afternoon. Then, we would use the Expires META tag as follows:

<META name = "Expires" content

= "Thu, 19 Jul 2012 14:00:00 GMT">

It should be noted that the Expires META tag uses dates that conform to RFC 1123.

For a second example of the use of META tags, let's turn our attention to the Refresh META tag. The use of this tag provides a mechanism to redirect or refresh users to another Web page after a delay of a specified number of seconds occurs. Because the Refresh META tag is used within an HTTP-EQUIV tag, let's first examine the format of the latter. This is shown as follows:

Table 5.2 Basic Types of META Tags

TAG	DESCRIPTION
Abstract	Provides a one-line overview of a Web page
Author	Declares the author of a document
Copyright	Defines any copyright statements you wish to disclose about your document
Description	Provides a general description about the contents of a Web page
Distribution	Defines the degree of distribution of the Web page (global, local, or internal)
Expires	Defines the expiration date and time of the document being indexed
Keywords	Provides a list of keywords that defines the Web page; used by search engines to index sites
Language	Defines the language used on a Web page
Refresh	Defines the number of seconds prior to refreshing or redirecting a Web page
Resource type	Defines the type of resource for indexing, which is limited to the document
Revisit	Defines how often a search engine should come to a Web site for reindexing
Robots	Permits a Web site to define which pages should be indexed

<META HTTP-EQUIV="varname" content="data"

Note that the use of the HTTP-EQUIV tag binds the variable name (varname) to an HTTP header field. When the varname is "Refresh," the HTTP-EQUIV tag can then be used in the HEAD section of an index.html file to redirect a browser user to another location. For example, to redirect a browser user to www.popcorn.com after a 5 second delay, you could code the following tag:

<META HTTP-EQUIV="Refresh" content="5;

url=www.popcorn.com">

Because we are discussing caching, we will conclude our brief review of META tags with the tag used to inform browsers and other products not to cache a particular Web page. That tag is the "pragma" tag, whose use is shown as follows:

<META HTTP-EQUIV="pragma" content="no-cache">

While META tags are relatively easy to use, they may not be effective. This is because they are only honored by browser caches that actually read HTML code, but may not be honored by proxy caches that very rarely read such code. In comparison, true HTTP headers can provide you with a significant amount of control over how both browser and proxy caches handle Web pages. Thus, let's turn our attention to HTTP headers and how they can be used to control caching.

5.1.5.2 HTTP Headers Through the use of HTTP headers, you can obtain a fairly substantial amount of control concerning the manner by which browser and proxies cache data. Although HTTP headers cannot be viewed in HTML and are typically generated by Web servers, it's possible to control some of their use based upon the server being accessed. Thus, in examining HTTP headers, we will primarily focus our attention upon cache control headers and their utilization.

5.1.5.2.1 Overview Currently, there are approximately 50 HTTP headers defined in the HTTP/1.1 protocol that can be subdivided into four categories: entity, general, request, and response. An entity header contains information about an entity body or resource, while a general header can be used in both request and response messages. A request header is included in messages sent from a browser to a server, while a response header is included in the server's response to a request. Because HTTP headers are transmitted by a server prior to sending HTML, they flow to any intermediate devices, such as a proxy cache that can operate upon the contents of the header as well as the browser. The HTTP header data are only viewed by a browser and are not displayed by the browser; thus they are transparent to the user.

The following illustrates an example of an HTTP response header transported under HTTP/1.1. In examining the header entries, note that the Date header is used to specify the date and time the message originated and represents a general type of header.

```
HTTP/1.1 200 ok
Date: Fri, 20 Jul 2012 14:21:00 GMT
Server: CERN/3.1
Cache-Control: max-age=7200, must-revalidate
Expires: Fri, 20 Jul 2012 16:21:00 GMT
Last-Modified: Mon, 16 Jul 2012 12:00:00 GMT
ETag: "4f75-316-3456abbc"
Content-Length: 2048
Content-Type: text/html
```

The HTTP header seen here—sent by the server in Figure 5.4— represents a response-type header that provides information about the software used by the server to respond to a request. Because revealing a specific software version can provide hackers with the ability to

Figure 5.4   A typical HTTP/1.1 response header.

match vulnerabilities against a server, many times only basic information is provided by this header.

Of particular interest to us is the cache-control header, as this header specifies directives that must be obeyed by all caching mechanisms along the request/response path. Thus, in the remainder of this section, we will focus our attention upon this header. However, prior to doing so, we need to discuss the Expires HTTP header, as its use controls cache freshness.

5.1.5.2.2 Expires Header   The Expires HTTP header provides a mechanism that informs all caches on the request/response path of the freshness of data. Because the Expires header is supported by most caches, it also provides a mechanism to control the operation of all caches along a path. Once the time specified in the Expires header is reached, each cache must then check back with the origin server to determine if the data have changed.

The Expires HTTP response headers can be set by Web servers in several ways. Web servers can set an absolute expiration time, a time based upon the last time that a client accessed the data, or on a time based on the last time data changed. Because many parts of a Web page contain static or relatively static information in the form of navigation bars, logos, and buttons, such data can become cacheable by setting a relatively long expiry time.

As indicated in Figure 5.4, the only valid value in an Expires header is a date in Greenwich Mean Time (GMT). Although the Expires HTTP header provides a basic mechanism for controlling caches, to be effective each cache must have a clock synchronized with the Web server. Otherwise, caches could incorrectly consider stale content as being fresh. Thus, a limitation associated with the use of the Expires header is the fact that the clocks on the Web server and the cache need to be synchronized. If they have different settings, the intended results from the setting of the Expires header may not be achieved, and a cache could incorrectly consider stale content as being fresh and cacheable. A second problem associated with the use of the Expires header is the fact that, once used, it will eventually expire. This means that it is possible to forget to update an Expires time, which will then result in every request flowing to the Web server instead of being cached, thereby increasing the delay or latency experienced by browser users as well as increasing bandwidth utilization.

5.1.5.3 Cache-Control Header The cache-control general header field within the HTTP/1.1 header specifies the manner by which all caching mechanisms along the request/response path should operate. The cache-control header includes one or more request and response directives that specify the manner by which caching mechanisms operate and, typically, override default caching settings. Our discussion of cache-control is mainly applicable to HTTP/1.1, as HTTP/1.0 caches may or may not implement cache control.

Table 5.3 indicates the cache-control header format and directives available under HTTP/1.1 for the cache-control header. Through the use of the cache-control header, a client or server can transmit a variety of directives in either a request or response message. Such directives will commonly override the default caching algorithms in use. Note that cache directives are unidirectional, in that the presence of a directive in a request does not mean that the same directive has to be included in the response. Also note that cache directives must always be passed through devices along the request/response path to the destination,

Table 5.3 Cache-Control Header Format and Directives

cache-control = "cache-control" ";" 1#cache-directive
cache-directive = cache-request-directive I cache-response-directive
cache-request-directive =
  "no-cache"
  I "no-store"
  I "max-age" "-" seconds
  I "max-stale" "=" seconds
  I "min-fresh" "{=" seconds
  I "no-transform"
  I "only-if-cached"
  I cache-extension
cache-response-directive =
  "public"
  I "private" ["=" <"> 1#field-name <"]
  I "no-cache" ["=" <"> 1#field-name <"]
  I "no-store"
  I "no-transform"
  I "must-revalidate"
  I "proxy-revalidate"
  I "max-age" "=" seconds
  I "s-maxage" "="
  I cache-extension

even if an intermediate device, such as a proxy cache, operates upon a directive. This is because a directive can be applicable to several types of caches along the request/response path, and at the present time there is no method to specify a cache directive for a specific type of cache.

Cache control can be subdivided into request and response headers. Each cache-control header can include one or more directives that define the manner by which cache control should operate. Cache-control requests were supported under HTTP1.0, while HTTP1.1 introduced cache-control response headers, which provide Web sites with more control over their content. For example,

Cache-control: max-age=7200, must-revalidate

Included in an HTTP response, this header informs all caches that the content that follows is considered fresh for two hours (7200 seconds). In addition, the must-validate directive informs each cache along the request/response path that they must comply with any freshness information associated with the content.

5.1.5.4 Directive Application Prior to describing the function of the directives associated with the cache-control header in detail, a few words are in order concerning the application of a directive. When a directive appears without any 1#field-name parameter, the directive then is applicable to the entire request or response. If a directive appears with a 1#field-name parameter, it is then applicable only to the named field or fields and not to the remaining request or response.

Now that we have an appreciation for the applicability of directives, let's turn our attention to the function of the specific directives that can be included in a cache-control header. In doing so, we will first examine the cache-request directives listed in Table 5.3.

5.1.5.5 Cache-Request Directives In examining the entries in Table 5.3, you will note that there are seven distinct cache-request directives as well as a mechanism that permits the cache-control header to be extended. The latter occurs through the use of assigning a token or quoted string to cache extension. As we review the operation of each cache-request directive, we will also discuss, when applicable, its use as a cache-response directive.

5.1.5.5.1 The No-Cache Directive The purpose of the no-cache directive is to force caches along the request/response path to submit a request to the origin server for validation prior to releasing a cached copy of data. This function can be used to maintain freshness without giving up the benefits of caching. In addition, this directive can be used along with the public directive to ensure that authentication is respected.

If the no-cache directive does not include a field name, this forces a cache to use the response to satisfy a subsequent request without a successful revalidation with the server. If the no-cache directive specifies at least one field name, then a cache can use the response to satisfy a subsequent request. In this situation, the specified field name(s) are not sent in the response to a subsequent request without a successful revalidation of the origin server, enabling the server to prevent the use of certain HTTP header fields in a response while enabling the caching of the rest of the response.

5.1.5.5.2 The No-Store Directive In comparison to the no-cache directive, the no-store directive is relatively simple. Its use instructs caches not to keep a copy of data under any condition. Thus, the use of the no-store directive can be used to prevent the inadvertent release or retention of sensitive information. The no-store directive applies to the entire message, and can be sent either in a response or in a request. If sent in a request, a cache will not store any part of either this request or any response to it. If sent in a response, a cache will not store any part of either this response or the request that solicited the response. This directive applies to both nonshared and shared caches.

The purpose of the no-store directive is to satisfy the requirements of certain users who are concerned about the accidental release of information via unanticipated accesses to cache data structures. Although the use of the no-store directive can result in an improvement of privacy, it should not be considered as a reliable or sufficient mechanism for ensuring privacy. For example, it is possible that malicious or compromised caches might not recognize or obey the no-store directive, while communications networks are vulnerable to a range of hacking methods, including eavesdropping.

5.1.5.5.3 The Max-Age Directive   The purpose of the max-age directive is to enable the client to indicate that it is willing to accept a response whose age is less than or equal to the specified time in seconds. That is, the max-age directive specifies the maximum amount of time that data will be considered as fresh. Unless a max-stale directive (described next) is also included, the client will not accept a stale response.

5.1.5.5.4 The Max-Stale Directive   The purpose of the max-stale directive is to enable a client to be willing to accept a response that exceeds its expiration time. If a max-stale directive is included, the client becomes able to accept a response that exceeds its expiration time by the number of seconds specified in the max-stale directive. By using a max-stale directive without a value, the client becomes willing to accept all stale responses.

5.1.5.5.5 The Min-Fresh Directive   The purpose of the min-fresh directive is to enable a client to accept a response whose freshness is equal to or greater than its current age plus the specified time in seconds. Thus, the use of this directive enables a client to specify that it wants a response that will be fresh for at least the number of seconds specified in the min-fresh directive.

5.1.5.5.6 The No-Transform Directive The implementers of proxy and other types of caches found it useful to convert certain types of data, such as images, to reduce storage space. This functionality makes it possible for a transformation to cause potential problems. For example, in the interest of reducing storage, the transformation of an X-ray stored as a lossless image into a lossy JPEG image could result in the loss of important medical information. To prevent this situation from occurring, the use of a no-transform directive is used, since its presence informs caches on the request/response path not to perform any transformation of data. Thus, if a message includes the no-transform directive, an intermediate cache or proxy will not change those headers subject to the no-transform directive. This also implies that the cache or proxy will not change any aspect of the entity-body that is specified by these headers, including the value of the entity-body itself.

5.1.5.5.7 The Only-if-Cached Directive The purpose of the only-if-cached directive is to enable a client to cache only those responses it has stored and not to reload or revalidate data with an origin server. This directive is commonly employed under poor network connectivity conditions, and its use informs a client cache to respond using either a cached entry applicable to the request or with a Gateway Timeout status.

5.1.5.5.8 Cache-Control Extensions The purpose of cache-control extensions is to enable the cache-control header field to be extended. The extension occurs through the use of one or more cache-extension tokens, each with an optional assigned value. There are two types of cache-control extensions: informational and behavioral. An informational extension does not require a change in cache and does not change the operation of other directives. In contrast, behavioral extensions operate as modifiers to existing cache directives. When a cache-control extension is specified, applications that do not understand the extension will default to complying with the standard directive. In comparison, if the extension directive is supported, this new directive will modify the operation of the standard directive. This permits extensions to the cache-control directives to be made without requiring changes to the base protocol.

Now that we have an appreciation for cache-request directives, let's turn our attention to cache-response directives.

5.1.5.6 Cache-Response Directives   As indicated in Table 5.3, there are nine cache-response directives as well as a mechanism to extend the cache-control header. Because we previously discussed several cache-request directives that are also applicable to cache-responses, we'll primarily focus our attention upon cache-response directives that are not applicable for use on a request path. However, as we review previously mentioned directives, we will briefly note whether the directive functions in a similar manner to its use in a request header.

5.1.5.6.1 The Public Directive   The purpose of the public directive is to indicate that a response can be cached by any cache. This cacheability holds even if data would normally be noncacheable. Thus, the public directive can be used to make authenticated responses cacheable even though such responses are normally noncacheable.

5.1.5.6.2 The Private Directive   The purpose of the private directive is to indicate that all or a portion of a response message is intended for a single user and must not be cached by any shared cache; however, a private nonshared cache can cache the response. Thus, an origin server can use this directive to indicate that specified portions of a response are only applicable for a single user. Note that if the private-response directive specifies one or more field names, the specified field names must not be stored by a shared cache; however, the remainder of the message may be cached. Also note that the usage of the word *private* only controls where the response may be stored; it does not ensure the privacy of the message content.

5.1.5.6.3 The No-Cache Directive   The no-cache directive functions in the same manner as in a cache-request directive. That is, its use forces caches to submit a request to the origin server prior to releasing cached data. Note that most HTTP/1.0 caches will not recognize or obey this directive.

5.1.5.6.4 The No-Store Directive Similar to the no-cache directive, the no-store directive also functions in the same manner as in
a cache-request directive. That is, its use instructs caches not to keep
a copy of data in cache. This directive applies to both nonshared and
shared caches and requires a cache to store the information in nonvola-
tile storage, as well as make a best-effort attempt to remove the information from volatile storage as promptly as possible after forwarding it.

5.1.5.6.5 The No-Transform Directive The no-transform directive
also functions in the same manner as previously described when we
covered cache-request directives. That is, the use of this directive does
not allow caches to transform data, such as changing a lossless image
into a lossy image to reduce its storage requirements.

5.1.5.6.6 The Must-Revalidate Directive The purpose of a must-
revalidate directive is to ensure that a cache does not use an entry
after it becomes stale. Thus, a cache will first revalidate an entry prior
to responding to a request when the must-revalidate directive is present. A common use of the must-revalidate directive is to support
reliable operation for certain protocol features. Another use of the
must-revalidate directive occurs by servers if, and only if, a failure to
validate a request could result in an incorrect operation, such as an
unexecuted financial transaction.

5.1.5.6.7 The Proxy-Revalidate Directive The proxy-revalidate
directive is similar in functionality to the must-revalidate directive. However, this directive does not apply to nonshared user-agent
caches. One common application for the proxy-revalidate directive
is on a response to an authenticated request. In this situation, the
proxy-revalidate directive enables a user cache to store and later return
the response without having to revalidate it, since it was previously
authenticated by the user.

5.1.5.6.8 The Max-Age Directive Similar to its use in the cache-request
header, the max-age directive specifies the amount of time data will
be considered fresh. That is, this directive indicates that a response is
to be considered stale after its age is greater than the specified number
of seconds.

5.1.5.6.9 The S-Maxage Directive   The s-maxage directive is similar to the max-age directive. However, this directive has one significant difference in that it is only applicable to shared caches, such as a proxy cache. Note that the maximum age specified by this directive overrides the maximum age specified by either the max-age directive or the Expires header.

5.1.5.6.10 The Cache-Extension Directive   In completing our review of cache-response directives, the use of cache extension is similar to that described for its use in a cache-request header. That is, its use enables the header to be extended.

5.1.6 Windows DNS Caching Problems

This author would be remiss if he did not mention a common caching problem associated with the use of Windows 2000 and Windows XP. Both versions of Windows cache unsuccessful DNS (Domain Name Service) lookup attempts. This means that failed attempts to contact a Web site are stored. Thus, you may not be able to view a particular Web site when using either version of Windows until the cached result expires.

By default, the Windows DNS cache expiration time is 5 minutes. Thus, you can wait 5 minutes and then retry to access a particular URL. For those who do not want to wait until the cached result expires, you can flush the Windows DNS cache. To do so, you would perform the following operations:

1. For Windows XP, in the Windows Taskbar, select the Start menu. Then, select Run.
2. In the textbox, enter *ipconfig/flushdns*. This will result in the DNS cache being flushed.
3. Now reload the Web-site URL.

5.1.7 Viewing HTTP Headers

There are several methods available for viewing the full headers contained in HTTP. You can manually connect to a Web server using a Telnet client activated using port 80. To do so, you would enter the command "open www.xyz.com:80." Once you connect to a particular site, you can then use the GET command to request the representation. For example, if you want to view the headers for http:/www.xyz.com/index.html, you would first connect to www.xyz.com on port 80. Then, you would type

GET/index.html HTTP/1.1 [return]

Host:www.xyz.com [return] [return]

You would then press the Return key once to display each line in the header. Unfortunately, due to security concerns, most Web-site operators do not support Telnet into their computers. Thus, a good alternative is to use an HTTP header viewer.

One interesting HTTP header viewer can be used at www.websniffer.com. Figure 5.5 illustrates the HTTP header viewer screen into which this author entered the URL of the U.S. Office of Personnel Management (www.opm.gov), which is a U.S. government agency. In examining Figure 5.5, you will note that the HTTP request header is shown followed by the HTTP response issued by the queried site, in this example www.opm.gov. From the response header, we can determine some interesting information about the queried site. First, the software operating on the server is identified. After the date and time is displayed, information about the use of ASP.net, connection, content length, and content type is displayed, followed by information about cache control. Once data concerning the HTTP response header is displayed, Web-Sniffer displays the content of the URL as source HTML code.

Because we are concerned with cache control, we will not discuss the other headers. Instead, let's turn our attention to the cache-control directive, which is shown as "private." This means that responses from this site are intended for a single user and must not be cached by any shared cache, although a private nonshared cache can cache the response.

Another interesting site to consider for viewing HTTP headers is www.webmaster-toolkit.com. In Figure 5.6, we entered the same URL, but note that the order of data in the headers does not match the prior example. This is probably due to the design of each program, since most users working with headers are concerned about the setting of cache control.

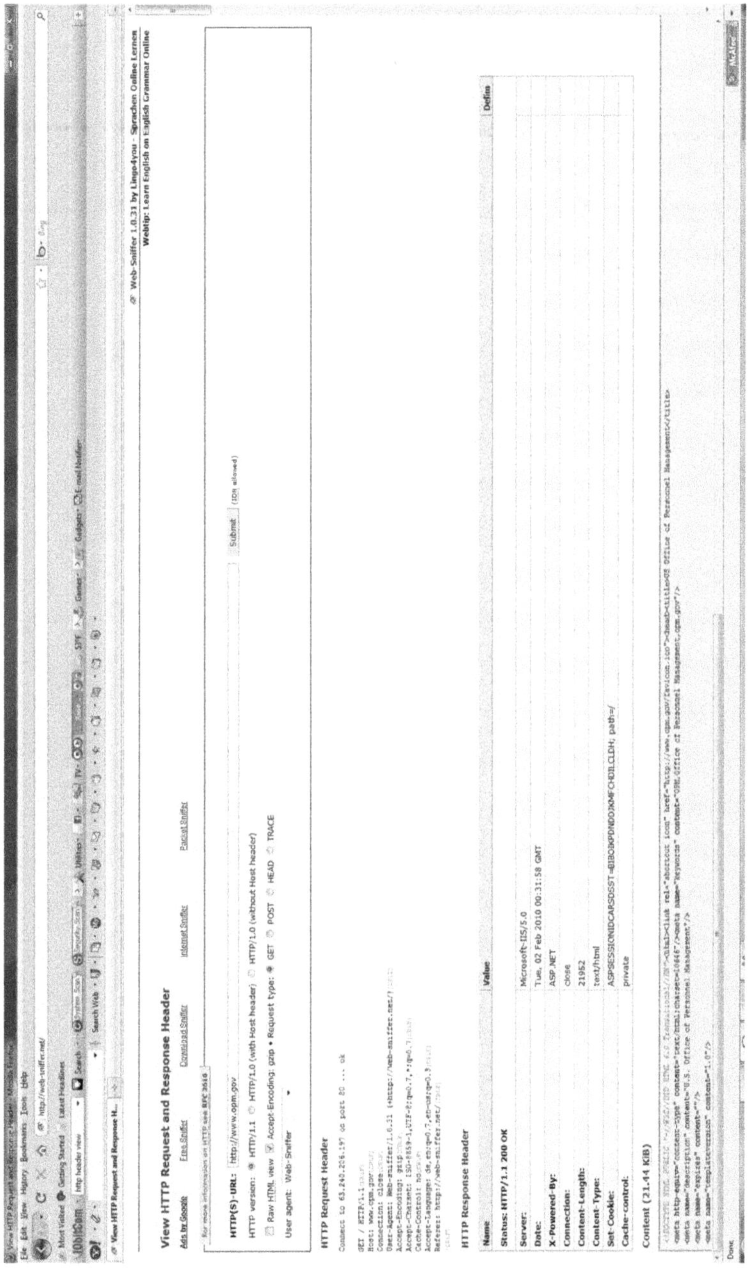

Figure 5.5 Using an HTTP header viewer.

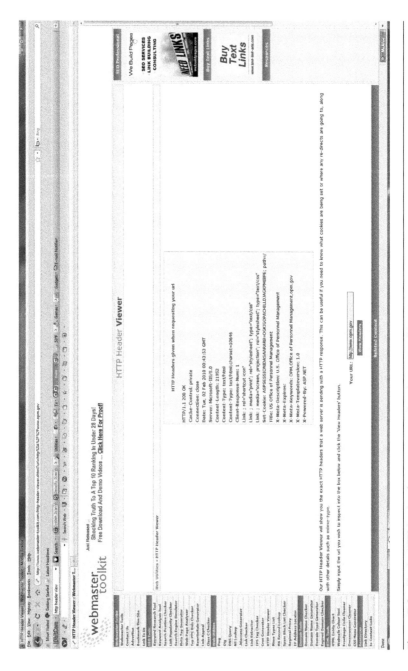

Figure 5.6 Viewing HTTP headers for www.opm.gov via webmaster-toolkit.com.

In concluding our use of an HTTP header viewer, let's view the headers of the *New York Times*. Figure 5.7 shows the headers for www. nytimes.com via the use of the webmaster-toolkit.com site. Note that this author scrolled down the resulting "headers" page so that readers could see that the URL nytimes.com was entered as the site to send a request that elicited a response. In examining Figure 5.7, once again let's focus our attention upon cache control. Note that the *New York Times* Web site uses a no-cache directive in its response, forcing caches to submit a request to the *New York Times* Web-site server prior to releasing cached data. As an educated guess, the reason behind the use of the no-cache directive is probably due to the fact that the *New York Times* changes its page composition quite frequently. In fact, the right side of its home page typically includes a Markets section showing stock averages for the Dow Jones index, the S&P 500, and NASDAQ, whose values are updated every few minutes when the financial markets are open.

5.1.8 Considering Authentication

In an electronic commerce environment, many Web pages are protected with HTTP authentication. In such situations, pages protected with HTTP authentication are considered private and are not kept by proxies and other shared caches. Some Web sites that wish such pages to be cached can do so through the use of the public directive. If a Web site wants those pages to be both cacheable and authenticated for each user, you would use both public and no-cache directives, shown as follows:

Cache-control: public, no-cache

This pair of cache-control directives informs each cache that it must submit client-authentication information to the origin server prior to releasing data from the cache.

5.1.9 Enhancing Cacheability

In concluding our discussion covering caching, let's focus our attention upon a core series of techniques that can be employed by Web-site operators to enhance the cacheability of their pages. Table 5.4 lists

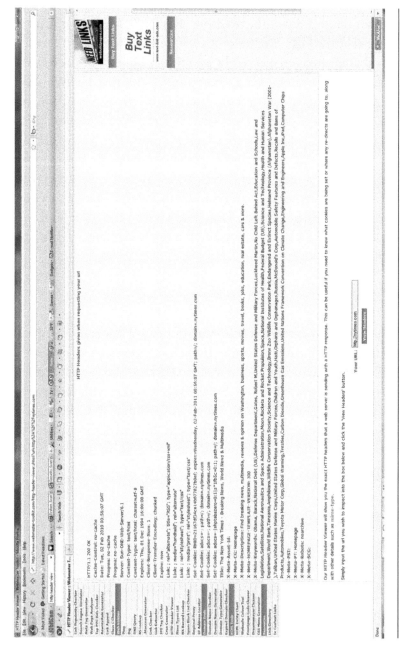

Figure 5.7 Viewing the HTTP headers for www.nytimes.com.

Table 5.4   Techniques for Enhancing Cacheability of Data

Minimize use of SSL/TLS
Use URLs consistently
Use a common set of images
Store images and pages that infrequently change
Make caches recognize scheduled updated pages
Do not unnecessarily change files
Use cookies only when necessary
Minimize the use of POST

eight techniques that you can consider to improve the cacheability of data. Although some techniques may be more obvious than others, let's discuss each in the order that they appear in Table 5.4.

- *Minimize use of SSL/TLS*: When SSL/TLS (secure sockets layer/transport layer security) is used, pages flowing between the client and server are encrypted. Because encrypted pages are not stored by shared caches, reducing the use of SSL/TLS pages enhances the overall cacheability of Web-site data.

- *Use URLs consistently*: Using the same URL can make your site cache friendly, enabling a larger percentage of pages to be cached. This is especially true when your organization provides the same content on different pages to different users.

- *Use a common set of images*: If your Web site uses a common set of images and your pages consistently reference them, caching can become more frequent.

- *Store images and pages that infrequently change*: If you carefully examine your Web-site content, you will more than likely note many images and Web pages that are either static or that infrequently change. By using a cache-control max-age directive with a relatively large value, you can make caches take advantage of infrequently changing or static data.

- *Make caches recognize scheduled updates*: As indicated earlier in this section, certain pages, such as the *New York Times* home page, regularly change when financial markets are open. You can make caches recognize the scheduled change of such pages by specifying an appropriate max-age or expiration time in the HTTP header.

- *Do not unnecessarily change files*: One of the problems associated with caching is that it is relatively easy for a Web site to associate a large number of files with falsely young Last-Modified dates. For example, when updating a site by copying every file instead of just files that have changed, each file will then appear to be recently modified and, as a result, adversely affect caching. Thus, Web-site operators performing backups and restores or other site-update operations should restrict file updates to those files that have actually changed.

- *Use cookies only when necessary*: The purpose of a cookie is to identify the prior action of a user. Thus cookies, when cached by a proxy server, provide no additional benefit than when cached by a browser. This means that more effective caching can occur if cookies are not used or their use is limited to dynamic pages.
- *Minimize the use of POST*: While information sent in a query via the use of POST can be stored by caches, the reverse is not always true. That is, responses to POST are not maintained by most caches. Thus, minimizing the use of POST makes your data more cacheable.

5.2 Load Balancing

In comparison to caching that can be performed at many locations on the request/response path, load balancing is usually performed at the location where servers reside. In this section we will examine the rationale for load balancing, the different algorithms that can be used to distribute HTTP requests among two or more servers, and the different types of load balancing available along with a discussion of their advantages and disadvantages. In addition, we will examine the configuration and operation of a relatively free method of load balancing that occurs through the use of DNS.

5.2.1 Types of Load Balancing

There are several types of load balancing used on the Internet. Two of the primary types of load balancing involve communications and servers. Concerning communications load balancing, the goal is to attempt to distribute the communications load evenly among two or more computer systems. In a computer environment, load balancing can occur at different places, with a main server distributing requests to multiple back-end processors representing a typical example of computer load balancing.

5.2.2 Rationale

Web servers are similar to other computers in that they have a set amount of processing power and RAM memory. Both the processing power and RAM memory as well as the speed of the server's network connection limit the number of pages per unit time that can be served to clients. Thus, when an organization has only one Web server, its ability to respond to all incoming requests may be degraded as traffic increases. Clients will begin to notice degraded server performance as requested pages load slowly or they experience timeouts and fail to connect to the server.

In an attempt to alleviate the previously mentioned problem, Web-site operators have two options. First, they can attempt to upgrade their facility through the addition of multiple processors if the platform used supports additional hardware. Next, they may be able to increase RAM memory, allowing more pages to be cached. However, an increase in traffic to the Web site can lead to the point where the continued upgrade of server hardware is no longer cost effective. At this point in time, one or more servers need to be added to enable the load to be shared among a group of servers. The distribution of the load to be shared among two or more servers is referred to as computer load balancing, which is the subject of this section.

5.2.3 Load Balancing Techniques

There are several techniques that can be employed to obtain a load balancing capability. Load balancing can occur through software or hardware or a combination of hardware. For example, when a software program is used for load balancing, it operates on a hardware platform in front of a series of Web servers used by an organization. The software typically operates by listening on the port where external clients connect to access a service, such as port 80 for Web traffic. The load balancer will then forward requests to one of the back-end servers, which will commonly respond via the load balancer.

This action enables the load balancer to reply to clients without their being aware of the fact that the site they are accessing has multiple servers. In addition, the client is precluded from directly accessing the back-end servers, which can enhance a site's security. Depending upon the type of load balancer used, the failure of a back-end server may be both alarmed to notify a system administrator of the failure as well as compensated for by the balancer. As an alternative to acquiring hardware or software for load balance operations, its possible to use the round-robin capability of the Domain Name Service (DNS). Unfortunately, as we will shortly note, there is no easy method to compensate for the failure of a back-end server under DNS load balancing. In the remainder of this section, we will briefly review several types of load balancing techniques prior to examining them in detail.

5.2.3.1 DNS Load Balancing   Perhaps the easiest technique used to implement load balancing is obtained through the modification of DNS entries. This technique, which is referred to as DNS load balancing, requires a site to have two or more servers, each running the same software. The address of each server is then stored in the site's domain name server (DNS) under one name. The DNS server then issues those addresses in a round-robin manner. Thus, the first client to access the site obtains the address of the first Web server, the second client obtains the address of the second server, and so on. Later in this section, we will discuss DNS load balancing in more detail.

5.2.3.1.1 IP Address Mapping   A second load balancing technique involves mapping the name of a Web site to a single IP (Internet protocol) address. That IP address represents the address of a computer or network appliance that intercepts HTTP requests and distributes them among multiple Web servers. This type of load balancing can occur through the use of both hardware and software. Although the use of a load balancing appliance is more expensive than DNS modifications, it enables a more even load balancing to be achieved. This is because a load balancing appliance can periodically check to see if each server it supports is operational and, if not, adjust its serving mechanism. In comparison, the DNS approach cannot check for the availability of servers and would then periodically forward client requests to an inoperative server, assuming a server in the DNS entry became inoperative. This explains why, when you attempt to access a Web site, you may first receive an error message when a subsequent access request results in the retrieval of the desired Web page. This is because the second request results in the DNS server returning the IP address of a different server on the second request. Thus, when multiple requests are required to access a Web server, there is a high probability that the site uses DNS load balancing and at least one server is off-line.

5.2.3.1.2 Virtual IP Addressing   A third load balancing technique involves the use of software to configure multiple servers with the same IP address, a technique referred to as virtual IP addressing. Under this technique, multiple servers can then respond to requests for one IP address. For example, suppose you have three Windows servers, each assigned IP addresses 198.78.64.1, 198.78.64.2, and 198.78.64.3, respectively. You could use virtual IP addressing software to configure all three servers to use the common virtual IP address of 198.78.64.5. You would then designate one server as the scheduler, which would receive all inbound traffic and route requests for Web content to the other two servers based upon the load balancing parameters you set. Under virtual IP addressing, the failure of the scheduler server would be compensated for by assigning backup scheduling duties to another server.

5.2.3.2 Load Balancing Methods   There are several load balancing methods that can be used to distribute HTTP requests among two or more servers. Table 5.5 lists three of the more popular methods of load balancing algorithms in use.

5.2.3.2.1 Random Allocation   Under the random allocation method of load balancing, HTTP requests are assigned in a random manner to servers. Although the random method of allocation is easy to implement, it's possible for one server to periodically be assigned more requests than another server, although on average all servers over time should have the same load.

Table 5.5   Types of Load-Balancing Algorithms

Random allocation
Round robin
Weighted round robin

5.2.3.2.2 Round-Robin Allocation   A second method that can be used to assign HTTP requests to multiple servers is on a rotating or round-robin basis. Typically, the first request is allocated to a server selected randomly from a group of servers so that not all initial requests are assigned to the same server. For subsequent requests, a circular order is employed. Although a round-robin allocation method divides requests equally among available servers, it does not consider server processing capabilities. That is, if one server has twice the processing capability of another server, a round-robin allocation method would result in the more powerful server having half the loading of the less powerful server.

5.2.3.2.3 Weighted Round-Robin Allocation   The weighted round-robin allocation method was developed in response to the fact that there are normally processing differences between servers. Under the weighted round-robin load allocation method, you can assign a weight to each server within a group. Thus, if one server is capable of processing twice the load of a second server, the more powerful server would be assigned a weight of 2, while the less powerful server would be assigned a weight of 1. Using the weight information, the more powerful server would be assigned two HTTP requests for each request assigned to the less powerful server. Although the use of a weighted round-robin allocation method better matches requests to server processing capability, it does not consider the processing times required for each request. In reality, the latter would be extremely difficult, since it would require every possible request to be executed on each server in the group. Then, the processing requirements would have to be placed in a database on the load balancer.

5.2.4 Hardware versus Software

There are several differences between hardware and software load balances that need to be considered prior to selecting a load balancing platform. A hardware load balancer is usually considerably more expensive than its software-based cousin. Although the hardware-based load balancer can provide a higher servicing capability, it may lack some of the configuration options available with software-based load balancers.

Today, a majority of load balances are software based. In fact, some Web server and application server software packages include a software load balancing module. Because one of the most popular load balancing methods, DNS load balancing, is software based and requires no additional hardware, we will conclude this section with a discussion of its operation.

5.2.5 DNS Load Balancing

As a review, the purpose of the DNS is to respond to domain name lookup requests transmitted by clients. In response to such requests, the DNS returns the IP address that corresponds to the requested domain name. For example, assume a client wants to access our illustrative site www.popcorn.com. Let's assume its IP address is 198.78.46.8. Then, when the client enters www.popcorn.com into the browser's URL field, the browser first checks its internal cache to see if the URL was previously resolved into an IP address. Assuming it wasn't, the Web browser communicates with a DNS server for the required IP address. In actuality, the browser may access several DNS servers, such as one on the local LAN, until it retrieves the applicable IP address. That address can be controlled by the DNS server associated with the domain popcorn.com, which in effect enables DNS load balancing to occur.

Under DNS load sharing, several IP addresses are associated with a single host name. For our example we will assume that the domain popcorn.com has a very active access history of clients purchasing goodies and that the domain now has four servers whose IP addresses are 198.76.41.1 through 198.76.41.4. Then, when a request flows to the DNS server to resolve a domain name, it responds with one of the four IP addresses that are served up in a round-robin or load-sharing manner. Thus, the use of IP addresses in a round-robin manner results in a form of load balancing.

5.2.6 DNS Load-Sharing Methods

There are two basic methods of DNS-based load sharing you can consider. Those methods include the use of CNAMES and the use of A records.

5.2.6.1 Using CNAMES One of the most common implementations of DNS is the Berkeley Internet Name Domain (BIND). Depending upon which version of BIND is used, you can implement load balancing through the use of multiple CNAMES or multiple A records.

Under BIND 4, support is provided for multiple CNAMES. Let's assume your organization has four Web servers configured with IP addresses 198.78.46.1, 198.78.46.2, 198.78.46.3, and 198.78.46.4. You would then add the servers to your DNS with address (A Names) records as shown here.

```
Web1   IN   A   198.78.46.1
Web2   IN   A   198.78.46.2
Web3   IN   A   198.78.46.3
Web4   IN   A   198.78.46.4
```

Note that the Web server names (Web1, Web2, Web3, and Web4) can be set to any name you want, but they need to match canonical names added to resolve www.popcorn.com in our example to one of the servers through the following entries.

```
www   IN   CNAME   Web1.popcorn.com
      IN   CNAME   Web2.popcorn.com
      IN   CNAME   Web3.popcorn.com
      IN   CNAME   Web4.popcorn.com
```

Based upon the preceding, the DNS server will resolve the wwww.popcorn.com domain to one of the four listed servers in a rotated manner, in effect spreading requests over the four servers in the server group.

5.2.6.2 Using A Records While the previously described method works under BIND 4, multiple CNAMES for one domain is not a valid DNS server configuration for BIND 8 and above. For BIND 8 name servers, you would include an explicit multiple CNAME configuration option such as the one shown here:

```
Options {
Multiple-cnames yes;
};
```

If you are working with BIND 9 and above, then you should use multiple A records as indicated below to effect load balancing via DNS.

```
www.popcorn.com    IN    A    198.78.46.1
www.popcorn.com    IN    A    198.78.46.2
www.popcorn.com    IN    A    198.78.46.3
www.popcorn.com    IN    A    198.78.46.4
```

As an alternative to the above, many times a Time To Live (TTL) field is added to A records. The TTL value indicates the maximum time that information should be held to be reliable. By setting a low TTL value, you can ensure that the DNS cache is refreshed faster, which will improve load sharing on your organization's Web servers. Unfortunately, the trade-off of this improvement is the fact that the load on your organization's name server will increase. The following example shows the use of a 60-second TTL value when A records are used.

```
www.popcorn.com    60    IN    A    198.78.46.1
www.popcorn.com    60    IN    A    198.78.46.2
www.popcorn.com    60    IN    A    198.78.46.3
www.popcorn.com    60    IN    A    198.78.46.4
```

The use of CNAMES or A records to obtain a DNS round-robin method of load balancing is transparent to clients. Because it employs existing hardware and software, it's very cost effective, requiring only a minimum of effort, and is popularly used by small- and medium-sized organizations. Unfortunately, as previously mentioned, there is no way for DNS to detect the failure of a server, which means that, upon the failure of a server, DNS will continue to route clients to that server. Thus, if there are four servers defined by the use of A records and one fails, then 25% of client requests will be sent to a server that cannot respond to client requests.

5.2.7 Managing User Requests

One of the problems you may have in the back of your mind is how to ensure that a particular server selected in a round-robin method via DNS load balancing knows the status of a client. After all, your Web site would rapidly lose surfers if each client had to reenter previously entered information each time they were directed to a different server. The technical term for keeping track of where a particular client is with respect to its use of a server is referred to as *server affinity*. Although DNS load balancing does not directly provide server affinity, it can use one of three methods to maintain session control and user identity via HTTP, which is a stateless protocol. Those methods include the use of cookies, hidden fields, and URL rewriting. While the use of cookies should be recognized by readers and was previously mentioned in this book, the use of hidden fields and URL rewriting has not been mentioned and deserves a bit of explanation.

5.2.7.1 Hidden Fields A hidden field is used to pass along variable data from one form to a page without requiring the client to reenter data. A hidden field is similar to a text field; however, instead of being displayed on a Web page, the hidden field, as its name implies, does not show on the page. In addition, a client cannot type anything into a hidden field, which leads to the purpose of the field, which is to provide information that is not entered by the client. Thus, a Web server can create and enter data into a hidden field, which enables a second server that is accessed via DNS load balancing to manage the user without having the client reenter previously entered data.

5.2.7.2 Settings The hidden field under HTML code is assigned by the use of the type attribute as shown here

<input type ="hidden" />

Through the use of the name and value settings, you can add a name and value to a hidden field. The name setting adds an internal name to the field, which enables a program to identify the fields, while the value setting identifies the data that will be transmitted once the form is submitted. To illustrate the use of a hidden field, consider the following HTML code shown in Table 5.6.

In the example shown in Table 5.6, the action attribute specifies the manner by which data will be submitted, which in this example occurs via a CGI script on the server. Next, the method=post entry represents a preferred method for sending form data. When a form is submitted POST, the user does not see the form data that was sent.

Table 5.6   Coding a Hidden Field in HTML

```
<html>
  <head>
    <title>Hidden Field Example</title>
  </head>
  <body>
  <form name="clientstatus"
  action="http://www.popcorn.com/clientstatus.cgi"
  method="POST">
  <input type="hidden" name="hidefield" value="Cart_ ID">
  ...
  </form>
  </body>
</html>
```

The use of the input type defines a hidden field that has the field names *hidefield* and value *Cart_ID*, which will be referenced and updated. Assuming that there are multiple servers using DNS load balancing and that they are, in turn, connected to a common back-end database that maintains cart status information, any server accessed by the DNS load balancer will allow the cart information to be retrieved from the back-end database without further action by the client.

5.2.7.3 URL Rewriting   In addition to the use of cookies and hidden fields, you can also consider the use of URL rewriting as a mechanism to provide server affinity. Simply stated, URL rewriting is the process of intercepting an incoming Web request and redirecting the request to a different resource. When URL rewriting is employed, the URL being requested is first checked. Based on its value, the request is redirected to a different URL. As you might expect, URL rewriting can be both complex and provide the potential for unscrupulous persons to learn more about your Web site than they need to know. Thus, cookies and hidden forms are the preferred methods used to obtain server affinity.

6

THE CDN ENTERPRISE MODEL

The purpose of this chapter is to examine content delivery with respect to the enterprise. Commencing with a discussion of when and why content delivery should be accomplished in-house, we will turn to several techniques that can be employed to facilitate the delivery of content to include audio, video, and text. Because the most effective method to determine an appropriate content delivery mechanism requires knowledge of where data must flow, and the quantity of data within each flow, we need knowledge of the enterprise's operating environment. This author would be remiss if he did not include a discussion of one of the built-in resources available for access on most Web servers: their traffic logs. Now that we have a general appreciation concerning where we are headed, let's proceed and turn our attention to investigating the Content Delivery Network (CDN) enterprise model.

6.1 Overview

The sizes of business enterprises can vary significantly. Some enterprises that host a Web site could be small retail stores, such as the mythical www.popcorn.com that this author has employed throughout this book. In comparison, other types of enterprises can range in size from Fortune 100 and Fortune 500 industrial organizations to large banks and insurance companies that were once considered too big to fail in competition with the so-called mom-and-pop stores that now are technically savvy and have effective Web sites to market their products. Thus, an enterprise model that may be well suited for one organization could be ill suited for a different-sized organization. Even if two organizations are similar in size, they may have differences in the type and location of customers that they attract, similar to the difference between an automobile manufacturer and a heavy-equipment manufacturer.

It would be very difficult, if not impossible, to discuss a series of CDN enterprise models that could be associated with different types of organizations. In recognition of this fact, the author has used a different approach to the topic of this chapter. Instead of attempting to match CDN enterprise models to organizations, a better approach, in this author's opinion, is to discuss such models in a structured order. The structured order will let readers consider one or more models that could be well suited to the operation of their organization, providing them with the ability to select the most appropriate model. As we examine different CDN enterprise models, we will commence our effort by discussing simple data-center models applicable to organizations that operate a single Web site. Then we will examine the more complex CDN enterprise models that are applicable for organizations capable of operating multiple data centers. For the purpose of this chapter, we will use the term *data center* quite loosely to describe a facility where one or more Web servers are located. To regress a bit, this author was one of the first Webmasters when he configured a desktop computer to function as a Web server. That server operated in a regular environment, and the room in which the server was located became the author's data center.

6.1.1 Rationale

Any discussion of the use of an in-house content delivery mechanism should commence with an investigation of the rationale for doing so. After all, for many organizations that lack the staff, time, or equipment, the simple solution is to outsource content delivery. However, in doing so, a distinction needs to be made between having your Web site hosted and having your Web site hosted with a content delivery capability. Concerning the former, there are many organizations that have data centers where your organization can have either a dedicated server or a virtual server, with the latter representing a Web site operating on a computer that runs many applications that can include other organizational Web servers, ftp servers, mail servers, and so on. While your organization will not have to obtain hardware and software as well as install and operate communications facilities, the use of a hosting facility does not mean that it employs the services of a CDN nor that it offers a CDN facility that matches the locations

Table 6.1   Rationale for Developing an In-House Content Delivery Capability

- Concentrated customer base
- Distributed locations available for use
- Knowledgeable staff
- Control
- Economics

where you expect clusters of clients to originate their access to your Web server. Thus, you need to ask applicable questions prior to having your Web site hosted to obtain information about their CDN capability or a lack of that capability.

Table 6.1 lists five key reasons that can justify developing an in-house content delivery capability. In the following paragraphs, we will turn our attention to each of the reasons listed in Table 6.1.

6.1.1.1 Concentrated Customer Base   Having a concentrated customer base can considerably facilitate the development of an in-house CDN capability. This is because a concentrated customer base—such as persons that utilize online ticket ordering for sports events at an arena in Macon, Georgia, or a similar activity that typically originates a vast majority of requests from the immediate geographic area—generates local traffic. While it's possible a person in Los Angeles or London may also need some tickets, you will not have any significant access requirements outside the middle Georgia geographic area. Thus, the operator of the Web site does not have to be concerned with reducing latency from potential Web clients originating traffic from areas outside the middle Georgia area to include areas outside the United States. Thus, the primary focus of such Web-site operators should be on maintaining availability to the site. Depending upon the traffic volume to the Web site, the site operator may consider operating multiple servers using a load-balancing technique to provide a high level of access to its facility.

6.1.1.2 Distributed Locations Available for Use   A second reason for considering an in-house content delivery capability is in the case where an organization has distributed locations available for supporting Web servers, thereby making it possible to create an organization-wide CDN. For example, consider an organization headquartered in

Stockholm, Sweden, that has branch offices located in New York City, Singapore, Sydney, Tokyo, Paris, London, and Moscow. Suppose that the organization currently operates a single Web server in Stockholm, and the use of a network traffic analyzer or Web-site statistics indicates that users accessing the server from Japan and Australia were experiencing significant latency delays that resulted in a number of terminated sessions. Because the Sweden-based organization has branch offices in Tokyo and Sydney, it may be possible to install servers at those two locations to enhance access from Australia and Japan. In addition, by using such latency tools as Ping and Tracert, you could determine if it was practical to enhance service to Singapore by having clients in that location access a server in Tokyo or Sydney. With appropriate programming, traffic directed initially to the Web server located in Sweden could be redirected to a server located either in Tokyo or Sydney, based upon the origin of the initial data flow to the server in Sweden. In this example, using two distributed locations outside the main office would enable locations that experience significant latency to obtain speedier access to data because the Web servers would be located considerably closer to the browser user. In addition, either or both new server locations could be considered to serve other potential clients in the Oceania and Pacific region.

6.1.1.3 Knowledgeable Staff It makes no sense to develop an in-house content delivery networking capability if an organization lacks experienced or trainable personnel to support distributed servers and the communications they require. The availability of a knowledgeable staff or the resources necessary to hire and/or train applicable personnel is a prerequisite for being able to develop an in-house content delivery networking capability. Thus, you need to examine the existing personnel skill set and their ability to tackle a new CDN project, as well as consider the availability of funding for additional personnel and the training of both current and, if required, additional employees.

6.1.1.4 Control A key advantage associated with in-house content delivery versus using a third party to provide a CDN capability is control. By assuming responsibility for content delivery, an organization becomes capable of reacting faster to changing requirements. In addition, your employees will develop skill sets that a third-party

CDN provider may not achieve, since your organization should know your customers better than a third party.

Another important area of control involves reacting to a changing environment. If you operate your own CDN, you can prioritize the work of your employees to satisfy changes that you or upper management deem important. In comparison, a third part may require a lengthy contract modification to have the service provider initiate one or more content delivery changes to satisfy changing organizational requirements.

6.1.1.5 Economics   One of the most important reasons for developing an in-house content delivery networking capability is economics. Can an organization save money by performing content delivery operations in-house instead of signing a contract that places the responsibility for content delivery in the hands of a third party? The answer to this question can be quite complex because so many factors need to be considered beyond a direct dollar and cost accounting. For example, although it may be more expensive for an organization to establish an in-house CDN, the ability to train employees and directly control the operation of the network could represent a rationale for deciding against a pure economic analysis where you compared your cost to the cost associated with the use of a third party.

Although economics is an important decision criterion, many times there can be other factors that, when considered, result in a decision that may not make sense from a pure economic perspective. Even if a decision does make economic sense, you may need to consider the availability of funds if your organization needs to borrow money to take a more economical route. During what is now referred to as the "great recession," many banks froze small- to medium-size organizations from obtaining loans no matter what their balance sheets looked like. Thus, the Web-site manager must consider a wide range of factors that are in the economic area—but that are beyond a pure economic analysis of in-house versus third-party CDN capability—to include the availability of funds and the terms if such funds are available.

6.1.2 Summary

Now that we have an appreciation for the main factors that can govern a decision to perform content delivery in-house, we need to determine whether our organization requires establishing a content delivery mechanism beyond operating a single Web server. We need a way to analyze the existing traffic flow that will allow us to recognize existing and potential bottlenecks that could be alleviated by establishing a content delivery networking capability.

6.2 Traffic Analysis

There are several methods an organization can use to determine the need for some type of content delivery networking capability. Those methods include the analysis of Web logs and the use of other networking logs that are built into many server operating systems, as well as the use of a network protocol analyzer that has a programming capability. You can even use cookies as a mechanism to track how many times a visitor returns to your Web site as well as to generate additional information that enhances your knowledge of the activities of clients accessing your server. Through the use of a network analyzer's programming capability, you can create a program that, for example, can count traffic origination by country and the time of day each access occurred, providing you with detailed information about the access habits of customers and potential customers. Although such information is valuable, there are numerous types of protocol analyzers, each with different programming constraints. On the other hand, Web logs and other programs built into several server operating systems, as well as the use of cookies, are more readily available without additional cost. Consequently, we will turn our attention to server operating-system programs and cookies in this chapter.

6.2.1 Using Web Logs

Regardless of the software used to provide a Web-server operating capability, each program will have at least one commonality: the ability to record Web activity into logs that can be analyzed to provide information about users accessing the server. Such information, at a minimum, will be able to inform you about the locations where traffic originated and the time the traffic originated, enabling you to literally open a window of observation concerning your client base. Because different Web-server application programs vary with respect to their capability, we will focus our attention on the type of logs generated by the Apache open-source solution for Web-site operations.

6.2.1.1 Apache Access Logs   Apache represents a popular Web-site solution that includes a very flexible Web-logging capability. In addition to supporting error logging of messages encountered during operations, Apache has the ability to track Web-site activity. Apache generates three types of activity logs: access, agent, and referrer. Information recorded into those logs tracks accesses to your organization's Web site, the type of browsers being used by each client to access the site, and the referring Uniform Resource Locators (URLs) of the sites from which visitors arrived. Using various configuration codes, it is possible to capture every piece of information about each inbound access request to a Web site. Table 6.2 lists examples of the Apache strings used to log information to the log file, and a short description of the data logged as a result of a particular configuration string.

Although referred to as an access log, in reality this log should be called an activity log, as it records activity occurring on the Web server being accessed. In its standard configuration, Apache records all access attempts by clients and all server-side errors, with the latter able to be adjusted through the use of a control parameter. In addition, you have the ability to create custom logs. For example, you can arrange to log data identifying the browsers used by clients, which might assist your development programmers to structure their efforts. Because logging of everything can rapidly expand the use of disk space when a server is popular, you should carefully select the data you really need to log. In comparison to the use of access logs, error logs can be used to identify problems with your site. Both logs, but especially the access log, can experience rapid growth when a server is heavily used. While you might be tempted to delete an access log with the expectation that Apache will start a fresh one, it's important to note that Apache keeps track of the access log file size and will continue to try to write at what it thinks should be the current end of file. However, there is a helper program in the /bin directory that allows you to "rotate" log files, whereby existing log files are renamed, and Apache is told to continue writing at the beginnings of the new log files.

Table 6.2 Apache Logging Scripts

STRING	DESCRIPTION
%a	Remote IP address
%A	Local IP address
%b	Bytes sent, excluding HTTP headers, in CLF format
%B	Bytes sent, excluding HTTP headers
%C	Content of cookies in request sent to server
%D	Time taken to serve the request (ms)
%e	Content of environmental variable
%f	File name
%h	Remote host
%H	The request protocol
%i	Contents of header line(s) in the request sent to the server
%l	Bytes received including request and headers
%J	Remote log name
%m	The request method
%n	The contents of a specific note from another module
%o	The contents of header line(s) in the module reply
%O	Bytes sent, including request and headers
%p	The canonical port of the server serving the request
%P	The process ID of the child that serviced the request
%q	The query string, if it exists
%r	The first line of the request
%s	The status of the original request
%t	The time that the server finished processing a request
%T	The time required to service the request
%U	The URL path request
%V	The canonical server name of the server servicing the request
%X	The connection status when the response is complete

6.2.1.2 Access Records An access record includes such information as the client's IP (Internet protocol) address; the date and time; a record of the request, such as a GET, POST, or PUT; the HTTP response code; and the size of the response message. In addition, it's possible to configure the Apache log file specifications so that a reverse lookup is performed on the client's IP address, enabling the host name and domain to be obtained and placed into the log file.

6.2.1.3 HTTP Response Codes Most of the HTTP status codes (see Table 6.3) will be 200s, which indicate the successful return of the requested data. However, there are other response codes that can be used to identify potential hacker attacks or client errors. For example,

Table 6.3   Meanings of the Most Commonly Encountered HTTP Status Codes

CODE	MESSAGE	MEANING
200	OK	Indicates a successful request resulting in a file being returned
206	Partial Content	Indicates that a file was only partially downloaded
301	Moved Permanently	The server indicated that the requested file is now located at a new address
302	Found	Indicates that the user was redirected; since it's not a Permanent redirect, no further action needs to be taken
304	Not Modified	Indicates that the browser made a request for a file that is already present in its cache; a 304 status code indicates that the cached version has the same time stamp as the "live" version of the file, so they don't need to download it; if the "live" file was newer, the response code would be 200
400	Bad Request	Indicates that the server could not make sense of the request
401	Unauthorized	Indicates that an attempt was made to access a directory or file that requires authentication by entering a user name and password; subsequent requests would contain a user name and password, resulting in either a 200 status code indicating a user was authenticated or a 401 status code indicating the authentication failed
403	Forbidden	Indicates that the server has blocked access to a directory or file
404	Not Found	Indicates that the requested file does not exist on the server; this status code normally indicates a broken internal or external link
408	Request Timeout	Indicates that the client/server connection process was so slow that the server decided to terminate the session
410	Gone	The server indicates that the requested file used to exist but has now been permanently removed
414	Request—URL Too Long	Indicates that the request was too long; this status code can indicate that an attempt has occurred to compromise the server using a buffer-overflow technique

a series of 401 responses used to indicate an "authorization required" challenge followed by requests with different user names can be used to indicate that someone is probably trying to guess entries into a password-protected file. Another interesting code, is code 404 which defines "resource not found." This error code could reflect an error by the client; however, the appearance of a series of 404 responses in the log could indicate the presence of bad HTML links in resources on your site. In addition, the response sizes could also indicate potential problems. If the recorded sizes are often less than the actual resource sizes, this indicates that your clients are breaking connections before downloads are complete. This could indicate that either your server does not have sufficient capacity to service users or that your communications connection to the Internet does not have sufficient bandwidth to service your client base.

The following log entry illustrates an example of a successful request logged into your server's access log.

> 198.78.36.8 - - [13/Jun/2009:17:42:18 +1000]
> "GET /images/mercadesauto.jpg HTTP/1.1" 200 1076

The previous log entry informs us that the client's IP address was 198.78.36.8; the request was for a static HTML image file named mercadesauto.jpg; the HTTP/1.1 protocol was used; and 1076 bytes of data was transmitted by the client. Note that the use of GET should not normally be used for operations that cause side effects, such as using it for taking actions in a Web application. This is because a GET may be used arbitrarily by Web robots, which do not need to consider the side effects of a request.

6.2.2 Using Logging Strings

To illustrate the potential of the Apache logging strings listed in Table 6.2, let's assume that your organization wants to log the remote host, the date and time of the request, the request to your Web site, and the number of bytes transmitted in the request. To accomplish this, you would enter the following commands:

> LogFormat: "%h %t %r %b" common
> CustomLog logs/access_log common

The string LogFormat starts the line and informs the Apache program that you are defining a log file using the name "common," which is then associated with a particular log format string. The string consists of a series of percent characters, which generates a single log file instead of individual access logs. Apache is then instructed to log access information in the file logs/access_log, using the format defined in the previous line. In addition to being able to create a single log file for large Web sites that have multiple servers, a Web-site operator can analyze the data flow to multiple servers located within a physical location or scattered around the globe.

For the previous example, the sequence of log entries will begin by including the IP address of the client that made the request to the server. This logging results from the use of the %h entry in the first line in the above example. Next, the %t entry results in the logging of the time that the server completed processing the request. The format of logging is day/month/year:hour:minute:second zone, where day is two digits; month is three letters; the year is four digits; the hour, minute, and seconds are two digits; and the zone is four digits prefixed with a plus (+) or minus (–) with respect to Greenwich Mean Time. The following is an example of the entry of data into an access log from the use of the %t string:

[14/Sep/2009:17:23:45 –0600]

The last entry in our example, %b, indicates the number of bytes returned to the client excluding the HTTP headers, in common log format (CLF).

6.2.3 Web-Log Analysis

Although Apache and other Web application programs can be used to create logs containing predefined activity, such activity represents raw data. To convert the raw data into a meaningful report requires a reporting tool. Although some Web application programs also include a reporting module that, when invoked, will operate against the log to generate a report, there are times when a Web-site manager will require additional information. This resulted in the development of a series of application programs and collection of scripts used to generate reports from Web logs. Although this author will leave it to readers to decide which application programs or collection of Web-log analysis scripts are most suitable for their operating environment, this author would be remiss if he did not mention how readers can access applicable software.

If you are operating the open-source Apache server, you can go to almost any search engine and enter the string "apache log analysis tool" or just "apache log analysis." In early 2010, this author entered the first string at bing.com, Microsoft's relatively new search tool. The result was 2,220,000 hits, as indicated in Figure 6.1. In examining Figure 6.1, in addition to the large number of hits on the search term "apache log analysis," note that if you move your cursor over the greater-than (>) sign, you can obtain additional information about

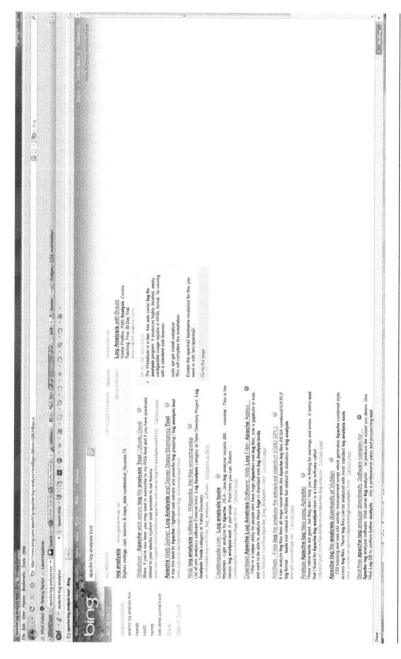

Figure 6.1   Searching bing.com for an Apache log analysis tool.

the page hit. In this example, Webalizer is a "fast, free Web server log analysis program," according to the additional information provided by the search tool. Although this author will leave it to the reader to select an applicable log-analyzer tool, it should be mentioned that some sites contain malicious software, which can be identified by having an up-to-date virus checker. You can see that the sixth entry was flagged by the virus checker used by this author as having what some people consider as adware, spyware, or other potentially unwanted programs. Although we will not discuss the use of Apache log-analysis tools, we can discuss some of the common reports generated by log-analysis programs and scripts. This will give us a solid indication of the type of data we can obtain from Web logs and why we need some additional tools to determine if our organization requires a content delivery capability.

6.2.4 Top Referring Domains

The Top Referring Domains is one of the more important reports provided by many application programs and Web-log analysis scripts. This report logs the URLs reported by browsers directing them to various Web pages on your server. Typically, application programs and Web-log analysis scripts lets the user configure the program or script to list the top 10, 25, 50, or another number of top referring domains.

Through the use of the Top Referring Domains report, you can note which sites are providing referrals to your organization's Web site. For example, consider the top ten referring domains report that is shown in Table 6.4. From an examination of the entries in the referenced table, you can note that the primary referring domains represent search engines. Although the three highest referring sites in our example (google.com, bing.com, and yahoo.com) are located in the United States, other search engines providing a referring service are located in the United Kingdom (uk), Canada (ca), Germany (de), and France (fr). While a majority of referring comes from the first three search engines in the United States that are listed at the top of Table 6.4, there is also a significant amount of referring occurring from search engines located in Western Europe in this example. Although the referring from search engines located in Western Europe could indicate that the placement of a server outside the continental

Table 6.4 An Example of a Top-10 Referring Domains Report

REFERRALS	DOMAIN
127,183	google.com
123,742	bing.com
114,784	yahoo.com
87,413	google.co.uk
67,137	google.ca
47,412	msn.com
46,193	yahoo.de
45,237	google.fr
39,762	yahoo.fr
12,756	cnn.com

United States might be warranted, the report does not indicate the delay or latency associated with the referrals. This means that we need additional information prior to being able to reach an intelligent and informed decision concerning the placement of a server outside of the continental United States. Unfortunately, we cannot obtain such information directly from Web logs. Instead, we can either examine the number of dropped sessions, which may indicate problems clients had accessing the Web site, or we can use a protocol analyzer or such built-in operating-system tools as Ping and Tracert.

One of the uses of the top referring domains that can affect the need for content delivery is advertising. For example, consider Figure 6.2, which illustrates the home page of Yahoo France during early 2010. Note that prominently displayed is an advertisement from ING Direct. ING is an abbreviation of Internationale Nederlanden Groep, which in English is referred to as the International Netherlands Group. ING is the owner of ING Direct, a virtual bank with operations in Australia, Canada, France, Italy, Spain, the United Kingdom, the United States, and other countries.

6.2.5 Considering Status Codes

To verify whether your organization is receiving the value associated with advertising expenditures, you can consider both the number of referrals from the Web site you are advertising on as well as the potential results from adding a content delivery capability. For example, assume your organization operates an Apache server. Further, assume

Figure 6.2   The Yahoo France home page during early 2010.

that you are searching the results of the Apache log files that you created to include the use of the %s parameter, which records the status code that the server transmits back to each client. In Table 6.3, some of the more commonly encountered status codes resulting from the use of the %s parameter are listed. Note that the codes can be subdivided into successful responses beginning at 200, a redirection beginning at 300, and client errors beginning at 400.

Returning to our Apache application, assume that an analysis of the log revealed that there were a large number of 408 status codes. Because the 408 status code indicates a request timeout that resulted in the server aborting the session, this would indicate that clients were having difficulty accessing the server. While this could be a bandwidth problem, your ISP usually provides graphs of your bandwidth utilization on a daily, weekly, and monthly basis. Thus, you might be able to quickly rule out bandwidth as the culprit. If you rule out bandwidth on your Internet access line, then you need to check latency from the general location of clusters of clients to the location of your server. If the latency is causing timeouts, then you need to decide if the cost of content delivery by placing one or more servers in Western Europe is worth the cost. While this could make advertising more fruitful, there are other factors that need to be considered, such as sales and marketing of any products your organization sells as well as an improvement in its image to the client population in Western Europe. Because each organization is literally unique, this author has presented the tools to allow readers to make the technical analysis while leaving the actual decision process to the reader.

Although we will shortly discuss how we can use a protocol analyzer to assist in our ability to obtain information for our decision-making process, let's first complete our discussion of Web-log utilization. To do so, we will continue by examining some of the statistics we can obtain from various logs.

6.2.6 Web-Log Statistics

Because Apache and other Web-server programs enable you to log most, if not all, of the contents of HTTP headers, it's possible to obtain valuable statistics by summarizing the contents of logs. Two of the more important statistics you can obtain from Web-server logs are access to your server based upon the country of client origination and the time zone from where access occurred.

A distribution of access to your organization's Web site by origination country provides you with a good indication of where traffic originated in its flow to your Web server. This information can be helpful for determining the general location of server requests and the effect of your organization's advertising and marketing efforts. However, since we are concerned with facilitating content delivery, we will leave advertising and marketing concerns to other publications.

6.2.7 Reverse Mapping

Prior to continuing our examination of origination country information, let's digress a bit and discuss how we can obtain the origination country and other domain information, since requests to a Web server include a source IP address. Thus, a mapping from an IP address to a domain address is required. This mapping is referred to as a reverse IP lookup. Reverse IP represents an easy way to determine all the .com, .net, .org, .edu, and other domains from which clients access your organization's Web server. There are many uses for a reverse IP capability that go beyond the ability to identify your client access base. For example, if your organization is considering the use of a large shared host computer operated by a third party, you can use a reverse IP capability to determine who is using the host prior to signing a contract. In addition, if we assume that your organization is a small biotechnological firm and that the server already hosts your primary competitor, you might not be able use the server regardless of its client base. Another possible use of a reverse IP capability is to identify phishing and scam sites, which often come in groups. If you locate one and do a reverse IP lookup, you might find several other scam sites hosted on the same server.

A reverse IP capability is built into most Web-server log-analysis programs. In addition, there are numerous third-party reverse IP lookup sites on the Internet that can be accessed via a search engine. When using a reverse-lookup program or program capability, you should carefully consider its effect upon the logging to your computer. This is because a reverse IP lookup is a time-consuming process and can slow down a busy Web server. Due to this fact, many organizations will copy the access log to another system to run a reverse IP lookup or will run the reverse IP lookup on the Web server during a slow evening shift to minimize its impact on clients accessing the server.

The reverse IP address lookup is typically accomplished through a reverse Domain Name Service (DNS) lookup, also known as a *reverse DNS resolution* or simply *reverse mapping*. Normally a DNS query takes the form "what is the IP address of host www in domain =abc.com." However, there are times when we need to determine the name of a host given its IP address, such as when we want to analyze a Web-server log to determine additional information about the clients accessing the server. Through reverse mapping, we can determine the domain name associated with a given IP address. The reverse DNS database of the Internet is rooted in the Address and Routing Parameter Area (ARPA) top-level domain of the Internet. For IPv4 addresses, the in-addr.arpa series of addresses records serve as pointers to applicable root servers for a reverse lookup. For IPv6 addresses, a series of ip6.arpa records function as pointers to applicable root servers for a reverse DNS lookup. From the applicable root server, the process of reverse resolving of an IP address occurs by searching for the applicable named.rev file that sets up inverse mapping. That file will contain the names of the primary and master name servers in an organization's local domain, plus pointers to those servers as well as any other nonauthoritative name servers. The names of the primary and secondary master servers are indicated by NS records, while the pointers are indicated by the use of PTR records. The file also needs a Start of Authority (SOA) record to show the start of a zone and the name of the host on which the named.rev file resides. Here, the term *zone* represents all of the hosts that constitute an entity. For example, consider the following extract from a DNS file shown in Figure 6.3. In this example, there are three hosts in the reversed mapped zone.

Although we are primarily concerned about the reverse IP lookup process, a few words describing the major entries in the DNS file extract shown in Figure 6.3 are warranted. The first entry in each of the zone files is the Start of Authority (SOA) resource record. The SOA record indicates the authoritative name server for this domain. Because the SOA record indicates the beginning of a zone, there can be only one SOA record for each zone.

zone	IN	SOA	origin contact (
	serial		
	refresh		
	retry		
	expire		
	minimum)		
zone	IN	NS	name server name
in-addr.arpa address	IN	PTR	host1.zone.
in-addr.arpa address	IN	PTR	host2.zone.
in-addr.arpa address	IN	PTR	host3.zone.

Figure 6.3   Extract from a DNS file.

6.2.8 SOA Record Components

The format of the SOA record is:

zone	**IN**		**SOA**	origin contact (
	serial			
	refresh			
	retry			
	expire			
	minimum/time to live			
)				

The components of the SOA record are described as follows:

zone: This is the name of the zone. Normally the SOA field contains an at sign (@).

IN: IN is used to state that the address class is the Internet class.

SOA: The type of resource record is SOA. All the information that follows this is part of the data field and is part of the SOA record.

origin: This is the host name of the primary name server for the domain, and it is normally written in the fully quali-fied domain name format with a trailing dot added, such as www.popcorn.com.

contact: This is the e-mail address of the person responsible for this domain. Note that the at sign (@) in the e-mail address is replaced by a dot.

serial: This number can be considered to represent the version number of the zone file. You need to change the serial number every time you update the zone data, as this field is used by secondary name servers to determine if the zone file on the primary server has been updated. That is, when the secondary server requests the SOA record from the primary, it compares the serial number received to the serial number in its cache. If the serial number received from the primary has increased, the secondary server requests a full zone transfer. Otherwise, the secondary server assumes it has the most current zone data.

refresh: This is the length of time (in seconds) that the secondary name server should wait prior to checking with the primary server to see if the zone data was modified.

retry: The retry time is the amount of time, in seconds, that the secondary name server should wait prior to attempting another zone refresh after a failed attempt. This number should not be set too low, as rapidly retrying to access a down system will consume network resources. A setting of one hour (3600) is commonly used.

expire: Expire defines how long (in seconds) the secondary name server should keep the data without receiving a zone refresh. If there has been no answer from the primary server to refresh requests after repeated retries for the amount of time specified in the expire, the secondary should discard its data.

minimum/time to live: This entry represents the amount of time (in seconds) that resource records from this zone should be held in a remote host's cache. It is recommended that this value be large, as a small or low value will force remote servers to repeatedly query for unchanged data. A commonly used value is 86400, which represents a 24-hour time period.

To illustrate an example of the potential entries in a named.rev file, let's assume that the domain popcorn.com consists of three hosts: a Web server, an ftp server, and a client host with the name baked.popcorn.com. Since the named.rev file sets up inverse mapping, it needs to include the names of the primary and secondary name servers in your local domain to include pointers to those servers. The names of the primary and secondary servers will be indicated through the use of NS records, while the use of an SOA record is required to indicate the beginning of a zone as well as the name of the host on which the named.rev file resides. Assuming that it's popcorn.com,

```
$ttl 2d          ; 17280 seconds
$origin 46.78.198. in-addr.arpa
@                IN   SOA   www.popcorn.com. root.www.popcorn.com. (
                 1.5 ; serial number
                 3600 ; refresh 1 hour
                 600 ; retry 10 minutes
                 3600000 ; expire 1000 hours
                 86400 ) ; minimum 24 hours
            IN   NS    ns1.popcorn.com.
            IN   NS    ns2.popcorn.com.
1           IN   PTR   www.popcorn.com.
2           IN   PTR   ftp.popcorn.com.
3           IN   PTR   baked.popcorn.com.
```

Figure 6.4 An example of a named.rev file.

whose IPv4 address is 198.78.46.1, that the ftp server is .2 on the subnet, and that the client with the name *baked* is at .3, then Figure 6.4 illustrates a more detailed named.rev file.

In examining the entries in the named.rev file illustrated in Figure 6.4, note that a reverse name resolution zone requires the first three blocks of the IP address reversed followed by .in-addr.arpa. This enables the single block of IP numbers used in the reverse name resolution zone file to be associated with the zone. Then, the NS records point to the name servers while the PTR records have the following format:

<last-IP-digit> IN PTR < fully qualified domain name-of-system>

As an alternative to the previously mentioned reverse lookup, some third-party vendors offer a table lookup process that is interesting. They convert an IP address into a decimal number and then search their database to provide a variety of information to include the domain and country of the associated IP address. The actual IP number conversion multiplies the first dotted decimal number by 256*256*256, which is added to the second dotted decimal number multiplied by 256*256, which is added to the third dotted decimal number multiplied by 256, which is then added to the fourth dotted decimal number. That is, assuming the IP address is a.b.c.d, then the IP number becomes:

$$X = a*(256*256*256) + b*(256*256) + c*(256) + d$$

Now that we have an appreciation for the reverse lookup process, let's continue our exploration of Web-log statistics and turn our attention to the origination country.

6.2.9 Origination Country

As we return our focus to the origination country information, note that some reports simply list the number of Web page views by originating country in descending order. While this type of report refines raw log data, you more than likely will have to take pencil to paper and use a calculator to further analyze this report. For example, assume that you need to group a number of Western and Eastern European countries, as your organization has offices in both general locations, and you are considering providing a content delivery capability in each area. Concerning Eastern European countries, let's assume that your organization markets farming equipment and that you already have branch offices in Prague, Warsaw, and Budapest. Let's also assume that your clients currently access your Web server in the United States but that your Web manager noted a high number of server-based timeouts occurring from Eastern Europe. Thus, you might then consider establishing a Web server in a branch office; however, the question now becomes one of selecting an applicable office. Since we will not investigate the cost of labor, office space, and communications—something that you would ordinarily perform on your own—we can focus our attention upon the client country of origin. However, since most Web-log analysis programs simply list total by country, you will need to consider grouping different countries together as well as using Ping and Tracert to determine, from a technical perspective, where the new server should be located.

6.2.10 Originating Time Zone

Another summary report available from most Web-server log-analysis programs groups page views according to the time zone of the browser user. This type of report usually lists page views in descending order based upon the time zone of origination. That time zone is stated in reference to Greenwich Mean Time (GMT) with a plus or minus hourly offset. For example, the Eastern time zone in the United States, which encompasses states from Maine in the north to Florida in the south, is GMT – 05:00. In comparison, Moscow, Russia, is located in GMT + 03:00, while Tokyo, Japan, is located in GMT + 09:00.

While a Top Time Zone report can provide valuable information, it's possible that this report could provide some misleading information. This is because a time zone covers an area of the globe between the North and South Poles. Thus, a large number of page views occurring from GMT – 05:00, which is the previously mentioned Eastern time zone, could originate from New York, Florida, or even Argentina, because each of those locations are all in the same time zone. This indicates that, in most cases, you need to supplement the report of Top Time Zone page views with knowledge about the locations from which the traffic originated. An exception to this is when considering system maintenance. In this situation, the use of the Top Time Zone page views could assist you in determining the impact upon taking down your Web server for periodic system maintenance.

6.2.11 Other Statistics

In addition to the originating country and originating time zone reports, a Web-log-reporting program or the use of a collection of scripts can be expected to generate a series of statistics. Table 6.5 provides a list of the general type of statistics you can typically obtain from the use of a Web-log analysis and reporting program or commercial script.

In examining the entries in Table 6.5, you will note that the statistical information provides general summary information about the

Table 6.5 Web-Log Analysis Statistics

MONTHLY, WEEKLY, OR DAILY STATISTICS

- Total page views
- Total visitors
- Unique visitors
- Hourly unique visitors
- Average page views per hour
- Page views per visit
- Busiest day in reporting period
- Busiest hour in reporting period

activities occurring at a particular Web site. Although this information may be suitable for examining the need to upgrade an existing Web server, the summary information is usually not suitable for deciding if an in-house content delivery mechanism is warranted based on existing traffic. The originating-country report supplemented by an originating-time-zone report can be used to consider the need for a distributed content delivery capability. In comparison, the summary statistics are usually better suited for evaluating the capacity and processing power of an existing Web server or group of servers against the current workload request flowing to the server or group of servers. For example, the average-page-views-per-second statistic can be compared with the capability of your server to generate Web pages. If this statistic increases over time and begins to approach the capacity of your server, this indirectly informs you that it's time to consider other options, such as upgrading your server, installing a load balancer and another server, or using the services of a third party.

While it's true that not all Web pages have the same composition—and that the variance in Web page composition will affect the pages per second (PPS) rate that a hardware platform can generate—working with an average page view per second and comparing that value to the average server page-generation capability provides a reasonable gauge concerning server performance. As the page-views-per-second value approaches the server's PPS generation capability, the load on the server increases to a point where the server must either be upgraded, a load balancer and additional server should be installed, or a third party with sufficient capacity must be considered.

6.2.12 Other Analysis Tools

Although you may not realize it, there are a variety of analysis tools you can consider, ranging in scope from commercial and freeware products to the use of cookies. Concerning commercial products, one of the earliest programs developed to analyze Web-server logs in a Windows operating environment—Webtrends—is still being marketed in its ninth incarnation. This commercial program provides users with the ability to obtain real-time updates for key metrics as well as receive real-time alerts. Marketed under the moniker Webtrends Analytics 9, this data-collection and -analysis program is both scalable and customizable. In the Apache server environment, one popular log-analysis tool is Webalizer, which can be downloaded from several sites. Because it is written in C, it is very fast, and its reports are usually sufficient for obtaining data about many important metrics, such as the number of hits and the pages that are being accessed.

If you have a commercial account on a number of Web sites, you may be able to access traffic reports that can provide you with information that can be used to consider if you should maintain what is essentially a third-party hosting service or use your own server. For example, this author operates an eBay store selling U.S. postage stamps. One of the perks of having an eBay store is the ability to obtain traffic reports, such as the report generated and shown in Figure 6.5.

If you examine Figure 6.5, you will note that the left column indicates the types of reports a store operator can obtain. In comparison, the right column on the page shows three graphs: page views, visits, and home-page views for the current month. A page view is counted every time a visitor views your listings, a page within your store, and other pages tracked by eBay. A visit is defined by eBay as a sequence of consecutive pages viewed by a single visitor for 30 minutes without a break, while the "storefront" displays the number of times a storefront home page was accessed. Because each report occurs on a monthly basis and compares the current month to the prior four weeks and a year ago, you can see a bar graph (current month) and two line graphs (prior 4 weeks and prior 52 weeks). Note that because the traffic report was executed on the 12th of the month, the bar graph terminates at that point, while the two line graphs continue till the end of the month. By clicking on "view full report," you can view the report in its entirety. Figure 6.6 illustrates an example of the full report concerning page views. Note that this report provides some very interesting information concerning activity of eBay users interested in U.S. postage stamps. In this example, you will note that the visits report indicates graphically that, up until the 12th of the month, the number of visits for the month, the prior 4 weeks, and the prior year was relatively stable in spite of the great recession. If you turn your attention to the lower portion of Figure 6.6, you will see that under the "details" heading you can view numeric quantities. Thus, the traffic reports can provide users of eBay and other commercial sites with valuable data.

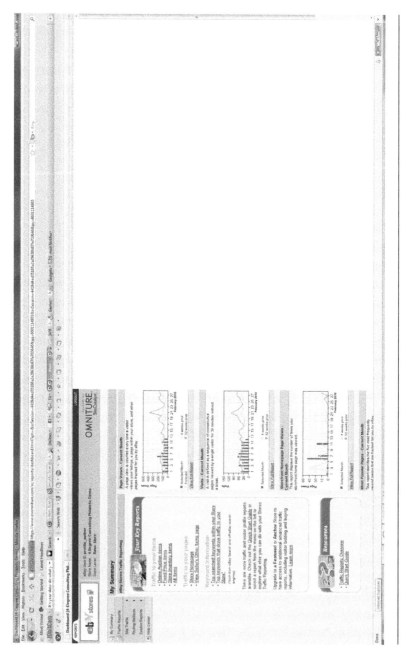

Figure 6.5 An example of a traffic report generated by E-bay for a store.

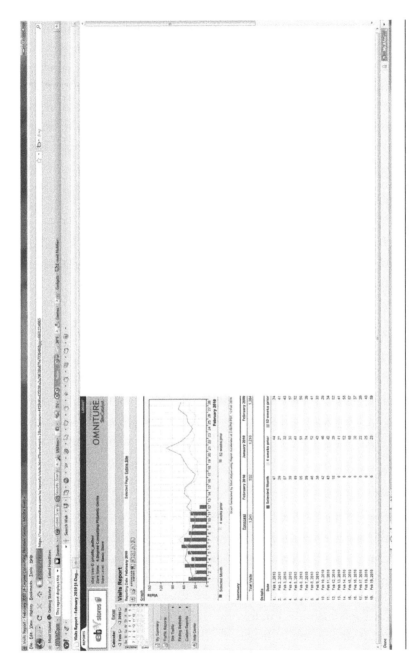

Figure 6.6 Viewing detailed E-bay-provided visit data.

6.2.13 Cookies

Although cookies have received some bad publicity due to their use by some Web sites, you can put them to practical use as a mechanism to track Web-server usage. Prior to discussing how this can be accomplished, let's first review what a cookie is and the different parameters that can be associated with them.

A cookie is a rather simple text message that can be placed in the client computer's memory or written as a file onto the hard drive on the client computer. Although the primary purpose of a cookie is to store state information concerning a client-server transaction, such as items in a shopping cart, the use of cookies has considerably expanded since its humble beginnings as a method to overcome the stateless nature of the HTTP protocol. Today, you can use cookies to determine the duration of user visits on different Web pages as well as generate other types of statistics without having to use a log-analysis program or to supplement the use of this type of program.

If you're using a recent version of Microsoft's Internet Explorer, you can view cookies by selecting the Internet Options from the Tools menu. Then you would select the General tab and click on Settings, then select Files, which will provide a view of all temporary files as well as cookies. You can also configure both Internet Explorer and most other modern browsers to either accept all cookies or to alert you each time a server attempts to provide you with a cookie. To do so, if you're using a modern version of Internet Explorer, you would select the Internet Options from the Tools menu. Then, by clicking on the Privacy tab, you can move a slider bar to the setting you prefer.

You can obtain an indication of the pervasive use of cookies by examining Figure 6.7, which illustrates the use of cookies by the Internal Revenue Service (IRS) when this author was using his Firefox browser. Of course, clients can configure their Web browsers to not allow cookies, but few users do so. In examining Figure 6.7, note that the left dialog box occurs by selecting the Options entry from the Tools menu in Firefox. By clicking on the "Show Cookies" bar, the left dialog box is displayed. Then, this author scrolled down to the IRS site and viewed the two cookies a visit to www.irs.gov deposited on his computer.

Figure 6.7 Viewing cookies on Firefox.

If you do not set the cookie's expiration, the cookie is created, but it is not stored on the user's hard disk. Instead, the cookie is maintained as part of the user's session information. When the user closes the browser, the cookie is discarded. This type of cookie is referred to as a *nonpersistent cookie*. A nonpersistent cookie like this is useful for information that needs to be stored for only a short time or that for security reasons should not be written to disk on the client computer. For example, nonpersistent cookies are useful if the user is working on a public computer, where you do not want to write the cookie to disk. It's important to note that users can clear one or more cookies on their computers at any time they desire. This is true regardless of the cookie's expiration date

6.2.13.1 Cookie Basics   When a cookie is transmitted from a server to a client's browser, an additional line is added to the HTTP headers. For example, consider the following:

Content-type: text/html
Set-Cookie: roasted=2; path=/; expires Wed, 11-Aug-2010
    14:42:00 GMT; domain=popcorn.com

This header results in a cookie named roasted that has a value of 2; perhaps the user visited popcorn.com and placed two roasted bags of popcorn in his or her shopping cart. The cookie has a path of /, which means it is valid for the entire site; however, the cookie expires on 11 August 2010 at 2.42 p.m. The domain=popcorn.com parameter tells the browser to send the cookie when requesting an arbitrary page of the domain popcorn.com, with an arbitrary path. Cookies are defined in several RFCs (Request for Comments), and when you develop cookies on the server side, you define their style as cookie based on RFC 2109 or cookie2 based on RFC 2965. Regardless of the style used, their names are case insensitive.

When a cookie is transmitted from the client browser to the server, its header is changed slightly. The following example illustrates the reverse transmission:

```
Content-type: text/html
Cookie: roasted=2
```

The preceding makes the server aware of a cookie named roasted whose value is 2.Thus, as long as the cookie hasn't expired, good old popcorn.com knows that the client's shopping cart had two roasted bags in it.

From the above examples, we can note that a cookie has at least five parameters. Those parameters include the name of the cookie, its value, its expiration date, and the path and domain for which the cookie is valid. In addition, a cookie can indicate the need for a secure connection to use the cookie. The first two parameters (name and value) are required, while the other four are optional and can be set either manually or automatically. Concerning the path, it sets the URL path the cookie is valid within. Pages outside of the specified path cannot read or use the cookie. If it is not set, the default is the URL path of the document creating the cookie. The use of the domain parameter extends the flexibility of the path parameter. That is, if a site has multiple servers, you can use the domain parameter to make the cookie accessible to pages on any server in the domain. To do so, you would use the domain parameter, assuming that our example site popcorn.com has multiple servers, as follows:

```
domain=www.popcorn.com
```

If the cookie requires a secure connection a flag is used to indicate this fact. A TRUE or FALSE value is used to indicate that a secure connection, such as SSL or TSL, is required.

6.2.13.2 Writing Cookies   Cookies are transmitted to a client's browser via the HttpResponse object (http://msdn.microsoft.com/en-us/library/system.web.httpresponse.aspx) that initiates a collection called Cookies (http://msdn.microsoft.com/en-us/library/system.web.httpresponse.cookies.aspx). You can access the HttpResponse object through the use of several programs, such as Perl or Javascript, or through the programming capability of your server. The browser is responsible for managing cookies on a user system, and any cookies that you want to send to the browser must be added to this collection.

When creating a cookie, you specify as a minimum a Name (http://msdn.microsoft.com/en-us/library/system.web.httpcookie.name.aspx) and Value (http://msdn.microsoft.com/en-us/library/system.web.httpcookie.value.aspx). Each cookie must have a unique name so that it can be identified when reading it from the browser. Because cookies are stored by name, naming two cookies with the same name will cause one to be overwritten. You can also set a cookie's date and time expiration. Expired cookies are deleted by the browser when a user visits the site that wrote the cookies. The expiration of a cookie should be set for as long as your application considers the cookie value to be valid. For example, a cookie that effectively never expires can result from setting the expiration date to be 20 years in the future; however, a user can still delete the cookie. A cookie can be quite complex, as it can be up to 4096 characters in length. Thus, a Web-server operator can create a cookie with time and date information as well as page of entry to the server that can be used as a mechanism for tracking client information.

6.2.13.3 How a Cookie Moves Data   Cookie data can be a collection of simple name-value pairs stored on your hard disk by a Web site. The Web site stores the data, and later it receives it back. A Web site can only receive data in the form of cookies that it previously stored on your computer. It cannot examine any other cookie, nor anything else on your machine.

When you type a URL into a Web browser, a Web server might look in your cookie file, resulting in the data moving as follows:

- When you enter the URL of a Web site into your browser, your browser sends a request to the Web site for the page defined by the URL.

- Your browser looks on your computer for a cookie file that the Web site previously sent. If it finds a cookie file, your browser will send all of the name-value pairs in the file to the server along with the URL. If it finds no cookie file, it will send no cookie data.
- The Web server receives the cookie data and the request for a page. If name-value pairs are received, the Web site can use them according to some predefined program.
- If no name-value pairs are received, the Web site employing cookies knows that you have not visited before. The server creates a new ID for you in its database and then sends name-value pairs to your machine in the HTTP header for the Web page it transmits. Your computer then stores the name-value pairs on your hard disk.
- The Web server can change name-value pairs or add new pairs whenever you visit the site and request a page.

6.2.13.4 How Web Sites Use Cookies The general purpose behind the use of cookies is to enable a server to store information on your computer. Such information allows a Web site to "remember" the "state" your browser is in, such as if you placed items in a shopping cart and what those items are. As a minimum, a cookie placed on your computer informs a server that you previously visited the site.

Because of the common use of caching, proxy servers, and DNS extensions, the only method for a site to accurately count visitors is to set a cookie with a unique ID for each visitor. Web sites can use cookies in many different ways. For example, a common use of cookies is to determine the number of visitors to a site, the number of new versus repeat visitors, and how often a visitor has visited the site. The first time a visitor arrives at a Web site, the site creates a new ID in its database and transmits the ID as a cookie. The next time the user returns, the site can increment a counter associated with that ID in the database, resulting in the ability of the site to know how many times that visitor returned to the site. By simply running through the database and comparing the counter value associated with each ID, a simple program can determine the total number of unique visitors.

6.2.13.5 Problems with Cookies This author would again be remiss if he did not mention some of the problems and limitations associated with cookies. Those problems include the fact that many computers are shared and that people use multiple computers, as well as certain privacy issues.

6.2.13.5.1 Shared Computers Any computer that is used in a public area, as well as computers in an office environment or at home, can be shared by multiple people. For example, assume you're at the public library and you use a computer to make a purchase from an online store. The store will leave a cookie on the computer. In the early stages of Web development, cookies sometimes included credit card information, which made it possible for someone to use the same computer to purchase something from the store using your account. Even though credit card information is not typically sent in cookies, at the very least it's a good idea to clear all temporary files and cookies after you use a browser on a computer accessible by other persons.

6.2.13.5.2 Multiple Computer Usage A separate issue from shared computers is the use of multiple computers. People often use more than one computer during the day. For example, I have a computer in my kitchen, another computer in my office, and two laptops that I frequently use. Unless the site is specifically programmed to solve this problem, I will have four unique cookie files sent from a site that I visit using each computer, one on each device. Thus, any site that I visit from each computer will track me as separate users, resulting in an extreme level of annoyance when you're forced to set your preferences over and over. Sites that allow registration and store preferences at a central locations, such as Amazon and eBay, make it easier for a user to use the same account on different computers.

6.2.13.5.3 Privacy Issues Although cookies can be considered as being benign text files, they provide lots of useful information about the habits of a user. When you visit a Web site, it's possible for the site to not only track the pages you view and the ads you click upon, but, in addition, if you purchase an item, they now have your name and address. Then it becomes possible for the site operator to market such information to others.

Different sites have different policies concerning the marketing of information. Unfortunately, you may have to carefully search through the contents of a site to determine its policy, which is why many persons use various "spyware" removal programs to remove certain types of cookies. One company, called DoubleClick, which is now owned by Google, is known for its banner ads on many Web sites as well as its ability to place small GIF files on sites that allow the company to load cookies onto your computer. DoubleClick can then track your movements across multiple sites. Because of this practice, DoubleClick is often associated with the controversy over spyware because some of their browser cookies are set to track users as they travel from site to site and record the commercial advertisements a client views and ads they click upon. Due to its cookie operations, DoubleClick deposits on client browsers are considered to be malware by several commercial organizations that detect their presence and provide the client browser operator with the ability to remove such cookies.

6.2.14 Other Logging Information

Previously, we noted the use of access logs and cookies to obtain information about the use of server resources. To ensure that readers have a solid understanding of server performance, we will conclude our discussion by turning to a tool built into server software. Because Microsoft's Windows operating system represents the dominant operating system used by Web application programs, we will look at the Performance Monitor tool built into Windows server to obtain an appreciation for how we can open a window to view the performance of a server's hardware platform.

6.2.15 Microsoft's Performance Monitor

Microsoft developed Performance Monitor to view, log, and chart the values of various performance-related counters. Performance Monitor can be used to spot trends that signify whether a hardware upgrade or replacement should be considered or is necessary. Performance Monitor is a tool for examining the ability of the operating system and its hardware platform to satisfy operational requirements. The name Performance Monitor was used by Microsoft to reference this tool when it was bundled with Windows NT. When Microsoft introduced the Windows 2000 server and the Microsoft Management Console (MMC), it changed the name from Performance Monitor to Performance. In later versions of Windows, the title of the product has reverted back to Performance Monitor, which will be used throughout the following discussion.

6.2.15.1 Activating Performance Monitor   Figure 6.8 illustrates how the built-in Performance Monitor can be activated using a Windows 2000 server. Although the Start menu has changed and will undoubtedly change again in the next release of Windows, this figure provides readers with a general indication of how to access the product. As shown in Figure 6.8 by the sequence of highlighted menu entries, you would select Programs>Administrative Tools>Performance to invoke the Performance Monitor. Although the graphic display will change based upon the version of Windows used, Performance Monitor can normally be found under Administrative Tools.

Under Windows 2000 server and other more recent Microsoft products, you access Performance Monitor via the MMC, as shown

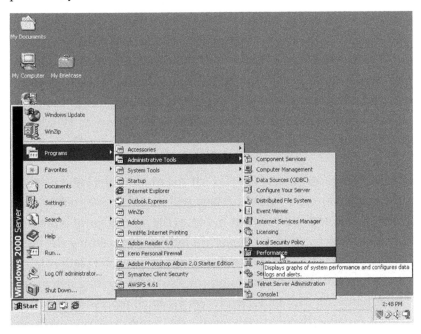

Figure 6.8   Accessing Windows 2000 server's performance monitor provides the ability to display graphs of system performance.

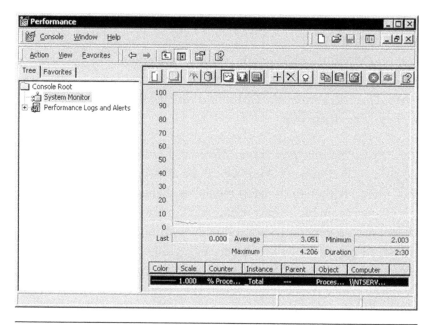

Figure 6.9 Windows 2000 server's performance monitor runs under the Microsoft Management Console.

in Figure 6.9. Note that the left portion of the display provides a tree of activities that can be invoked. The right portion of the display provides a graph of the objects you previously selected. After you select one or more objects, the display will show each object in a different color during the selected time period and indicate, for each graphed entry, its latest value (last) as well as average, maximum, and minimum values. Note that similar to other windows in Microsoft Windows, you can easily resize the display.

6.2.15.2 Adding Counters and Instances   If you examine the lower portion of the graph shown in Figure 6.9, you will note that one counter was previously selected. That counter indicates the percentage of processor utilization, which can be an important indicator concerning the need to either upgrade or replace an existing server hardware platform.

In a Microsoft Windows environment, a server's operating system can support hardware with multiple processors. Each processor is referred to as an *instance*. By right-clicking on the graph, you can select an applicable counter or group of counters to be plotted, thereby displaying a dialog box labeled "Add Counters," as illustrated in Figure 6.10.

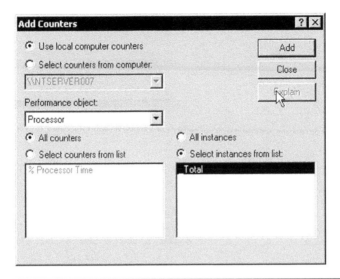

Figure 6.10 System overview properties: the add counters dialog box provides a mechanism to define the counter whose values you wish to monitor.

Note that, through the use of Performance Monitor, you can select one or more counters for each instance or processor. In the example shown in Figure 6.10, the "% Processor Time" counter was selected when the button Select Instances from the "Select counters from list" labeled box was selected. Because the hardware platform (computer) operating Windows Server had only one processor, the right area of the display shows Total selected when the button labeled "Select Instances from list" was clicked. Otherwise, if there were multiple processors on the hardware platform running Windows server, the counter could be selected for an individual processor or for all processors.

A second method you can use to select counters to monitor performance is by clicking on the Performance Logs and Alerts entry in the tree portion of the window. Three sub-branches display when you explode the Performance Logs and Alerts branch. Those sub-branches are shown in the left portion of Figure 6.11. In this example, the Counter Logs entry is shown as selected, displaying two previously defined logs in the right portion of the window. A dialog box labeled System Overview Properties is displayed when you right-click on either entry or a blank display. That dialog box is shown in the right foreground of Figure 6.11. Note that there are three tabs in the System Overview Properties dialog box. Those tabs are labeled

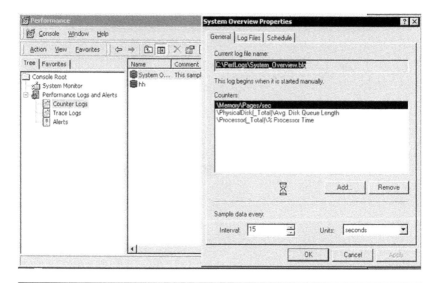

Figure 6.11 Double clicking on a log results in the display of the system overview properties dialog box, showing the counters in the log.

General, Log Files, and Schedule, with the tab labeled General shown positioned in the foreground.

The General tab indicates the name and location of the current log file. You can add or remove counters and define the sampling interval. The tab labeled Log Files lets you control various aspects of a log file, such as its format, the amount of storage to be used, and the assignment of a comment to the file. In comparison, the Schedule tab lets you define when logging occurs.

6.2.15.3 Working with Performance Monitor To better illustrate some of the functionality and capability of the Performance Monitor, let's modify the previously selected log file. You can use the buttons labeled Add or Remove to do so. If you want to add some counters, click on the Add button shown in the General tab located in the System Overview Properties dialog box, which displays a Select Counter dialog box.

The left portion of Figure 6.12 illustrates the selection of the Add button, while the right portion of the display shows the Select Counters dialog box. If you focus on the three buttons in the Select Counters dialog box, you will note a gray-colored button labeled Explain, which was selected by this author. Selecting that button displays a textual explanation about each highlighted counter. In the example shown in

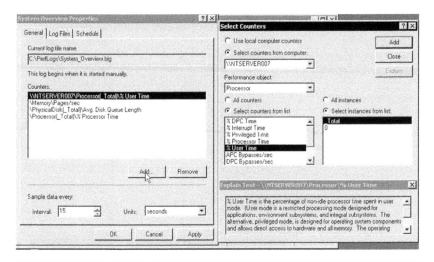

Figure 6.12 Obtaining an explanation about a highlighted counter.

Figure 6.12, the "% User Time" counter was highlighted, which displays an explanation concerning what the counter signifies. As indicated by the explanation, "% User Time" represents the percentage of non-idle processor time spent in user mode. The term *user mode* references applications, environment subsystems, and integral subsystems operate that do not require direct access to hardware or all memory. As the "% User Time" value increases, the load on the processor increases.

Once you select the counters to be monitored and select a schedule, you can view the effect of logging via the Performance Monitor's graphing capability. To illustrate the graphing capability, the selected counters shown in the left portion of Figure 6.12 were plotted as a line chart and as a bar chart. Figure 6.13 illustrates the plot of the selected counters in a line chart format, with the five counters listed at the bottom of the graph as textual data. The vertical bar above the A in Average indicates the current time of the plot as the vertical line moves from left to right across the display.

To change the composition of a graph, you select an icon above the graph. If you look at the cursor arrow shown in Figure 6.13, you will note that it is positioned on a line graph icon, the fifth icon from the left in the series of icons. When this icon is selected, it results in the display of a line graph of the selected counter values. If you move the cursor to the fourth icon from the left, your cursor will be positioned on a bar chart icon. Clicking on that icon will result in the

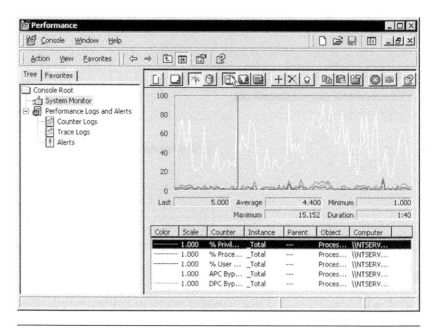

Figure 6.13 Viewing a line graph of the values of five selected counters.

type of graph being changed from a line chart to a bar chart format, as shown in Figure 6.14.

In examining Figure 6.14, note that only the display of the graph changed when a different graph icon was selected. The lower portion of the graph, which contains the color legend for each counter, remains as is. Thus, the use of icons representing various types of graphs provides users with the ability to select a type of graph that satisfies their requirements. If you compare Figures 6.13 and 6.14, in this particular example of the values of five counters, the line graph appears more meaningful. While you would probably prefer the line graph in this situation, in other situations a bar graph may be the preferred graph to use. Because changing graph types is no more than a click away, users can easily experiment with displaying the different types of graphs supported by Performance Monitor

6.2.15.4 Summary Windows Performance Monitor and other tools can be valuable for determining the utilization of hardware, processor, memory, and disk resources. In addition, its use can assist you in spotting trends that will provide you with a mechanism to plan upgrades rather than react to problems.

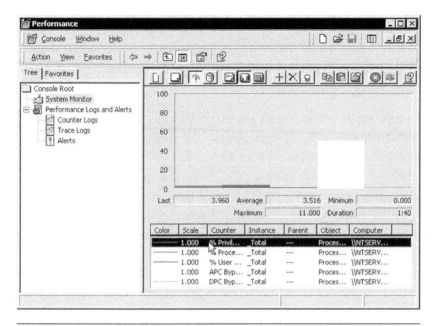

Figure 6.14   Viewing a bar graph of the values associated with five counters.

By carefully monitoring counters associated with the utilization of processors, memory, and disk activity, you can obtain a valuable insight to potential utilization problems prior to those problems actually occurring. This in turn will provide you with the information to consider several options to improve the content delivery capability of your organization's Web server or servers. These options can include adding processors, memory, and more or faster disk storage to existing hardware, adding servers, or even replacing existing hardware with more capable equipment. Regardless of the option you select, having the ability to view key performance metrics provides you with a detailed insight concerning the operation of your organization's server hardware platforms and represents a key tool you can use to facilitate content delivery.

Now that we have an appreciation for the use of server operating-system tools, we need to concern ourselves with the flow of data across the Internet. Although Web logs provide a good indication concerning the locations from where data is arriving, these logs do not indicate if browser users are encountering abnormal network delays that would justify the distribution of servers beyond an organization's primary data center. To obtain an insight into the network, we need to turn to a different set of tools. One of those tools is a network analyzer; other tools, such as the Ping and Traceroot (Tracert) programs, are built into most modern operating systems.

6.2.16 Using a Network Analyzer

An appropriate network analyzer, also commonly referred to as a *protocol analyzer*, makes it possible to observe the flow of data between your organization's server and browser users. Most protocol analyzers include a timing chart, which indicates the interaction of packet flow between your organization's server and individual browser users or groups of such clients by time. By examining the interaction of the requester and server by time, you can determine if there are abnormal delays that would warrant the installation of one or more servers at areas around the globe to facilitate access to your organization's Web site. Obviously, such information can also be used to determine the use of a third-party content delivery networking capability as well as the general locations where the CDN network should have a hosting capability.

To illustrate the use of a network analyzer, this author will use a commercial product marketed under the name Observer. Network Instruments of Minneapolis, Minnesota, developed Observer, which supports both wired and wireless Local Area Network (LAN) analysis at data rates from the 10 Mbps of legacy Ethernet to the 10 Gbps of more modern Gigabit Ethernet networks.

Similar to other protocol analyzer products, you use Observer to capture and analyze certain types of data packets. For example, assume that your organization has a LAN connected to the Internet and also operates a Web server that is connected to the LAN. If you have several workstations connected to the LAN, you could create several filters to record traffic routed to the server instead of all traffic routed to your organization's LAN. To do so, you would set up a filter to record traffic that flows to the Internet Protocol (IP) address of the server. If the server supports several applications in addition to operating as a Web server, you could also add a filter to limit the data capture to inbound packets flowing to port 80, which represents HTTP traffic. If you wanted to capture secure traffic, you would then filter data using a protocol analyzer's AND capability to also filter on the SSL (Secure Sockets Layer) port number. By filtering an IP address and one or more port numbers, you can define the type of

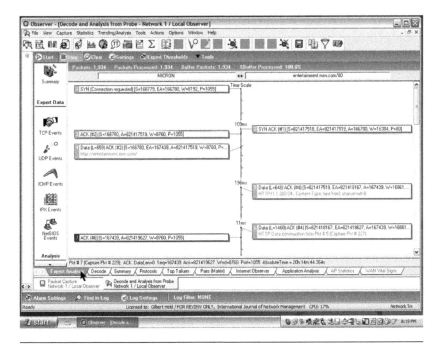

Figure 6.15 Through the use of Network Instruments Observer software-based protocol analyzer, you can examine the delays associated with the flow of packets between devices.

packet capture to a specific hardware interface as well as one or more applications operating on the hardware platform.

Once you capture relevant packets, you can perform one or more operations on the captured data. Perhaps one of the more interesting tools provided by the use of Observer is its Expert Analysis option, which decodes the data flow between two devices, such as a browser and a Web server.

Figure 6.15 illustrates an example of Observer's Expert Analysis option. In this example, the screen is shown subdivided, with a time scale in milliseconds (ms) used for the subdivision. The left portion of the screen shows the flow of packets from a Web browser to a Web server, while the right portion of the screen shows the response from the server. In this example, the Web browser was assigned the computer name Micron. That computer is shown accessing the MSN Web server, whose host address is entertainment.msn.com on port 80.

In examining Figure 6.15, you can observe the three-way initial Transmission Control Protocol (TCP) handshake issued by the computer named Micron to the Web server. The initial SYN in the three-way handshake occurs at the top of the time scale, with the server's initial response occurring slightly after 109 ms on the time scale. The server responds with a SYN ACK, which results in the computer named Micron completing the three-way handshake by transmitting a SYN packet. After completing the three-way handshake, the computer named Micron transmits a data packet further down the time scale, with the server responding at a time slightly after 196 ms on the time scale. For this particular example, the interactions between the client and server are rapid, and no substantial network delays would warrant any adjustment to the geographic placement of a server. However, by using the Network Instruments Observer or a similar product on a periodic basis, you can obtain the capability to examine the data flow between devices and note any abnormal delays that could justify the redistribution of servers to facilitate content delivery.

6.2.17 Other Tools to Consider

In concluding our discussion of traffic analysis, a word about Ping and Tracert is warranted to either supplement or replace the use of a network analyzer. If you know the distribution of access originators to your organization's Web site, you can use either tool to determine the delay from your network to a distant device that will closely mimic the delay to the location where clusters of remote users are geographically located. For example, assume that, through an analysis of Web logs, you note that a large number of page views to your organization's Web server in Boston occurs from Romania, Bulgaria, and several other Eastern European countries. While the geographic distance between Eastern Europe and Boston is considerable, if browser users access the Internet via service providers that have a fiber-optic link to a major Western European peering point, the transmission delay to the server located in Boston may be minimal and not warrant the distribution of content delivery outside the Boston area.

Because you would have to either dynamically view Web logs or use a network analyzer in real time to determine the IP addresses of remote users in order to run Ping or Tracert, a better method is to select a server located within the general area where access requests are initiated to your organization's Web server. Then, you could ping the server to determine the round trip delay to the distant computer or you could run Tracert to examine the delay on each path to the distant server. For either situation, the resulting display will indicate the network-associated delay between your organization's Web server and the general area of access from clusters of browser users. Based on the results obtained from the use of Ping and Tracert and the value of browser user requests to the server, you can then make an informed decision concerning either the distribution of servers to remote sites to enhance content delivery or using a third party to provide a content delivery service.

6.3 Content Delivery Models

In concluding our discussion of content delivery performed by the enterprise, we will examine a series of CDN models. As indicated earlier in this chapter, some models may be better suited to one organization than another. However, since the number of offices, the activity of an organization's Web site, and the location of browser users accessing the Web site can vary considerably between organizations, our focus will be on Enterprise CDN models, leaving the selection of an appropriate model to the readers of this book. In this section, we will commence our investigation of CDN models with an elementary single-site, single-server model. Using this model as a base, we will proceed to discuss more complex models, examining single-site, multiple-servers; multiple-sites, single-server per site; and multiple-site, multiple-server per site models. As we discuss each model, we will examine its advantages and disadvantages as well as discuss the model's operation.

6.3.1 Single-Site, Single-Server Model

The simplest model of content delivery over the Internet is the single-site, single-server model. This model results in an organization configuring a single hardware platform at a single location to provide Web services to both customers and potential customers around the globe, regardless of the location of browser clients.

6.3.1.1 Advantages The key advantage associated with the single-site, single-server model is its cost and efficiency. A single hardware platform reduces both hardware and software costs, including licensing fees for certain products. With respect to hardware cost, not only do you reduce the cost associated with requiring additional servers, but in addition, you eliminate the cost associated with a load balancer or similar hardware product. Concerning software costs, because there is only one server, the organization does not have to purchase multiple operating systems or application programs, nor are multiple licenses for certain products necessary, reducing software costs to a minimum. In addition, the single server requires less support than multiple servers do. For example, running a simple log-analysis program on a single server might take a few hours each week. In comparison, when you have multiple servers at a site, you may have to first rotate and move logs and then run a program against a series of logs. The time involved in rotating and moving logs could exceed the time to run a program against a single log, while the application program you use against multiple logs may require an additional license fee.

6.3.1.2 Disadvantages There are several disadvantages associated with the single-site, single-server content delivery model. The most obvious disadvantage is the failure of the server, which results in the removal of the presence of an organization from the Internet. Another problem is the occasional need for hardware and software modifications, which could temporarily render the site inoperative. Last, but not least, a single-site requires browser users who may be located around the globe to have their requests flow through one or more common telecommunications circuits and peering points to the site. If one or more of those circuits or peering points should become inoperative, a large number of potential users could have their access to the Web site blocked. If a circuit failure occurs within the network of the ISP used by the organization hosting the Web site, it's possible that all access to the site could be blocked even though the server is operational. Thus, the single-site, single-server model results in some key potential operational deficiencies.

Another problem associated with the single-site, single-server model is the fact that all browser user access flows to a common server location. This means that browser access from one location could be relatively rapid, with minimal delay encountered by the user client. In comparison, browser access from other locations could traverse

multiple peering points as well as have the data flow routed over relatively low-speed communications circuits or high-speed circuits with
lots of traffic and very high occupancy levels. Concerning the latter,
routers are designed to drop packets when necessary, which means that
retransmission requests will occur, which can result in latency increasing to the point where browser users either access your competitor
Web sites or simply abandon your organization's Web site. For either
situation, this represents a potential loss of revenue and goodwill.

6.3.1.3 Considering Server Options   Although many times in this book
we have noted that a single server represents a point of failure that
can make your organization's Web site inoperative, a few words are in
order concerning how to increase the level of server availability and
why, after doing so, a single server can be more reliable than the use of
multiple servers. The key to raising the availability level of a server is
redundancy and cutover capability. The more redundancy a server has,
the greater its reliability can become, assuming a cutover mechanism
exists to replace a failed device by an operational one. For example,
many servers can be obtained with dual power supplies where, in the
event of the failure of one, the second takes over. Similarly, in the
area of disk drives, the use of different RAID (Redundant Array
of Independent Disks) levels can be used to add redundancy to disk
storage. While it is up to the reader to determine the need for and
level of redundancy, by adding applicable levels of redundancy you
may be able to enhance the availability level of your organization's
Web server to the point where it provides a similar availability level to
that obtained from multiple servers.

6.3.1.4 Considering Network Operations   If your organization purchases
redundancy for your Web server or servers, you probably analyzed
the need to have a high level of availability. Unfortunately, the high
level of availability can be compromised by using a single Internet
access line, even if that line operates as a T3 facility at approximately
45 Mbps. To obtain a high level of Internet availability, you need to
install multiple access lines to the Internet. In addition, such lines
should be routed to your organization's location through different Internet Service Provider (ISP) points of presence (POPs) and,
if possible, by different ISPs. This author can testify to the value of

the latter when, during a rather large rainstorm, a bridge over which a SONET optical fiber was routed eastward from Macon, Georgia, to Atlanta washed away. While one connection to the Internet was terminated until the fiber was restrung weeks later, a second access line to Jacksonville, Florida, that went west stayed operational.

6.3.2 Single-Site, Multiple-Server Model

A second CDN model retains the single-site location but adds one or more clusters of servers to a single-site, single-server model. Referred to as a *single-site, multiple-server model,* the use of multiple servers can usually provide more processing capability than a single server. In addition, depending on the way multiple servers are connected to the Internet, this model could provide multiple connections to the Internet, increasing the availability of access to the content presented by the organization.

The ability to effectively use multiple servers at a single site is based upon having the capacity to balance the load on the multiple servers located at the site. To do so, this requires either the programming of DNS or the use of a load balancer. While either method can be used to make more effective use of your organization's Web servers, as previously described in Chapter 5, there are disadvantages associated with each method, which we will shortly discuss.

6.3.2.1 Advantages Using two or more servers enables the failure of one server to be compensated for by the remaining operational devices. In addition, the effect of hardware and software upgrades can occur on one server at a time, resulting in the other servers in the cluster having the ability to serve customers without having to be placed offline or having their performance degraded. If multiple connections to the Internet are used, the availability of server content is increased.

6.3.2.2 Disadvantages Using a single site maintains the disadvantages associated with browser users located around the globe accessing a common location. Data traversing across many peering points, or the routing of data over relatively low-speed data circuits or heavily used high-speed circuits, can result in significant delays. Such delays can result in browser users abandoning your organization's Web site or even accessing a competitor, either action resulting in the potential loss of revenue to electronic commerce Web sites. For example, consider a user accessing the Web site of an airline, attempting to purchase two round-trip tickets from New York to Los Angeles. This is not a highly unusual route, and there are many airlines as well as travel-oriented Web sites that are more than happy to provide a response to a browser user's request. Thus, if browser users encounter difficulties in accessing the Web site of one airline, there is a good possibility that they will move on and access the Web site of another, resulting in a considerable loss of revenue to the first site. While every Web site is different, you need to assess the potential loss associated with an inoperable or inaccessible Web site and act accordingly. For example, you can usually compute a retail organization's Web-site sales history on an hourly basis. You may also be able to determine the number of outages and the total outage over a period of time. Then, you can compute the cost of each outage and use this data as a mechanism to determine the value of adding certain types of redundancy to your organization's Web site.

Although the old adage that two is better than one applies to multiple servers, you need to determine a method for distributing traffic among multiple servers. This means that your organization will require some type of load-balancing mechanism to distribute the traffic load in an equitable manner among the servers in your organization's server cluster. Although you can use the Domain Name System (DNS) load-balancing capability without any additional cost, as previously noted in Chapter 5, a DNS server has no capability to check the status of other servers in its tables. For example, using a programmed DNS to balance loads will work rather well as long as all servers are available. If one out of five fails, then 20% of service requests would be forwarded by the DNS server to a failed machine, and the client would receive an error message after a timeout period occurs. If the client tries again to reach a server, he or she has an 80 percent chance of being successful; however, the client might simply decide not to try again and abandon the access attempt. In the event that a load balancer is used and the hardware platform fails, this would cause the site to become unreachable, which is why such network appliances typically can be obtained with redundant memory and power supplies.

6.3.3 Multiple-Sites, Single-Server per Site Model

To alleviate potential delays associated with browser users accessing a central site, your organization can consider placing servers at one or more office locations within a country, or scattered in different countries, based upon an analysis of client locations. This action will result in a new CDN enterprise model involving multiple sites. When a single server is located at each site, we obtain a multiple-site, single server per site enterprise model.

The primary reason for a multiple-site model will be based on the need to distribute content closer to existing and potential customers. Assuming that you use one or more of the tools previously mentioned in this chapter to determine that a multiple-site model is more appropriate than a single-site model, you need to consider the number of locations where servers should be installed and the number of servers to be installed at each location. The multiple-site, single-server per site model represents the simplest type of geographically distributed content distribution.

Under the multiple-site, single-server per site model, an organization examines both actual and potential data flow to its primary Web site. By observing where customers and potential customers are geographically clustered, and noting delays associated with Internet access and data flow from those clustered areas, an organization can determine where one or more servers should be installed outside of the main data center. Thus, the multiple-site, single-server per site model represents a way to distribute servers to geographic locations where their installation can enhance browser user access.

6.3.3.1 Advantages The primary advantage associated with the multiple-site, single-server per site model is the fact that it enables content to be placed closer to browser users. This can reduce latency, which should result in a decline in site abandonment, which in turn can result in an increase in customers and customer revenue. A second advantage associated with this model is the fact that servers are now placed at two or more distinct locations. Thus, the failure of a communications circuit, an electrical outage, or another type of impairment may not cause an organization's entire Web presence to disappear.

6.3.3.2 Disadvantages   The comparison of any multiple-site model to a single-site model will result in differences in hardware, software, and support costs. Unless the single-site model employs a large number of clustered servers, the cost of a multiple-site model can exceed the cost of a single-site model.

Another disadvantage associated with the multiple-site model is the way browser users are directed to one of the multiple servers located at geographically dispersed areas. If the direction occurs through the central site, that location becomes a weak link. If that site experiences a power outage or if a circuit linking that site to the Internet fails, then its possible that the redirection facility will fail. You can overcome this problem by setting up separate domains for each distributed server so that the distant user requests flow directly to an applicable server. The key problem associated with this method occurs when content updates are managed from a central site. If that central site should lose its Internet connection, there will be a delay in updating distributed servers. In addition, if the organization maintains its database servers at the central site, which results in the distributed servers having to access the central site, a failure at that location will adversely affect the ability of browser users around the globe to access information or purchase products that rely upon checking the database at the central site. Under this scenario, the solution to the problem is to increase the level of availability of access to the central site.

There are two good ways to do this. First, the central site could install redundant communications links to the Internet so that the failure of one circuit would be compensated for by the ability to use a second circuit. As previously discussed, to provide an even higher level of availability, the central site could use the communications facilities of two different ISPs. A network problem experienced by one ISP would then be compensated for by the ability of data to reach the central site via the network of the second ISP. However, if you decide to employ two different ISPs, it is important to ensure that they provide Internet access over two diverse paths. Earlier in this chapter, this author mentioned a flood that washed away a bridge that included a high speed fiber-optic circuit routed from Macon to Atlanta. If both ISPs aggregated their service in Macon and routed data to Atlanta via the washed-away fiber, redundancy would fail. Thus, it is extremely important to consider the routes via diverse circuits flow.

A second method that can be used to raise the level of availability of the central site is obtained by using two or more servers at that location. The CDN model is then modified into a new category that we will refer to as the *multiple-site, multiple-server model*.

6.3.4 Multiple-Site, Multiple-Server per Site Model

As its name implies, the multiple-site, multiple-server per site model results in an organization placing two or more servers in at least one location in addition to its central site. The goal behind this model is to provide highly reliable access to content distributed closer to the user. Although this model is both costly and complex to implement, it is used by many multinational organizations that have established e-commerce businesses on two or more continents or have a large number of users located in geographically dispersed locations. In addition, there are various versions of the multiple-site, multiple-server per site model that warrant discussion. While the basic multiple-site, multiple-server per site model may imply that initial data flow is directed to a central site, it's possible to set up independent domains. For example, browser users located in Europe would access a data center located on that continent, while browser users located on another continent would be directed to a data center located on that continent. At each data center hosting multiple servers, a load-balancing mechanism would distribute the workload over those local multiple servers. In this example, each location functions as an autonomous entity, and there is no need for communications between server locations.

The opposite end of the autonomous entity operating model is a nonautonomous entity model. In this situation, each location outside the primary data center communicates with the data center to obtain the dynamic content or other types of information, such as daily price changes for different products. Between the autonomous and non-autonomous entities are partial autonomous entities, where one or more distributed sites only have a requirement to periodically access a central site. Now that we have an appreciation for the potential variances associated with the multiple-site, multiple-server per site model, let's conclude our discussion concerning this model by turning to the advantages and disadvantages associated with this model.

6.3.4.1 Advantages   There are several advantages associated with a multiple-site, multiple-server per site model. The primary advantage is reliability and availability of access. Using multiple servers per site reduces the probability of a site being down. In addition, because there are multiple locations with multiple servers, it is highly unlikely for the presence of the organization on the Internet to go dark. Because access to each location can be further enhanced by multiple connections to the Internet, it becomes possible to create a very reliable and highly available presence on the Web while moving content closer to the ultimate requester.

6.3.4.2 Disadvantages   Similar to the multiple-site, single-server per site model, the key disadvantage of the multiple-site, multiple-server per site model are costs and complexity. Because multiple servers will be installed at multiple locations, costs can easily become a major issue. In addition, because a load-balancing mechanism will be required to distribute the load at each location, the complexity of this model is far above the level of complexity of the other models mentioned in this chapter. When you add development and operational costs, this model is both the most expensive to implement and the most expensive to maintain. However, for some e-commerce multinational organizations, the benefits associated with having a direct presence at many locations where Web content can be tailored to the area far outweighs the cost of the effort.

6.3.5 An In-Between Model

One mechanism you should consider for your organization is what this author refers to as an in-between model. Because no two organizations are the same, chances are high that your organization needs something that doesn't quite fully fit into a single model. Thus, you might end up with some multiple sites, some with single servers, some with redundant servers with a load-balancing mechanism, and other sites with a single server that has a high degree of built-in redundancy.

In concluding this chapter, an observation by this author is warranted. If you travel and access the Internet from several countries, you will probably note that you can access the Web sites of major booksellers, home improvement stores, as well as major appliance and electronics type stores that are native to the country you are traveling in, but which are branches of multinational firms headquartered in another country. When you access the local Web site, you are accessing either a multiple-site, single-server per site, or a multiple-site, multiple-server per site Web model.

7

WEB-HOSTING OPTIONS

Until now, we have subdivided the ability to obtain a presence on the Internet into two basic categories: Do it yourself, or employ the services of a content delivery provider. Although the content delivery provider can be viewed as a form of Web-hosting organization, in actuality the term *Web hosting* can denote a range of organizations, including content delivery providers. The use of a third party for hosting an organization's presence on the Internet represents a content delivery option, and we now focus on this topic.

In this chapter, we will turn our attention to third-party Web hosting. We will initially discuss the rationale for using a third-party Web-hosting facility. Once we understand the major reasons for considering this method of establishing a presence on the Internet, we will discuss the different categories of Web hosting available for consideration, the variety of tools provided by third-party vendors to facilitate an organization's presence on the Internet, and evaluation factors that can separate the suitability of one Web-hosting vendor from another with respect to meeting your organization's operational requirements.

7.1 Rationale

There are a variety of factors an organization will consider when determining if a third-party Web-hosting arrangement should be used either in place of, or as a supplement to, an in-house Web-hosting arrangement. While cost is normally an important consideration, there are also other factors that can have a heavy weight when an organization compares the development of an in-house system to the use of a Web-hosting facility. Table 7.1 lists some of the more important factors an organization should consider, with each factor having the ability, either alone or in conjunction with other factors, to form the rationale for obtaining the use of a Web-hosting facility.

Table 7.1   Rationale for Using a Web-Hosting Facility

Cost elements and total cost
Performance elements
Server-side languages supported
Web service tools available
Back-end database support
Facility location(s)

To illustrate the variety of choices you have concerning obtaining a Web-hosting provider, consider the example shown in Figure 7.1. In this example, this author used the Microsoft Bing Web site located at www.bing.com to search for Web-hosting providers. Note that the referenced figure shows only 10 of 202,000,000 hits. While it is highly unlikely that anyone will have the time or inclination to examine even a fraction of the resulting hits, this vividly illustrates that you have a significant number of choices that you can narrow down by refining your search. For example, if your organization was located in a specific city and wanted to be able to deliver disks without being at the mercy of the Postal Service or an express organization, you could search for Web hosting in that city. Chances are rather high that you will find one or more Web-hosting organization that meet your criteria. That said, let's examine the reasons associated with using a Web-hosting facility.

7.1.1 Cost Elements and Total Cost

Today, most Web-hosting services bill clients based upon several usage-related elements. Those elements can include processor requirements, disk space requirements, total data transfer, and bandwidth utilization. In addition, if your Web-hosting service provides an e-commerce site that includes the processing of credit cards, your organization can expect one or more fees per credit card usage in addition to a credit card processing fee.

To ensure a valid comparison between the use of a third-party Web-hosting service and an in-house effort, you need to consider each and every cost associated with these two options. For example, one cost commonly overlooked is electricity, which may be significantly reduced when you require the use of a third party. Instead of paying a

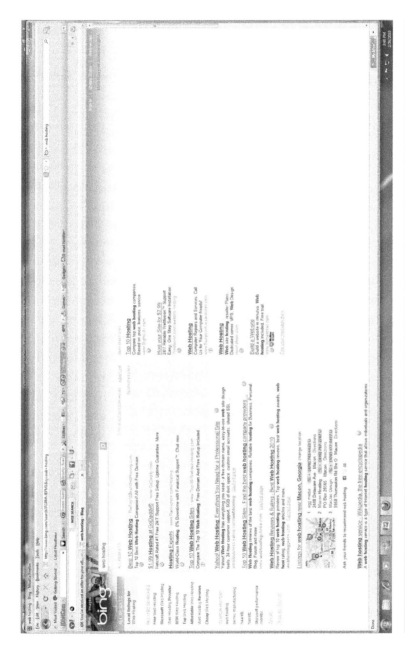

Figure 7.1 Using a search engine to locate Web-hosting providers.

direct cost for electricity when your organization operates an in-house Web site, a third-party Web-hosting facility will normally factor in the cost of electricity, building maintenance, and personnel into their hosting fee structure. In addition to the elimination of the cost for electricity by outsourcing Web hosting, you need to consider the additional cost associated with heat removal via a chilled or conventional air-conditioning system. This is especially true in certain locations, such as in Georgia, where the temperature during four to five months of the year hovers beyond 80 degrees with high humidity. In this case, the direct cost of operating a Web server is only a portion of the cost of electricity due to operating the server. Because the server generates heat, you have to consider the removal of the extra British Thermal Units (BTUs) that result from the operation of the server.

Other costs associated with operating a Web server that are often overlooked include training and maintenance when you operate an in-house Web server. Typically, but not always, the savings associated with using a third-party Web-hosting service will be less than the costs associated with a do-it-yourself approach. However, in spite of economics favoring the use of a Web-hosting service, many medium to large organizations will elect the do-it-yourself approach, as this action provides them with a higher degree of control. This is especially true for the larger e-commerce merchant Web sites, where prices can change very rapidly for certain merchandise and the organization needs to exercise full control over when maintenance and backup operations occur. In addition, when the third-party Web-hosting service operates a shared hosting facility where two or more organizations share the use of a common hardware platform, security considerations need to be examined. Although each organization is provided with a virtual Web server and in effect cannot view or change the operational parameters of the other virtual servers operating on the common hardware platform, many times organizations are very reluctant to use this type of Web service. This is especially true if one or more organizations on the shared hosting platform are competitors. For example, this author highly doubts that Walmart would agree to have its Web servers hosted by a third party that might be hosting a competitor, such as K-Mart. Although security might preclude one company from determining in advance price changes posted by another company, there is always the chance that the third-party provider could make a mistake that results in the flow of information that should not be disclosed. Thus, even though cost can be an important rationale for using a Web-hosting facility, it may not be the governing factor.

7.1.2 Performance Elements

The category of performance elements is a broad term that references the various factors that govern the operation of the Web-hosting facility. Such factors can include the operating system and application software provided by the vendor, the type of hardware platform the Web service will operate upon, uptime guarantees for both the hardware platform and communications to and from the Internet, the Internet connection or series of connections supported by the Web-hosting facility, and the type of support the facility provides. In the next few paragraphs in this section, we will take a more detailed look at each of these performance elements.

The operating system and applications supported by a Web-hosting facility govern your organization's ability to have a particular type of Web site placed into operation. That is, you would not select a vendor that could not provide support of on-line credit card billing if your organization required that capability. Similarly, if your organization is a parts supplier and the Web-hosting facility would need an interface to your organization's mainframe database, vendors that could not support the required interface would not be considered. Similarly, if your organization previously developed a Web server that operates under the Sun Unix operating system and you were looking for a hosting site in Australia, you would more than likely give preference to hosting sites in that country that can provide Sun UNIX platforms.

The type of hardware platform provided by the Web-hosting facility in conjunction with the operating system and application programs will govern the capability of the facility to respond to browser user requests. When examining the hardware platform, an organization needs to consider random access memory (RAM), the number of processors and their operating rate and data-path width, disk controllers, and disk drives. In addition, you need to consider the use of a virtual server versus a dedicated server. If the hosting provider operates virtual servers, this means that your organization will be one of many operating on a common hardware platform. While this may not necessarily be bad, the use of a virtual server more than likely will depend upon the policies of your organization and the clients already operating on a virtual server. This author remembers the old adage that "Macy's is not Gimbels" from a time when the two department stores competed with one another, prior to the rise of the Internet. Even if the latter had survived, it is highly doubtful if the two competitors would ever have their Web sites on a common virtual server.

Concerning RAM, you need to consider the current amount of RAM, whether RAM can be expanded, and, if so, the maximum amount of memory that can be supported. When considering the type of processor used by the hardware platform, it's important to note whether the platform supports more than one processor and, if so, how many are presently installed. Doing so will provide you with an indication of the upgradeability of the hardware platform. Similarly, investigating the capacity of disk drives, current storage used, and the ability to add additional drives will provide you with an indication of the upgradeability of online storage. Because a Web-hosting facility typically operates numerous hardware platforms, this option may provide more capacity and capability than if your organization acquired a single hardware platform for operation at your facility.

One of the more important performance elements provided by some third-party Web-hosting organizations is a very high uptime guarantee. Because the Web-hosting facility can amortize the cost of backup servers, redundant power, and redundant Internet connections over many users, they can usually afford to spend more on maintaining access to servers under adverse conditions than an individual organization can afford. However, not all uptime guarantees refer to the same component. Some uptime guarantees reference Internet availability, with a high uptime guarantee usually associated with sites that have multiple connections to the Internet. Other uptime guarantees refer to the hardware platform. While a Web-hosting facility will usually provide higher communications and processor uptime than affordable by small- and medium-sized organizations, it is important to examine both. Otherwise, a 99.999% processor uptime level, which sounds really exciting, may not be all that great if Internet availability is at a much lower level. In this situation, the hardware platform is almost never down, while the Internet connection is problematic.

Two additional performance elements that need to be considered, and which usually favor the use of a Web-hosting facility, are their Internet bandwidth and their help desk or assistance facility. Because the Web-hosting facility provides a service for many customers, it more than likely provides more bandwidth as well as more Internet connections than a single Web site could normally afford. Thus, the Internet connections provided by a Web-hosting facility, especially if the connections occur via two or more Internet Service Providers, can provide a higher level of availability than most organizations can afford when constructing an in-house Web site. Similarly, a Web-hosting facility that provides a hosting service for one or more sites with heavy international traffic may operate a 24/7 help desk, a luxury for many small- and medium-sized organizations.

To facilitate the reader's consideration of performance elements, Table 7.2 provides a checklist of those elements. Although the proverbial Vendor A and Vendor B are listed at the head of two columns, you

Table 7.2 Comparing Performance Elements

PERFORMANCE ELEMENT	VENDOR A	VENDOR B
Type of server		
Dedicated	_____	_____
Virtual	_____	_____
Operating system	_____	_____
Server hardware platform		
Processor(s)	_____	_____
RAM	_____	_____
Disk storage	_____	_____
RAID level, if required	_____	_____
Server software capability		
Credit card processing	_____	_____
Database interface	_____	_____
Applications required	_____	_____
Backup server availability	_____	_____
Internet connectivity		
Primary connection	_____	_____
Secondary connection	_____	_____
Diversity routing	_____	_____
Help-desk facility		
Operation 24/7?	_____	_____
Toll-free support	_____	_____

can compare any vendor against another or extend the comparison to additional vendors by simply duplicating the columns to consider more vendors.

7.1.3 Server-Side Language Support

For most organizations considering the use of a Web-hosting service, the support of server-side languages may be more inclusive then they could support with their existing personnel structure. However, although most Web-hosting facilities support a core set of server-side languages, they more than likely do not support all such languages. This means that, while a Web-hosting facility may provide support for more server-side languages than your organization could support independently, you still need to examine those languages the facility vendor supports. In doing so, you need to ascertain whether all of the languages your hosted Web site will require are supported, and, if not, whether it's possible to use an alternative language or whether your organization should consider a different Web-hosting facility whose language support better matches the requirements of your organization.

7.1.4 Web-Service Tools

Another reason for considering the use of a third-party Web-hosting facility concerns the Web-service tools they provide to customers. Those tools can vary considerably between hosting vendors. Some vendors may provide Web-page construction tools, while other vendors may add one or more promotion tools to their literal "bag of tools." Table 7.3 provides a list of major Web-hosting facility tools commonly offered as well as a mechanism to compare those tools against the requirements of your organization. In addition, space is provided for you to compare the offerings of two vendors against your organization's requirements. You can also duplicate the table as a mechanism to compare the tool offerings of additional vendors against the requirements of your organization.

7.1.5 The Importance of Images

In examining the list of common Web-hosting tools listed in Table 7.3, a few words need to be mentioned concerning the image formats

Table 7.3   Common Web-Hosting Facility Tools

CATEGORY/TOOL	ORGANIZATIONAL REQUIREMENT	VENDOR A	VENDOR B
Site construction tools			
Web templates	_____	_____	_____
HTML editor	_____	_____	_____
HTML version	_____	_____	_____
CSS support	_____	_____	_____
JavaScript	_____	_____	_____
ActiveX	_____	_____	_____
PHP support	_____	_____	_____
XML Support	_____	_____	_____
Image formats	_____	_____	_____
File manager	_____	_____	_____
Blog builder	_____	_____	_____
Photo album	_____	_____	_____
Calendar	_____	_____	_____
Counters	_____	_____	_____
URL redirect	_____	_____	_____
Guestbook	_____	_____	_____
E-mail forum	_____	_____	_____
Message forums	_____	_____	_____
Password protection	_____	_____	_____
Chat room	_____	_____	_____
Audio clips	_____	_____	_____
Headline news tools			
Today in history	_____	_____	_____
News headline feed	_____	_____	_____
Sports headline feed	_____	_____	_____
Promotional tools			
Daily cartoon	_____	_____	_____
E-cards	_____	_____	_____
Links	_____	_____	_____
Site ring	_____	_____	_____
Site searches	_____	_____	_____

supported by a hosting site and how they can possibly affect your organization's monthly cost. Many Web-hosting facilities include either a direct or indirect cost based upon downloads from a Web site in terms of the number of kilobytes or megabytes downloaded per month. While the goal of most organizations is to have an attractive and popular Web site where a high percentage of visitors are converted into paying customers, at the same time another goal is to minimize the cost of operating the Web site. We might think that these goals are mutually exclusive, but they are not. We have the technical ability to minimize costs while increasing the desirability of viewing our Web pages by optimizing the images sent to browser users. The key to minimizing or containing cost is obtained through the appropriate use of images and the recognition that the JPEG (Joint Photographic Experts Group) format can provide a visually pleasing image that cannot be differentiated from the same image stored and transmitted in other formats (or in JPEG formats that have not been optimized), which can impose a significantly higher burden on bandwidth costs. This key is obtained by having an image-manipulation program that controls the Q factor of a JPEG image.

The Q or quality factor normally ranges on a scale from 1 to 100, with 100 representing the highest quality and lowest compression. Unfortunately, some programs have developed alternative scales, such as the popular Lead Tools program, which uses a scale ranging from 1 (no compression, a sort of lossless JPEG) to 255 (lowest quality and highest level of compression).

To determine the value of compression, assume that your organization has a Web site that displays an image of your corporate headquarters on its home page that was compressed using JPEG at a default Q factor of 80 (used by many programs), resulting in 125,000 bytes of data downloaded each time your organization's home page is accessed. Let's assume a moderate level of activity that results in 100,000 hits per month. This level of activity then results in a cumulative download of 12,500,000,000 bytes per month just for the image. Now let's assume that you use an image tool offered by the Web-hosting vendor that allows you to manipulate images and, by using a lower Q factor, obtain an image that requires 87,000 bytes of data and, to the naked eye, looks exactly like the other image. Assuming the same number of Web home-page hits, this results in 8,700,000,000 bytes downloaded just for the image, or a difference of 3,800,000,000 bytes per month. Because many Web-hosting organizations have a monthly bill that includes a communications fee in terms of kilobytes or megabytes downloaded per month, by simply modifying the image on your organization's home page, you are able to reduce transmission by 3,800,000,000/1024, or 3711 Mbytes per month. At a typical cost of 10 cents per Mbyte, the simple use of a program that lets you adjust the Q factor of JPEG images could result in a monthly savings of $371, month after month after month.

7.1.6 Back-End Database Support

It's important to note that a back-end database is accessed indirectly by clients of your Web-hosting provider. Thus, the manner by which client data is entered and passed to a database is an important consideration. After all, it's not a trivial job to rewrite many thousands of lines of code if your organization previously developed its own Web site that included one type of back-end database and now you are faced with rewriting software to use a Web-hosting provider that supports a different back-end database. In addition to directly considering the type of back-end database supported by the Web-hosting provider, it may be important to investigate the scripting language you use and its ability to support the provider's back-end database. For example, the use of some scripting languages supports issuing generic commands that could manipulate a range of back-end databases. In comparison, other scripting languages may be more limited in scope.

7.1.7 Facility Location(s)

The last major factor that you can consider in justifying the use of a Web-hosting facility is the location or series of locations where the hosting facility resides. Some Web-hosting organizations have several server farms located on different continents. In comparison, other vendors may be limited to operating a single facility. By carefully examining the location or locations of Web-hosting vendors, it becomes possible for your organization to use those facilities as a mechanism to move content closer to groups of browser users that either currently access or have the potential to access your site. For example, assume that your organization operates a Web site in Los Angeles and you noted that a large number of page hits occur from browser users located in Western Europe. Further assume that through the use of Web logs supplemented by the use of a network analyzer programmed with appropriate filters, you notice that those browser users are experiencing significant transmission delays that appear to result in a high level of server abandonment. In this situation, you might consider the use of a Web-hosting facility located in Western Europe, whose utilization could reduce transmission delays experienced by browser users accessing your organization's Web site from that general geographic area.

To facilitate traffic from Western Europe flowing to the hosted server, your organization would register a new domain name with a country suffix corresponding to the location of the Web-hosting facility. Then, you could modify your existing Web server located in Los Angeles to redirect browser user requests originating from Western Europe to the hosted server.

Now that we have an appreciation for the key reasons for examining the potential use of a Web-hosting facility, let's turn our attention to the types of hosting facilities available.

7.2 Types of Web-Hosting Facilities

There are several ways that we can categorize the type of Web-hosting facility. These include their ability to support e-commerce, credit card, and/or PayPal usage; the operating system used (Windows, Unix, Linux); geographic location (United States, Canada, Western Europe, etc.); or the manner by which outside customers use Web-hosting facilities. For the purpose of this section, we will consider the type of Web-hosting facility to be defined by the way outside customers use Web-hosting facilities.

There are three basic types of Web hosting you can consider: dedicated hosting, shared hosting, and colocated hosting.

7.2.1 Dedicated Hosting

A dedicated hosting facility means that a server is dedicated to operating a single organization's presence on the Internet. This type of Web hosting should be considered if your organization needs to run customized software and applications instead of standard software provided by the hosting organization. A dedicated server is also preferable if there is a need for a high level of security or if your hosted server is expected to receive a high level of traffic that warrants the use of a hardware platform for the exclusive use of your organization. Because only one organization uses the resources of a dedicated server, its cost will be higher than when two or more organizations share the resources of a single server, a situation referred to as a *shared server*.

7.2.2 Shared Server Hosting

A shared server means that an organization's Web site operates on a hardware platform that one or more additional Web sites also operate on, in effect sharing the hardware platform. The ability to share the use of a common hardware platform is commonly obtained by a Web server program supporting multiple Web sites. Examples of Web server programs that provide this capability include Microsoft Windows 2000 Server, Windows 2003 Server, and Apache.

This author will turn to Microsoft's Internet Information Services (IIS) to show how multiple servers can be supported on a common Web platform. Under IIS, you can right-click on the server name (shown with an asterisk in the top of the left-hand side of Figure 7.2) established after the program was installed. This action results in the display of a pop-up menu that includes the option New. Selecting that option allows you to define a new Web site or a new FTP site.

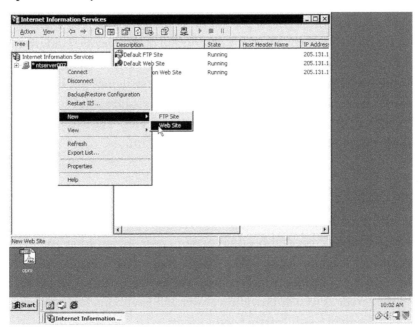

Figure 7.2 Right-clicking on the server name in the Internet Information Services box enables you to create a new server.

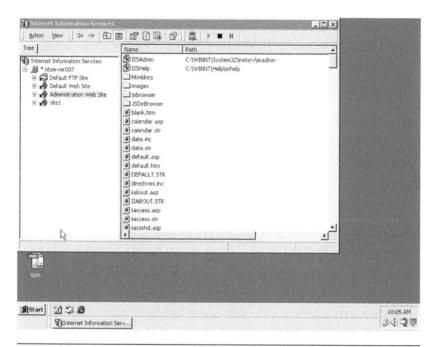

Figure 7.3 Viewing IIS after another Web site was added to the common hardware platform.

This action will result in the display of a Web-site creation wizard that walks you through the process for defining a new Web site. The wizard will request you to enter a description of the site, its IP address, and the port field to be used. Next, you can enter the domain name for the site. Assuming that we simply entered the name "site 1" for the new Web site, it would appear in the IIS box, as shown in Figure 7.3. Thereafter, we could again right click on a Web-site entry to add another site onto the common hardware platform.

7.2.3 Colocated Hosting

A third type of Web-hosting arrangement is referred to as *colocated hosting*. Under a colocated-hosting solution, your organization becomes responsible for purchasing a Web server. That server is then located at the third-party facility, which is then responsible for physically housing the server as well as providing power and environmental controls, security, support, and Internet connectivity.

The goal behind using a colocated hosting arrangement is that it provides an organization with the ability to obtain required hardware that may not be available from the hosting organization. It also provides an opportunity for an organization that has one or more excess hardware platforms to have them used by the hosting facility instead of having to be billed for additional hardware usage. Of course, such an arrangement can create problems if the hosting organization is not familiar with the hardware. In addition, selecting a customized hardware solution can create backup problems. Thus, the use of a colocated hosting method needs to be carefully analyzed based upon the hardware you select and the hosting organization's ability to support the hardware.

7.3 Evaluation Factors

In concluding our discussion of Web-hosting options, it's important to consider the manner by which you evaluate this option against the offerings of different vendors. If you type in the term *Web hosting* in Google, Yahoo, or another search engine, you will be inundated with responses. Google alone provides over 26 million responses.

When evaluating the suitability of a Web-hosting organization, we need to examine a large number of quantifiable metrics. We also need answers to questions that may be rankable but are not quantifiable. A number of quantifiable metrics were previously noted in this chapter. For example, Table 7.3 includes a list of Web-hosting facility tools you can consider by matching your organization's requirements against a comprehensive list of tools. Table 7.4 contains a list of Web-hosting evaluation factors that includes a reference to Table 7.3 for comparing hosting-facility tools. Similar to Table 7.3, Table 7.4 provides a list of features you may wish to evaluate. In the second column, you can specify your organization's requirements for a specific feature. In the third and fourth columns, labeled Vendor A and Vendor B, you can compare the offerings provided by two vendors to the features required by your organization. Of course, you can include additional vendors in your assessment by adding columns for Vendors C, D, etc.

Although most of the entries in Table 7.4 are self-explanatory, a few words of discussion are warranted with respect to service and support. For many organizations, it's important to ascertain the types of existing customer sites being hosted by a Web-hosting facility. Obtaining this information will provide a valuable insight concerning the ability

Table 7.4 Web-Hosting Evaluation Features

CATEGORY/FEATURE	ORGANIZATIONAL REQUIREMENT	VENDOR A	VENDOR B
Internet connection			
Bandwidth	_____	_____	_____
Type of connection			
T1	_____	_____	_____
T3	_____	_____	_____
Other	_____	_____	_____
Redundancy	_____	_____	_____
Uptime guarantee	_____	_____	_____
Type of server			
Dedicated	_____	_____	_____
Shared	_____	_____	_____
Cohosted	_____	_____	_____
Server operating system			
UNIX	_____	_____	_____
LINUX	_____	_____	_____
Sun OS	_____	_____	_____
Windows 2000	_____	_____	_____
Windows 2003	_____	_____	_____
Other	_____	_____	_____
Server capacity			
Processor speed	_____	_____	_____
Number of processors	_____	_____	_____
On-line storage	_____	_____	_____
Tape storage	_____	_____	_____
Other	_____	_____	_____
Server software			
Apache	_____	_____	_____
Microsoft IIS	_____	_____	_____
O'Riley	_____	_____	_____
Other	_____	_____	_____
Server-side software			
ASP	_____	_____	_____
C++	_____	_____	_____
Jscript	_____	_____	_____
Perl	_____	_____	_____
PHP	_____	_____	_____
Microsoft SQL	_____	_____	_____
VBScript	_____	_____	_____
Other	_____	_____	_____

Table 7.4 (continued)   Web-Hosting Evaluation Features

CATEGORY/FEATURE	ORGANIZATIONAL REQUIREMENT	VENDOR A	VENDOR B
Server security			
Certificates	_____	_____	_____
Authentication type	_____	_____	_____
Firewall	_____	_____	_____
Router access lists	_____	_____	_____
SSL	_____	_____	_____
Other	_____	_____	_____
Server backup			
Content backup	_____	_____	_____
Upon change	_____	_____	_____
Daily	_____	_____	_____
Weekly	_____	_____	_____
Other	_____	_____	_____
Redundant power	_____	_____	_____
Uptime guarantee	_____	_____	_____
Other	_____	_____	_____
Web-hosting facility tools (See Table 7.3)			
Server statistics			
Events logged	_____	_____	_____
Other	_____	_____	_____
Service and support			
Types of customers	_____	_____	_____
Opinions of customers	_____	_____	_____
Stability	_____	_____	_____
24/7 technical support	_____	_____	_____
Help desk	_____	_____	_____
Other	_____	_____	_____

of the third party to host your organization's Web site. For example, if you are considering a hosting facility that operates Web sites for clients who require credit card payments, then the hosting facility should be familiar with the process required. However, to ensure that it is, you should ask for references and obtain the opinions of existing customers concerning the performance of that function as well as functions that may be required in the future.

Index